PROPERTY INVESTMENT APPRAISAL

SECOND EDITION

Since the early 1970s, the techniques used by valuers to assess the value of investment properties have come under increasing scrutiny. These criticisms have been reinforced in the recession of the early 1990s, leading to a variety of high-level calls for change.

The first edition of this text, published in 1988, provided the most detailed account of this debate ever prepared and put forward the case for change. The new edition has been substantially altered to provide a detailed account of valuation in the market conditions of the mid-1990s, while expanding the number of examples and illustrations of the way valuation methods may be applied.

The text builds on the research-based critical analysis unique to the first edition, exploring the relationship between property and alternative investments; it explains the development of conventional approaches, putting current applications into their historical perspective; and it looks at the issues involved in assessing price and worth in both rising and falling markets.

Andrew Baum is Professor of Land Management at the University of Reading, and Managing Director of Real Estate Strategy, a division of Henderson Real Estate Strategy. **Neil Crosby** is Professor of Land Management at the University of Reading. Both are very well known authors and researchers in the field of property.

PROPERTY INVESTMENT APPRAISAL

SECOND EDITION

ANDREW BAUM
and
NEIL CROSBY

INTERNATIONAL THOMSON BUSINESS PRESS
I ⓣ P® An International Thomson Publishing Company

London • Bonn • Boston • Johannesburg • Madrid • Melbourne • Mexico City • New York • Paris
Singapore • Tokyo • Toronto • Albany, NY • Belmont, CA • Cincinnati, OH • Detroit, MI

Property Investment Appraisal

 A division of International Thomson Publishing Inc.
The ITP logo is a trademark under licence

British Library Cataloguing-in-Publication Data
A catalogue record for this book is available from the British Library

First edition 1995
First Published by Routledge
Reprinted 1996, 1997 and 1998 by International Thompson Business Press

Typeset by Mathematical Composition Setters, Wilts
Printed in Croatia by Zrinski

ISBN 1-86152-396-3

International Thomson Business Press
Berkshire House
168–173 High Holborn
London WC1V 7AA
UK

http://www.itbp.com

We would like to dedicate this book to Martin Newell, who tragically died in 1991. His contribution to this subject area is greater than is generally known and we owe him a debt of gratitude for his advice which we will greatly miss.

Contents

Figures

Preface

The debate regarding property investment valuation techniques has raged in earnest since the property crash of the early 1970s. Techniques used in appraising the value of investment properties, seemingly beyond debate, have come under the scrutiny of many observers and commentators, not all of them property valuers.

We have set out in this text to investigate many of the questions raised by this debate. One of the most important questions is the role of the valuer, which must be defined before any technique utilized in his or her work can be properly examined. The distinction between pricing (exchange value) and valuation (appraisal of worth) is therefore a continuing theme throughout the text.

We see property investment appraisal in crisis. The initial manifestation of this crisis is the apparent divergence of market value and investment worth, an indication of an inefficient market. If valuers were to perform their natural role of making the market more efficient, the distinction would reduce. We hope this text represents a philosophy which will help the acceleration of this very process.

We set out to investigate conventional techniques in both their historical and present day contexts. We attempt to identify their logical base and consider whether they remain logical in today's market. We then proceed to examine new alternatives, which are also investigated with a logical basis as the paramount criterion.

The text has been organized in an attempt to put both sides of the argument concerning pricing valuations in an objective way. This has proved extremely difficult: each of us is convinced that modern alternatives do represent a significant step forward and should be adopted by the valuation profession without delay. As regards techniques for the assessment of worth, we feel there is no debate. The rationale of this book is that the same basis may be used for all appraisals, and in this respect it is difficult to disguise our preferences.

We base our conclusions not only on the theoretical foundation of logic. We make use of considerable empirical research in tracing the fall from grace of conventional valuation techniques. We believe that progress will only be made by the adoption of a logical technical base and a continuing effort to examine the behaviour of the market. It is time to shift the emphasis away from theoretical, and towards empirical, research.

To a limited extent this text is complementary to Routledge texts, *The Income Approach to Property Valuation* and *Statutory Valuations*: it is intended as an undergraduate and postgraduate text which presumes an understanding of financial mathematics, some statistics and basic conventional valuation techniques. Equally importantly, we would like this book to change the approach of practitioners and to found a platform for research in property investment appraisal. At the very least, it must make a contribution to a continuing and vital debate.

The use of the male gender throughout is not meant to imply that property ownership and analysis is restricted to males.

Preface to the Second Edition

For this second edition, we have taken the opportunity to amend, add and, most importantly, simplify much of the central part of the book. In response to the pleas of our students, we have added to the text by including many more examples of the application of contemporary growth-explicit market valuation techniques to a variety of practical situations. We have also included a substantial amount of new material relating to the valuation of property investments in a falling or fallen market. To reinforce both of these additions, we have included a detailed case study (Chapter 9). We hope that these additions will help understanding and ultimately lead to implementation of our preferred solutions in practice.

We are encouraged by the progress made in UK practice since the first edition was published. Over the last four years, a number of influential practitioners have taken on board the limitations of conventional market valuation approaches and the advantages of the growth explicit alternatives. It would be ungracious to suggest that the adoption of some of the techniques argued for in this text has been solely because of the collapse in the property market in the early 1990s, but there is no doubt that it has been a very powerful catalyst for change, mainly because the limitations of the conventional techniques have been exposed.

For this second edition, we would also make the point that, while rapid progress is being made in portfolio strategy, risk measurement and performance analysis, this book concentrates on the appraisal of individual property investments, until recently something of a Cinderella in property research.

However, recent developments in research into property markets, forecasting and risk analysis suggest that the information needs of the property investment appraisal models argued for in this text are being better serviced now than ever before. This is a vital element in the process of change towards these models, which both authors still believe is the right way forward.

Part one

INTRODUCTION

1

Property investment appraisal in its context

WHAT IS APPRAISAL?

The subject of this book is the appraisal of property investments. In choosing the term 'appraisal' we have two distinct applications in mind. By 'appraise' we mean:

1 to fix a price for;
2 to estimate the amount, or worth of.

The first of these meanings implies what is known in the UK as the valuation process and in the USA as the appraisal process: the estimation of open market value or the prediction of the most likely selling price. This is (AIREA 1984: 194)

> The most probable price in cash, terms equivalent to cash, or in other precisely revealed terms, for which the appraised property will sell in a competitive market under all conditions requisite to fair sale, with the buyer and seller each acting prudently, knowledgeably, and for self-interest and assuming that neither is under undue duress.

or (RICS 1992)

> The best price at which an interest in a property might reasonably be expected to be sold by private treaty at the date of valuation assuming:
>
> (a) a willing seller;
> (b) a reasonable period within which to negotiate the sale has already taken place prior to the valuation date;

(c) the nature of the property and the state of the market are as at the valuation date;

(d) the property will be freely exposed to the market;

(e) no account is to be taken of an additional bid by a special purchaser.

The second of the two meanings, the estimation of worth, is not necessarily market based. It is conceived in this book as the estimation of worth to an individual, given certain objectively measured variables and his/her subjective estimates of other relevant factors. 'Worth' may be a value expressed as a price; it may alternatively be a rate of return expressed as a percentage of the outlay necessary to secure the acquisition of an investment property.

We use the term 'appraisal' to cover either meaning. In the UK, valuation is sometimes used to cover both meanings. Either is a source term from which the two specific applications are derived. We would encourage the use of the term 'market valuation' or 'valuation for pricing' for the former (prediction of the most likely selling price); and we would prefer to use 'valuation of worth' for the latter (the estimation of worth, or non-pricing valuation).

We hope this will not cause too much confusion. The possibility of confusion is grounded in the fact that the property world is divorced from the securities markets by terminology. There is no doubt regarding the meaning of valuation in the securities markets: it means the estimation of worth. Pricing is a function which is carried out by buyers, sellers and market makers. In property, however, there are no market makers. The price at which a transaction will take place has to be influenced by an expert opinion – a 'valuation' – because there is both insufficient market evidence and insufficient homogeneity of product for mere traders to be able to fix prices.

Coupled with this we have the mismatch between North American and British Commonwealth practice, whereby appraisal and valuation are the respective terms used to define the same – pricing – process.

To repeat, we suggest a compromise. While we would prefer to use the term 'pricing' to mean the estimation of the most likely selling price, we recognize the need to use the term 'market valuation'. We would like to use the term 'valuation' to mean the estimation of worth, but we recognize the need to clarify this by using the term 'valuation of worth' (see Figure 1.1).

This book attempts to encourage better practice in the appraisal of property investments. Market valuations should be accurate, that is, they should closely predict selling price. Valuations of worth, on the other hand, should be rational in order to facilitate decision-making. We shall argue in

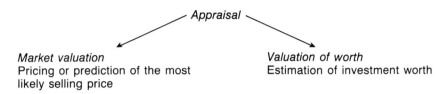

Figure 1.1 Appraisal and valuation

this book that *all* appraisals should be rational; if they are, accuracy is likely to follow.

It has been concluded many times (see, for example, Trott 1980) that the conventional method of appraising property investments is irrational. We examine the basis of this suggestion and the consequent possibilities of inaccuracy in Part 2 of this book. Nonetheless, charges of appraisal inaccuracy are much less common. Is it not true (as is often stated) that, if a market uses irrational or illogical methods in the fixing of price, appraisal techniques must mirror such irrationality in order to be accurate? Is it not also true that the accuracy of conventional property investment appraisals is proven by the lack of conclusive evidence to the contrary?

We answer both questions in the negative, and it is our response to these common beliefs that prompts us to produce this book. First, appraisals can rarely be proved to be inaccurate. Second, even if they were to be, a rational foundation is essential in the exercise of professional expertise.

Appraisals can rarely be proved inaccurate for many reasons. All market valuation is hedged by a series of assumptions. Special purchasers are excluded from consideration; a full exposure to the market, which is not defined, is assumed; no price movements over the marketing period are contemplated, even though full exposure may require a lengthy marketing period in an era of changing prices; and so on.

Predictions of the most likely selling price will only be shown to be wrong when prices achieved are revealed, and this is rarely the case. Overpricing is often justified in time in a rising market, and in any event vendors will rarely sell significantly below the asking price, avoiding proof of an overestimate. Estimations of individual worth – valuation of worth, in our terminology – would be impossible to prove inaccurate (by what criteria?); and in the fixing of a price in order to attract a sale (a variation on the pricing theme) the valuer is protected from criticism except where an auction is conducted formally or informally between a vendor and eager potential buyers and a high price results. An undersell is rare (reserve pricing ensures this in auctions); private treaty sales rarely permit an oversell (and in any case the purchaser may have been special).

It is therefore no accident that there have been relatively few reports of proven cases related to valuation negligence. Reports of variations in market valuations between valuers (for example, Hager and Lord 1985; Miles 1987) are interesting: there may be wide errors in samples of market valuations but none are suggested as being inaccurate.

Finally, the market valuation process is not, as is usually supposed, divorced from the operation of the market in fixing the selling price of an investment. Valuers often influence price rather than perform an independent and objective prediction. This is a result of the process by which properties are valued (priced) for sale. Valuations of this type are, within the larger practices, carried out by those actively involved in marketing (agents). This results in the confluence of the market valuation process and the market pricing mechanism. It is no justification of market valuation accuracy that prices paid are close to valuations when negotiations are carried out by valuers. This invalidates tests of market valuation accuracy and seriously questions beliefs in market efficiency based on an apparently objective comparison of market valuations and prices paid (see, for example, Brown 1985; Drivers Jonas/IPD 1988, 1990; and Venmore-Rowland and Lizieri 1992).

Even if a proof of appraisal accuracy were to be possible, irrational techniques which produced such accuracy should not necessarily be defended. It should be the aim of an appraisal to achieve accuracy by means of rational techniques. If buyers or sellers were to become aware of an inefficient sub-sector of the property market, prices will inevitably change and market valuation based on irrational techniques will immediately become subject to dangerous inaccuracy. The short leasehold market (see Baum and Butler 1986) is an example of the breakdown of conventional techniques, of the lack of confidence in market valuations for pricing leading to the use of tender sales and of the gradual, continuing adoption of an explicitly rational cash flow model for short leasehold appraisals.

Pricing follows valuation in the appraisal process. Fraser's suggestion (Fraser 1985a) that 'if the market is irrational, the last type of model appropriate for market valuation is a rational model' appears to ignore this fact. It presumes a separation of the valuer from the market. It also appears to presume that an irrational market will continue to be irrational and inefficient and that with its continuation goes the protection of irrational valuations. But surely any semblance of market efficiency will produce a shift in prices, so that irrational market valuations will always be outdated and potentially inaccurate. The case of over-rented properties in the early 1990s is a clear example (see Chapter 9).

Rational valuation does not necessarily imply a questioning of market price, but instead allows changes in observed prices to be reflected in changes in meaningful variables, permitting the accurate revaluation of other assets. We hope to show that conventional appraisal models do not permit this to happen.

Lack of rationality is increasingly inappropriate in today's de-regulated and international capital markets. A change to rational valuation will facilitate increased market efficiency and the rapid assimilation of any observable changes in equilibrium price into appraisals.

INVESTMENT

We are concerned with the appraisal of real property investments. More specifically, we are concerned with the prediction of the most likely selling price of a real property investment in the market, or with the estimation of the worth of such an investment to a prospective purchaser.

What is it that distinguishes a real property investment from other types of real property? The most useful distinction we can employ is that between property acquired for occupation and that acquired for investment. The desire for shelter or a place to do business or to enjoy recreation may be contrasted with the desire for 'a vehicle into which funds can be placed with the expectation that they will be preserved or increase in value and/or generate positive returns' (Gitman and Joehnk 1984).

Investment is 'the sacrifice of something now for the prospect of later benefits' (Greer and Farrell 1984). How does an investment 'generate positive returns' or 'later benefits'? It can do this in three ways:

1 by generating a flow of income (or reducing income tax);
2 by generating a return of capital (or reducing capital tax), whether it be less than, equal to or in excess of the initial sacrifice; or
3 by producing a psychic income, a positive feeling induced by investment ownership.

Investment return is therefore a function of income, capital return and psychic income.

Appraisal of the latter is neither vital nor straightforward and will not concern us greatly (but see page 30). Consideration of the first two factors is the essence of investment pricing and valuation.

INVESTMENTS

Property investments cannot be appraised in isolation, although the education and development of the valuation profession in many countries may suggest that this is so. By its nature, appraisal is a comparative or relative process, and property investments must at some stage be appraised in comparison with alternative investment vehicles (see pages 19–22). It is necessary in property investment appraisal to understand something of the nature of alternative outlets and their relative strengths and weaknesses. Four broad investment types will be briefly considered and analysed in comparison with property investment vehicles. These are:

1 bank deposits;
2 fixed interest securities;
3 index-linked gilts; and
4 equities, or ordinary shares.

The following analysis is rudimentary: further detail is provided by Rutterford (1993).

Bank deposits

Because cash is regarded as an alternative outlet for investment funds otherwise divided between fixed interest securities, equities and property, bank deposits are a useful starting point for a basic comparative investment analysis.

The common distinction between savings and investment does not help. As Sharpe (1985) puts it:

> A distinction is often made between investment and savings. The latter is defined as foregone consumption, with the former restricted to 'real' investment of the sort that increases national output in the future. While this distinction may prove useful in other contexts, it is not especially helpful for analysing the specifics of particular investments or even large classes of investment media. A deposit in a 'savings' account at a bank is investment in the eyes of a depositor.

In the UK, and for our purposes, bank deposits are identical in principle to building society accounts of the more common type. Each is characterized by the setting aside of cash in return for regular interest. This may be annual, six-monthly (as is typical with many building society accounts) or more regular. While the capital invested may appear to grow in such an account, it is important to note that what is really happening is that compound interest is being added to a fixed (in monetary terms) capital sum.

Rates of interest are typically not guaranteed for any substantial period and may vary with no specified limits. Consequently, a summary of the means of generation of return in a bank deposit investment (see page 7) can be stated as follows.

(a) *Capital* the investment provides a return of capital of an amount exactly equal in money terms to the original investment.

(b) *Income* the investment provides a return in the form of interest which may vary upwards or downwards over time.

Fixed interest securities

Conventional gilts and other fixed interest securities which are not index-linked are typically a major component of the portfolios of major investors (for our purposes this means insurance companies or pension funds (institutions)). Conventional fixed interest securities may be divided into gilt-edged securities (gilts), which are UK government fixed interest securities, and others, typically corporate fixed interest securities (debentures, loan stocks and preference shares, the latter strictly being fixed income securities providing dividends rather than interest). Our discussion and generalizations focus upon the particular characteristics of the much more common gilt, although the majority of comments made relate to all fixed interest securities. A suitable generic term for this type of investment is 'bonds'; the term 'stocks' is often used for ordinary shares (see pages 13–15).

Bonds are a means of borrowing cash. The UK government has in the past issued gilts for specific nationalization programmes and named the gilt accordingly. Currently, gilts are issued for general financing of government responsibilities. The modern names are Treasury, Exchequer and Funding.

Gilts are usually issued in amounts of £100 nominal value and will normally sell upon issue at a price close to this figure. By this means, the issuer assumes immediate use of the capital which changes hands in return for a commitment to pay interest in two equal 6-monthly instalments on two pre-specified dates, and to repay the nominal value at a specific date in the future (except in the case of undated gilts, which carry no commitment to repay the capital invested).

The amount of interest is fixed and determined by the coupon, decided before the time of issue of the gilt. The coupon is a rate of interest; the amount of interest per annum is the product of the coupon and the nominal value of, usually, £100. The amount of interest per 6 months is therefore given by

$$\text{Interest per 6 months} = \frac{\text{coupon} \times \text{nominal value}}{2}$$

For example, Exchequer $12\frac{1}{4}\%$ 1999 pays interest of

$$\frac{12\frac{1}{4} \times 100}{2} = £6.13 \text{ per 6 months}$$

The payment of interest continues until redemption of the gilt. Short-dated gilts are identified by a redemption date within 5 years; mediums by redemption within 5–15 years; longs by redemption over 15 years away; and undateds by unspecified redemption. For all apart from the latter types the redemption date is specified, like the coupon, at the date of issue; Exchequer $12\frac{1}{4}\%$ 1999, for example, is redeemed at a specified date in 1999. As time goes by, longs become mediums, mediums become shorts and shorts disappear as they are redeemed. Undateds continue unchanged, and are likely to remain so. While the government has the option to redeem after a given date, the six undated gilts which remain unredeemed all have coupons of between $2\frac{1}{2}$ per cent and 4 per cent, and no government will choose to replace these loans unless interest rates fall to very low levels.

Thus for redeemable fixed interest gilts held until the redemption date the cash flow to be produced by the investment can be predicted with certainty. Market prices will not, however, remain constant. Immediately after issue the stock market price-fixing mechanism will begin to operate, and market prices will fluctuate. Simplistically, if interest rates rise immediately after issue, the coupon is likely to become low in relation to new issues, the payment of interest will be comparatively less and the price of the bond will fall. The opposite would occur if interest rates fell as they did in 1982 and the early 1990s, producing large capital gains for many bondholders.

The market value of a gilt (as quoted in the financial press on a daily basis) represents a midpoint price around which gilts can be bought and sold. Given this readily available information and the certain income flow, the internal rate of return on fixed interest securities held to redemption can be accurately computed.

Table 1.1

Date	£
1 October 1995	(114.59)
22 March 1996	6.125
20 September 1996	6.125
22 March 1997	6.125
20 September 1997	6.125
22 March 1998	6.125
20 September 1998	6.125
22 March 1999	6.125 + 100 = 106.25

Take again Exchequer $12\frac{1}{4}$% 1999. This has a redemption date of 22 March. Let us assume that on 1 October 1995 £100 nominal value of this stock can be bought for £114.59. The timing and amount of expected cash flows are given in Table 1.1. (Note that tax deductions are ignored; in addition, this example ignores accrued interest, which must be considered when the date of purchase does not coincide with an interest payment date.)

This cash flow produces a half yearly rate of return of 3.72 per cent; annualized, this represents a before-tax internal rate of return or gross redemption yield of 7.58. Note, however, that this would normally be quoted in nominal terms, i.e. 2 × 3.72 per cent: see Figure 1.2.

This certainty is removed by the possibility of sale before redemption. As values move up and down, the prospect of selling the gilt to make a capital gain or loss arises. Given that future prices cannot be predicted, no certain calculation of internal rates of return can be made without an assumption that the gilt is held to redemption. It is, however, possible to be a little more positive by concluding that while future prices (and therefore gains and losses) cannot be predicted, there is a tendency for the value of the gilt to approach £100 plus the last interest payment as the redemption date approaches. Over time, interest payments become less important and the redemption value becomes more important. The value of a gilt with 6 months to run should thus be close to £100 plus the final interest payment.

The financial pages of national newspapers quote gross redemption yields on the nominal basis noted above. They also quote *interest yields* expressing the relationship between the current price and the annual interest payments.

1995								
High	Low	Stock			Price £	+ or −	Interest yield	Redemption yield
$118\frac{1}{2}$	$111\frac{1}{4}$	Exch.	$12\frac{1}{4}$ pc	1999	114.59	$+\frac{3}{4}$	10.69	7.58
Highest trading price in 1995	Lowest trading price in 1995	Stock	Coupon	Redemption year	Price	Price movement since last quote	Interest only yield	Nominal gross redemption yield

Figure 1.2 Typical gilt price information, British Funds

For irredeemable gilts only the latter is, of course, presented. Figure 1.2 shows a typical (mythical) extract.

The generation of return from government bonds can therefore be summarized as follows:

(a) *Capital*:   the investment provides a return of capital in an amount which may be more or less than the original investment. If held to redemption, the return will be the nominal value of £100; in any case, as the redemption date approaches the return of capital will tend towards this price.

(b) *Income*:   the investment produces an income in the form of interest, paid half yearly in arrears. Being determined by the coupon and the nominal value, this never varies: a bond is a fixed interest investment.

Index-linked gilts

Index-linked government bonds are a relatively recent innovation and their effect on the market is limited by their availability. Broadly speaking, they offer an income which is fixed in real, rather than monetary, terms and a redemption payment which is again fixed in real terms.

Parity with real values is attempted by tying interest payments and the redemption to the retail price index, albeit lagged by eight months. (This is to cope with the problem of accrued interest, which is included in the price of all gilts. Without lagging the interest payment, given that it could never be predicted, the price could not be calculated.) The coupon is the nominal interest, around 2–3 per cent to date.

The return on index-linked gilts is therefore the product of a nominal interest rate, an inflation-linked interest payment and an inflation-linked return of capital, normally a gain. While the calculation of the gross redemption yield is complex (see Rutterford 1993), it can be broadly estimated as $(1 + d)(1 + i) - 1$, where d is the inflation rate and i is the real return. Thus a 2 per cent index-linked stock, unless resold within a short period, has an unknown redemption yield in nominal terms, as this will depend upon the inflation rate between the time 8 months prior to purchase and the time 8 months prior to sale or redemption; but if inflation is expected to average 3 per cent, if the stock is held to redemption and if it is purchased at close to its nominal value of £100 then the expected redemption yield will be around $(1 + 0.03)(1 + 0.02) - 1, = 0.05060$ or 5.06 per cent. If compared with fixed interest gilts producing a known 6 or 7 per cent when held to redemption, these index-linked gilts would not be purchased in these conditions unless purchasers were greatly concerned with inflation risk (see Chapter 2).

The return generated by index-linked gilts is summarized below.

(a) *Capital*: the investment provides a return of capital in an amount which may be more or less than the original investment. However, given positive inflation, a monetary capital gain would be expected. The return of capital depends on the rate of inflation intervening between dates 8 months prior to purchase and 8 months prior to redemption. Assuming that the gilt is purchased at par on issue, the capital gain matches inflation, so that the price is maintained in real terms.

(b) *Income*: the investment provides a varying income equal to the nominal interest rate plus (minus) the lagged inflation (deflation) rate.

Ordinary shares

Ordinary shares, or equities, represent a share of ownership in a company. While they may or may not carry voting rights, all imply a fractional share in the equity value (total assets less debt) of a company. They are commonly issued with a nominal or par value of 25p.

Income is normally paid twice-yearly and is in the form of dividends (interim and final), which are determined by the company's profits and management policy, each of which may change from year to year. The income from shares, therefore, while it may have some relationship to the last declared dividend, is unpredictable.

An equity is 'irredeemable' in normal circumstances, other than by sale. The resale price is market determined and may be higher or lower than the purchase price. Again, therefore, capital return is unpredictable. Experience shows that the volatility of profits and dividend policy (among other factors) is reflected in the volatility of share prices. It should be borne in mind that there is no safety net as there is in the case of gilts with a guaranteed redemption; on the other hand, capital gain prospects are similarly unlimited.

Yield measures for ordinary shares are, as a consequence, largely unhelpful (although they are used a great deal by analysts). An internal rate of return, always the most complete return measure, can only be estimated given a prediction of resale date, resale price and all intervening interim and final dividends, or by projecting dividends to infinity (see page 14). This is so hazardous that it is rarely attempted. The only yield measure in common use is the relationship of last year's interim and final dividend to the current quoted price. Even next year's dividend yield can only be an estimate.

Dividend yield is no measure of total return. Low dividend yields may imply expected increases in dividends, expected capital gains or both. They are relatively volatile and do not form the basis of sound investment decision-making without the addition of a considerable volume of extra information. The price–earnings (P/E) ratio, a comparison of price per share with earnings per share, is a standard additional measure of the quality of the share, where a high P/E ratio may imply anticipated growth in earnings and therefore in share values. It can be used in the estimate of resale price in attempts to forecast holding period return, or IRR. Resale price is a product of earnings per share and the P/E ratio at the resale point, which may show cyclical fluctuation and be capable of some qualified estimation. More usually, however, the predicted IRR of an ordinary shareholding reflects the rationality that the value and therefore sale price of a share must ultimately reflect all future anticipated dividends. Assuming annual dividends,

$$P_0 = \frac{D_1}{1+e} + \frac{D_2}{(1+e)^2} + \frac{D_3}{(1+e)^3} \; \cdots$$

where P_0 is the price in year 0, D_1, D_2 and D_3 are expected dividends in years 1, 2 and 3 and e is the overall required return (target rate). If dividends are expected to increase in a common ratio (g), the series becomes

$$P_0 = \frac{D_1}{1+e} + \frac{D_1(1+g)}{(1+e)^2} + \frac{D_1(1+g)^2}{(1+e)^3} \; \cdots$$

Summing this geometric progression gives

$$P_0 = \frac{D_1}{e-g}$$

(Those familiar with common presentations of property valuation mathematics (see, for example, Baum and Mackmin 1989) may recognize '$e - g$' as a capitalization rate and the above formula as the income approach or investment method: of that, considerably more will follow.)

Such a model may be employed for valuation (estimation of a likely selling price for a share which has never traded on the stock market, for example) or analysis (estimation of anticipated return e). In either case it is instructive to note the effect of anticipated dividend or income growth.

For example, shares available at £1.25, last year's total dividend being 8p and expected to increase at a rate of 7 per cent per annum, would produce an estimated IRR of

$$1.25 = \frac{0.08}{e - 0.07}$$

$$e - 0.07 = \frac{0.08}{1.25}$$

$$e = 13.4\%$$

Such a model is naive, to say the least. It does, however, reveal a vital factor in property investment appraisal: anticipated growth in income and capital, g, and its effect upon initial yield. The initial or dividend yield in the example is low in comparison with the overall yield: this is fundamental and provides a central point of reference in this book. Chapter 2 develops this model further.

The return from ordinary shares is generated as follows.

(a) *Capital*: the investment may produce a return of capital which may exceed or be less than the original investment. All capital may be lost, however: at the same time, there is no limit on the possible amount or timing of redemption.

(b) *Income*: the investment provides a varying income dependent upon earnings and management policy.

Property

Property (in the UK and many Commonwealth countries) or real estate (in North America, Australia and elsewhere) may be acquired for many purposes other than investment. Broadly speaking, a distinction may be made between property owned for occupation (although there may be a simultaneous investment service performed by that property) and property owned for investment *per se*.

Property owned as an investment may be either freehold, connoting effective superior ownership, or leasehold, connoting an inferior form of ownership subject to a superior landlord, either leaseholder(s) or leaseholder(s) and freeholder. (For fuller details of UK land tenure, see Gray and Symes (1981).) The distinction between freehold and leasehold property considerably complicates a generalized view of property investment returns. While ownership of a freehold interest indicates perpetual ownership of indestructible land together with the more transient structure built upon it, ownership of a leasehold indicates a wasting asset. Yet this is too simplistic:

some leases retain their value after the lease end due to the phenomenon of key money (see Fraser 1984; Baum 1985) and the automatic renewal ensured by the operation of the 1954 Landlord and Tenant Act, and some freeholds exhibit a declining quality. Nonetheless, it is fair to generalize the permanent nature of a freehold and the temporary nature of a leasehold. It is in these two forms that property investments are almost universally held in the UK, especially by larger scale investors. Figure 1.3 shows the general relationship of the capital values over time of freehold and leasehold investments in a period of inflation.

It can be seen from Figure 1.3(a) that in a period of inflation a freehold property investment may be expected to show a profit upon resale. Obsolescence may contribute to a declining (although difficult to measure) building component value, so that refurbishment or redevelopment may be necessary to maintain performance, but the general trend of value is upward.

A leasehold interest in the same property, on the other hand, would peak in value and enter a period of rapid decline to zero by the end of the lease. The same is broadly true of an investment in leasehold commercial property.

Nonetheless, the problem of building depreciation or obsolescence of freehold buildings should not, as has usually been the case in the property

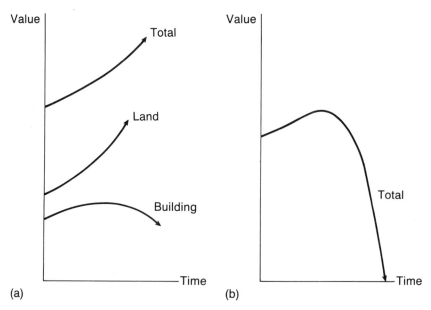

Figure 1.3 Term structure of property investment values: (a) freehold;
(b) leasehold

world, be understated. Poorly designed buildings located in low land value areas will produce a more rapid fall off in performance than carefully restored and refurbished buildings in the City of London. Not to distinguish between these vastly different investment types would be most dangerous, and in this text we suggest approaches to the problems.

The income produced by a property investment is in the form of rent reduced by operating expenses of various types. While operating expenses will be incurred both regularly (management, service provision) and infrequently (repairs), rent will normally be received at regular intervals, quarterly in advance being typical in the UK. Analogous to the stock market and its differentiation between cum-dividend and ex-dividend investments is the apportionment procedure applied to rents received in advance in respect of a full rent period during which the property is sold. Apportionment of the rent which relates to the period between completion and the next rent date is in the favour of the purchaser and is in effect deducted from the purchase price (see Bornand 1985).

The payment of rent is governed by the provisions of the lease. There is no standard arrangement in the English speaking world: US leases are of varying types but are rarely for longer than 10 years and often for 3-year periods; Australian leases of offices are typically for 9 years; Singapore and Hong Kong leases are usually for 3-year periods; and the UK has a standard (although increasingly questioned) 25-year lease which appears to favour UK landlords and to suggest their peculiar strength in the market.

In continental Europe, 5- and 10-year leases are very common, and the UK lease is clearly at odds with standard practice elsewhere (see Lofstedt and Baum 1993; and Crosby et al. 1993).

It is apparent that there is little conformity. The regularity with which rents may be increased, however, is slightly more standard. While the USA, Hong Kong and Singapore 3-year lease is usually at a fixed rent and the Australian 9-year lease incorporates 3-yearly reviews, the UK lease usually fixes rents for 5-year intervals with upward only reviews while only a minority of European leases often have rents indexed annually. (Longer North American leases may have rents tied to the rate of inflation or, more often, to tenant's turnover; this is rare in the UK.) The pattern of rental in the typical prime UK investment property is therefore stepped upwards (in a period of inflation or growth) at 5-yearly intervals. Rents at each review point are renegotiated in line with the open market rental or estimated rental value (ERV). It is arguable that ERVs reflect the fixed nature of the review period and are higher than their annual equivalents would be, but there is no published empirical proof for this. Where longer review periods arise (7-yearly, 14-yearly and 21-yearly reviews still appear in continuing

UK leases) the principle of 'uplift' may be applied to increase the rent beyond the equivalent ERV for a 5-year review pattern.

In summary, therefore, the return from property is generated as follows.

(a) *Capital*: the investment may produce a return of capital by resale which may exceed or be less than the original investment. In freehold investments there is an effective limit (land value) to any loss; in leaseholds, a decline to nil value must eventually be suffered.

(b) *Income*: the investment provides a varying income depending upon rental values, themselves a product of the demand for use of the property and the supply of alternatives. Variance of the income is reduced by leases and long review periods; upward only reviews will produce, at worst, a level income.

Summary

To summarize this broad overview of five investment types, it is useful to identify similarities.

Ordinary shares and property are fundamentally different from bank deposits and fixed interest securities in two major respects. First, ordinary shares and property are both what Sharpe (1985) calls real or equity investments, representing ownership of tangible assets. Bank deposits and fixed interest securities are not real investments.

This difference gives rise to a second difference: broadly speaking, equity or real investments perform well in periods of inflation (they are inflation proof to some degree), while money investments perform badly (inflation prone). The period of significant inflation witnessed in the UK from the 1950s until recently was a major cause of a rise in property and share prices in relation to alternative non-equity investments.

Sitting uncomfortably between these pairings is the relatively new index-linked gilt which is not a real investment, but which will perform well in inflationary periods. Table 1.2 illustrates this.

Table 1.2 A classification of investments

	Real investments	Monetary investments
Inflation proof	Equities Properties	Index-linked gilts
Inflation prone		Bank deposits Fixed interest securities

There are, of course, many other examples of investments which demonstrate or question these classifications. Leaseholds producing a fixed profit rent are inflation-prone real investments, as are fixed freehold ground rents, for example. During the first part of the 1990s these inflation-prone property investments were joined by the large number of over-rented (partially fixed interest) properties, let on long leases with upwards only rent reviews. So this limited list of five investment types is neither finite nor comprehensive. It does, however, serve to set property investment in a context of alternative investment opportunities.

COMPARATIVE INVESTMENT APPRAISAL

The context of alternative investment types within which property may be appraised is justified by the investment policies of the UK's major investors, the larger insurance companies and pension funds, which have in recent decades pursued a policy of portfolio diversification by retaining a mix of ordinary shares and fixed interest gilts but increasing holdings of property and, more recently, of index-linked gilts. The theoretical basis of such a diversification policy is considered later (see Chapter 2); the progress of institutional investors in the property market over the last two decades, when for many funds property holdings were built up from nominal levels to around one-quarter of all assets, is described in Chapter 4 and is well charted elsewhere. (See Plender 1982; Darlow 1983; Fraser 1984; McIntosh and Sykes 1984; DTZ Debenham Thorpe 1994.)

More critically, the property valuation profession has in recent years and now over a very long period been the subject of scrutiny by outside specialists as a result of this growing involvement in the property market by institutional investors. An early example is a report published by stockbrokers W. Greenwell & Co. in 1976, commonly referred to as 'The Greenwell Report' (Greenwell & Co. 1976). This report contains a critique of property investment appraisals and was regarded as displaying remarkable temerity in recommending a change in appraisal techniques. It can hardly be said that Greenwell & Co. were misguided by a lack of understanding of the art: the very methods they promoted (equated yield/discounted cash flow (DCF) appraisals) are now being practised more consistently by valuers. And the need for this questioning arose out of the secondary banking collapse fuelled by the property crash of 1973–4 for which, according to John Plender, valuers must accept some responsibility: 'blind faith in the wisdom of the valuer will leave the British banking system vulnerable to collapse if property investment bubbles over into speculation'

(Plender 1982). The property crash of the early 1990s appears to have proved him right.

Greenwell & Co. must take some credit for the appearance in 1980 of the interim report of a major research project into property appraisal methods (Trott 1980), which repeated the main Greenwell appeal for DCF-based valuation techniques. At the same time, other outside forces with either a general interest or expertise in the practice of investment were (and are) making inroads into the valuer's old areas of influence.

Valuers' reputations are endangered particularly by a belief that their methods are incorrect, illogical and, by deduction, capable of leading to inaccurate appraisals. The Greenwell Report insinuated that valuations were often too high as a result of blind reliance on an over-simple methodology. The main aim of the valuer, therefore, must be to ensure accuracy.

However, as argued in the first section of this chapter, this is not enough. Appraisals must also be rational. While institutions view property as an investment, most valuers and surveyors view property as bricks, planning permissions and legal interests. The more important clients are mobile between all types of investments: while numbers can be compared with numbers, bricks cannot be compared with share certificates.

In 1983, M. J. Patrick made a plea for greater cross-media awareness:

> Senior decision-makers, with overall responsibility for all investment, including property, are not surveyors but have backgrounds as actuaries or accountants. Understandably they are not necessarily impressed with statements that property is 'different' and incapable of being reported in a manner similar to that used for fixed interest and equity funds ... as investment becomes more competitive there are a growing number of advisers attempting to make inroads into areas which, traditionally, have been the preserve of professional surveyors. These advisers have already demonstrated considerable skill with other investment media. They bring with them new (to property) and more analytical approaches to property investment. Consequently if surveyors are to maintain their position they must, at the very least, attune themselves with alternative approaches. ...

Illustrative of this problem is the manner in which the UK property valuer appraises leaseholds. Comparison is the valuer's main tool, but rather than comparing a 10-year leasehold with (for example) 10-year dated bonds, the traditional valuer goes through a tortuous route (see Chapters 3 and 4) by which he attempts to make the leasehold appear to be broadly comparable with the freehold by perpetualizing the terminable income. He does this in order to compare property investment with property investment rather than with alternative investment media. This is no longer appropriate (see Chapter 8).

To restate the problem, valuers are increasingly required to provide analytical, defensible and accurate valuations that are capable of comparative interpretation. Traditional training within the surveying profession can hinder the development of valuers into investment specialists.

Yet valuers are being placed under specific pressure to come up with answers to problems which, we suspect, have already been addressed by outside professions. Two examples of this are the current unanswered questions in DCF-based investment valuations – what discount rate should be applied, and how should we forecast future income flows? In the solution of each of these a lateral approach, taking us into the stock of knowledge concerning the appraisal of other investments, will lead to a greater awareness of the place of property in the investment spectrum. Valuers and property analysts need to be able to develop such an awareness for three reasons:

1 The return on other investments may be a measure against which a property investment should be appraised. For example, should the redemption yield on conventional gilts be generally accepted as an indication of the equated yield which should be used in DCF-based property appraisals?

2 The return on other investments may be a guide to the future value of property. If conventional gilts yield 16 per cent when prime shops yield $3\frac{1}{2}$ per cent, when no rental growth is currently exhibited and little is expected (as in 1982), it is possible to conclude that prime shops will fall in price, as indeed they did. Advice to a vendor or purchaser should reflect that view.

3 Subject to (1) above, the return on other investments may be a guide to the implied necessary future performance of property. For example, levels of implied rental and capital growth can be computed given information regarding redemption yields on bonds and initial yields on property. Such information will aid the investor's choice between alternative property investments and improve the quality of professional advice.

Richard Ratcliffe (1965) summarizes our views, and our reasons for producing this book.

In the upward push of the appraisal fraternity toward the cherished professional goal, an essential reform is the rationalisation and updating of conventional valuation theory and methodology. We need to understand the valuation process as a form of economic analysis or research leading to a prediction of the most probable selling price of the property under conditions of uncertainty. We must shake off the older view of appraisal as the measurement of an inherent quality of real estate. We must recognise that 'the' value of a property cannot be expressed in a single unchallengeable figure. The appraiser must frankly admit that his predictions are fraught with various degrees of dependability. Thus he is responsible for giving to his client the benefit of his opinion of the degree of certainty of his findings, expressed as a probability qualification to the value figure in his report. We must view real estate valuations as investment analysis, a counterpart to security analysis.

THE IMPORTANCE OF VALUERS AND VALUATIONS

It may be thought that property valuers in the UK value property – in other words, they estimate what a property is worth. In fact they rarely do, because what they usually do is pricing, or estimating the most likely selling price of a building.

In the 1930s, property valuers were able to give investment advice. They were good at valuation in its best sense – they estimated the value of something to a buyer.

Today, they do not give investment advice. Valuation has become something else, specifically the estimation of the most likely selling price of a property, whether or not it makes sense. They know less than many would like them to know about the other markets, and property is sidelined from the mainstream investment world partly because valuers talk a different language.

The larger institutional investors have been forced to take the lead and to invest in solutions, largely because they are exposed to the other markets. Valuation in the stock market means estimating the value of a stock to a buyer. It does not mean estimating price, because the screen gives away that information to anybody and the *Financial Times* publishes it daily. Property valuation, on the other hand, is now a mysterious art/science devoted to the practice of estimating market price subject to a series of often ridiculous assumptions. Property valuers rarely value property.

None of this would matter if it had no impact on the property market and the wider economy. But it does. It is increasingly realized that the property market affects the economy (University of Aberdeen 1994). The boom and bust of the 1980s and early 1990s, and to some extent the depth of the later recession, is usually blamed on the developers, banks and investors. One common thread links these players: they were all advised by valuers. Is it enough for valuers to answer the question of value with a single snapshot in time or should they be asked for and provide the context of the valuation? Uninformed clients, however, make important decisions based upon the 'value' information provided by valuers. It has been informally suggested to one of the authors that 90 per cent of bank lending transactions in the late 1980s were decided by non-property professionals based upon a market value. Should bankers have asked for more information on future trends in values or should the expert valuers have informed the clients of the questions they should have asked?

Informed clients are fully aware of the limitations of pricing and pricing techniques. What are now collectively called conventional valuation techniques are not forward looking (and are thought to be essentially backward looking by some, based on comparisons of old transactions). It has to be assumed that during the (usually long) marketing period there is no change in values (!). The so-called valuations are essentially adaptive. As things happen, valuers adapt the inputs into the model; yields (and capitalization rates) fall as the market improves.

Adaptive models are very good at explaining the rise of the stock market through the early mid-1980s. But they fail to pick up shocks, like the crash of October 1987. They persuade investors that the world is continually new, that trends exist, that the market 'is doing well'.

Rational models, on the other hand, look forward. They failed to explain the rise of the stock market through early 1987, which is to their credit. They question price levels which are difficult to explain in terms of expectations. Trends do not exist, and the market cannot be 'doing well'. Instead, it has done well — but that probably means it will do very badly.

Using adaptive models, valuers over-priced property in 1980. They underpriced it in 1986. They over-priced it in 1989.

It is not suggested that changing to rational models (cash flow forecasts) will solve this problem overnight. However, the following should be noted.

1 Even without perfect foresight it is possible to demonstrate that rational valuations would not have allowed the same exaggeration of under- and over-pricing over the 1980s.
2 The property world is now full of complexities like short leaseholds, reversions and froths. Over-rented properties in particular are here for a very long time, and the only way they can be properly valued is by using a rational model. Some valuers are either unable or unwilling to attempt this.
3 If valuers do not question market prices, who is advising the sellers, the buyers, the developers and the lenders of the rationality of prices?
4 Finally, do valuers contribute to property booms and busts? It is possible

to argue that they are forced to reflect moods of euphoria or depression, perpetuating a market state until it explodes. This is bad for valuers, it is damaging for the property market, and it is a disaster for the economy.

This book attempts to encourage the irresistible drift to rationality in property investment appraisal. Through the development and application of rational techniques, valuers will once again be able to provide valuable investment advice.

Chapter 2 progresses our aims by introducing the general foundations of investment analysis.

2

Principles of investment analysis

QUALITIES OF INVESTMENTS

What is a good investment? A simple answer to this seemingly simple question is 'one which produces a high return'. Previously we have identified returns as deriving from three sources: income, capital return and psychic income. A good investment is one which produces high levels of these in comparison with the price paid.

Most investments are traded in an atmosphere of uncertainty. It is not possible to predict with accuracy what the level of return will be. Even fixed interest gilts held to redemption produce a return which is uncertain in real terms and dependent upon future inflation levels for purchasing power value.

Investors will attempt to reduce uncertainty to its minimum by market research and other means. Information which is freely available is impounded into prices, so investments promising a high return will (all other factors being equal) sell for more. Jacob and Pettit (1984) describe this 'efficient market hypothesis' as follows.

Market participants, acting in their own self-interest, use available information to attempt to secure more desirable (higher returns, *ceteris paribus*) portfolio positions. In doing so they collectively ensure that price movements in response to new information are instantaneous and unbiased and will 'fully reflect' all relevant information. Competition among participants to secure useful information will drive security prices from one equilibrium level to another so that the change in price in response to new information will be independent of the prior change in price. Price changes will be a random walk in response to the information.

Investors in the five categories summarized in Chapter 1 will typically hold some information which is not uncertain. This will be:

1 the price of the investment;
2 the current income produced — for bank deposits, this is the current interest rate; for fixed interest gilts, the coupon; for index-linked gilts, the next interest payment (based on the retail price index already published); for ordinary shares, the last dividend payment; and for property, the current contract rent.

Absolute certainty over the current income level leads to the use of the *initial yield* as a common market measure by which investments can be related. This is given by

$$\frac{\text{net current income}}{\text{price}}$$

The level of this initial yield will be determined by several factors which determine the quality of an investment. A high-quality investment is expected to produce a low initial yield because the market would bid a high price in relation to the level of current income. This initial yield depends upon a series of considerations or features which are largely unrelated to the current income level, and which are considered below.

Income and capital growth

The current income level may not be a good indicator of future income levels. Consequently, the initial yield may not indicate the continuing income yield that will be produced by an investment over its holding period. Where that yield is expected to increase over time, the initial yield will be low and a higher price will be paid.

Fixed interest gilts produce a fixed income. The price should reflect that fact. There is no prospect of income growth or, conversely, of monetary income loss. The initial yield is a perfect indication of the continuing income yield ('running yield').

Index-linked gilts, on the other hand, produce an index-linked income. As long as inflation is expected to be positive, income growth may be anticipated and the initial yield should therefore be lower, *ceteris paribus*, than for fixed interest gilts.

Ordinary shares produce dividends which depend upon:

1 profits, and
2 management dividend and reinvestment strategy.

The latter is often used to smooth away variations in the former, so that a broad relationship between inflation and dividends may be theorized via profit levels, and in an inflationary era the monetary profits of an average company might be expected to increase (except in the curious circumstances of 'stagflation': see Fraser (1984)).

For property, a similar long-term relationship between inflation and rents may be discernible. For example, the Investors Chronicle Hillier Parker (ICHP) Rent Index (May 1985) shows that over the period 1977–85 inflation was accurately matched by rental values as measured by the index (ICHP Rent Index adjusted for inflation, 1977 = 100, 1985 = 101).

Other causes of income growth may be considered additionally to inflation. There may be prospects for real growth in addition to inflation (see, for example, the period 1965–73 in the ICHP Rent Index adjusted for inflation, in which 1965 = 87, 1973 = 155). These possibilities for real growth may be discernible above the normal cyclical nature of the market. Particular sectors of the market, by type or region, may demonstrate this particularly well (for example, shops in the ICHP Rent Index adjusted for inflation, 1977 = 100, 1994 = 176). One of the major problems of this type of analysis is the quality of data. There are no such things as definitive rental value indices and it was not until the mid-1960s that any indices of rental value movements were published. One study (Crosby 1985) constructs shop rental value indices for Nottingham City Centre for 1910–81. The results from 1910 to 1960 are set out in Chapter 3 (Table 3.1) and show that between 1910 and 1960 a real growth rate above inflation of 1.25 per cent per annum was achieved. Theorizing over-simplistically, a supply artificially restricted by planning controls may be set against increasing demand as behaviour patterns change and population increases to cause real rental growth. A similar effect may be translated into real dividend increases for ordinary shares; it is not present for fixed interest (conventional) gilts.

There may also be monopoly profits which accrue to property owners. Property interests are unique: although the impact of heterogeneity will vary according to circumstances, extra gains may be made by exploiting the resulting monopoly position. An extreme example of this is marriage value. The owner of a mid-length leasehold interest will almost certainly be unable to sell to an investor at a price which matches the gain which the freehold reversioner could make by its surrender. Monopoly profits may accrue as a result to both freeholder and leaseholder. Other 'special purchasers' may appear: funds which are especially keen to buy a south-east prime shop, for example, for portfolio balance.

Less clear-cut is the gain made upon re-zoning or betterment. This may be diluted by competition, but the siting of a new motorway or the reallocation of land planned for commercial development may well produce capital gains in excess of inflation and a reasonable real growth. These can also be termed monopoly profits: they may be the product of the exploitation of monopolistic information or of monopolistic land ownership.

Finally, gearing or leverage, the use of borrowed funds to exaggerate capital and income growth, is particularly suited to property investment. Simple house purchase illustrates this strategy. Suppose a house purchaser has a choice of an all cash buy for £50,000 or a £30,000 interest-only 10 per cent loan and £20,000 equity input. Suppose prices increase by 50 per cent over 3 years. The comparison given in Table 2.1 emerges.

A 75 per cent capital increase resulting from gearing may be compared with an ungeared 50 per cent gain. Such gains can be maximized by increasing the gearing level in times of high price increases, where interest rates are low and where taxation rules are favourable. The risk of financial failure resulting from interest rate increases or falling prices is at the same time increased by such a policy (a risk cruelly exposed over the first 3 years of the 1990s for those borrowing high percentages of outlay at the peak of the market pricing cycle); but the general inflationary trend since the Second World War and the particular experience of 1960–72, when many massive gains resulted from such policies (see Marriott 1967; and Rose 1985), provides an example of a sustained period which demonstrated the benefits of gearing. While equities may be geared (for example, by the use of options), property is the perfect asset in this respect.

These four constituents of growth have produced many valuable property companies and helped to underpin the popular nature of property investment during the 1970s and 1980s. Income growth was directly translated

Table 2.1

	All cash	60% mortgage
House value in 3 years	£75,000	£75,000
Equity in 3 years	£75,000	£45,000
Less initial equity	£50,000	£20,000
Less interest payments (compounded)	£0	£9,930
Equity gain (t)	£25,000	£15,070
Equity gain (%)	50%	75.35%

into capital growth, and it might be surmized that (*ceteris paribus*) the geared purchase of property in an improving area close to a new development or traffic improvements in a period of inflation is an excellent investment, examples of which have been common over the last 25 years.

Operating expenses

Once the purchase of an investment has been completed, the investor must face the prospect of continued expense necessitated by ownership. For bank deposits, such operating expenses are nil, apart from the investor's own time spent in checking accounts. For securities, the management of a given investment (rather than a portfolio) is again reduced to keeping an eye on the financial pages. For property, on the other hand, operating expenses derive from several sources. Repair and maintenance costs, insurance premiums, rent review fees, management (rent collection, periodic inspection, services management) fees, shortfalls in service charges, rates (in some circumstances), re-letting fees, refurbishment costs, dilapidations claims and various legal expenses arising out of disputes with the public, tenants or adjoining owners contribute to a potentially high annual expenditure for the property investment owner, and may increase required initial yields.

Liquidity, marketability, transfer costs

Liquidity (for our purposes) is the ease and certainty with which an asset can be converted to cash at, or close to, its market value. Bank deposits are almost perfectly liquid; gilts are usually convertible to cash within one day; equities may be transformed to cash within a week to a month. Property, on the other hand, is illiquid. A quick sale will not usually be possible unless a low price is accepted. Even then, the period between a decision to sell and receipt of cash can be expected to exceed 3 months.

Contributing to property's illiquidity are a trio of factors. *Marketability* describes the reserve of potential buyers for an investment and the speed and ease with which they may be contacted. For large property investments – buildings worth more than £20 million, say – the number of potential buyers may be small. For unusual investments (for example, Land's End) the potential market may be difficult to target and advertising may be highly inefficient. On the other hand, the stock exchange ensures the marketability of most gilts and equities.

The *indivisibility* of property as an investment contributes to its lack of marketability and therefore to its illiquidity. The possibility of sale of part of an investment reduces the impact of this problem and enables flexible financial management. Property can be physically divided, divided into freehold and leaseholds, or split into time shares, but it remains in general a fundamentally indivisible investment, with a high minimum outlay. This explains the drive towards a unitized property market in the late 1980s. However, until a unitized market becomes established or syndication becomes acceptable and popular in the UK, the purchase and sale of small units of a property investment will not normally be possible. This is not true of the alternatives.

The *transfer costs* necessitated when a decision to sell is finally translated into cash are higher than those associated with the alternatives. Stamp duty, conveyancing fees and agents' fees on purchase are nearly matched by conveyancing fees and agents' fees on sale: these may total 3 per cent and 2.5 per cent respectively. A more likely transfer cost for equities is around $\frac{1}{2}$ per cent for a reasonable volume and is likely to be less for gilts.

Illiquidity and its associates may therefore be said to be highest for property in comparison to the chosen alternatives. It has been argued (Fraser 1985b) that the infrequency of property trading as compared with trading frequency in the stock market reduces the importance of this factor: but infrequency of trading probably results from illiquidity. The fact remains that cash tied up in property is, pound for pound, less liquid than cash tied up elsewhere. This has two implications: first, it increases the chances of a company becoming financially embarrassed and put out of business by lenders (see page 37); second, it decreases the chances of attractive alternatives being acquired. For property companies, the illiquidity of property may be said to be much more of a problem than it is for the larger institutions. In any case, it should increase required initial yields.

Psychic income

For many smaller investors property has an appeal unmatched by the alternatives. For some, this may be a prestige value: for others, it may be the opportunity for exercising positive management and, while perhaps increasing return, offering self-employment. Driving past farmland may hold more appeal for some (even fund managers) than reading the financial pages; building naming rights may be a more tangible example of the psychic income which may be derived from property ownership. Whatever its effect – noticeable in some cases, non-existent in others – psychic income is a positive input into the quality of property as an investment, which may reduce the required initial yield.

Tax efficiency

The tax efficiency of an investment refers to the degree to which a gross return is reduced to a net return for the individual investor. Given the different and complex tax positions of individuals, institutions and companies alike, it is impossible to generalize regarding the relative appeal of a real estate investment. However, it warrants thorough attention in each individual analysis.

Risk

Introduction

Of very great importance is the degree of risk attached to an investment. Some finance texts view risk as the major determinant of return; modern portfolio theory contributes to this importance by regarding the investment decision as a trade-off between expected returns and risk (see Brigham 1985). Branch (1985) is more circumspect, suggesting that 'investors will generally trade off some expected return for a reduction in risk'. A simple conclusion may be drawn: risk increases the required initial yield.

But what is risk? Reilly (1985) suggests that it is 'uncertainty regarding the expected rate of return from an investment'. Is there anything intrinsically unattractive about uncertainty when the expected rate of return may be much higher, or much lower, than expected? The answer to this question is supported by empirical rather than theoretical evidence. The typical investor is demonstrably risk-averse.

Experiments carried out in university classes usually bear this out. Despite the unreality engendered by the lack of real money in such an environment the following game is a useful test of risk-aversion. The tutor offers for sale ten tickets, each of which gives the right to a cheque. Five cheques for £50 and five cheques for £100 are to be distributed on a random basis with a 50:50 chance of each being handed over in return for a ticket in any one case. The class holds 15–20 students. Tickets are sold by means of sealed tender, so that only the ten highest bids are successful. Unsuccessful bidders lose no money.

The prices obtained for tickets always indicate risk-aversion. £75 would not be an unrealistic offer, balancing a chance of £25 profit with an equal chance of £25 loss. But students rarely bid up to £75. One such series of bids from 15 students was as follows:

£80	£70 ⎫		£50 ⎫		
£75	£65 ⎪		£50 ⎪		
£74	£60 ⎬ offers accepted		£50 ⎬ offers refused		
£74	£50 ⎪		£40 ⎪		
£70	£50 ⎭		£40 ⎭		

In a more competitive market place, the successful £50 bidders would be less fortunate. The £80 bidder showed some property market optimism and a confidence in his luck. The £75 bid was, as suggested above, a neutral offer but the other bids illustrate risk-aversion. They equated the 50 per cent chance of a considerable gain with the 50 per cent chance of a much smaller loss. The median bid of £60 equated a £40 gain with a £10 loss. The two £40 bids show an excessive degree of suspicion over the sincerity of the tutor.

Uncertainty regarding the expected rate of return from an investment is seen as unattractive and results in devaluation. Ten certain £75 returns would have produced £750; the tickets offered netted only £668 for the same eventual cost to the offerer. Risky investments are less valuable.

Sources of risks

The sources of property risk are manifold, and many are unique to this investment form. They may be distinguished as follows.

1   *Tenant risk* is the chance that the tenant will affect returns by his actions. The most serious concern of the investor will be the chance of voids, that is, the possibility of the tenant vacating the premises and paying no rent. Even where long leases are signed by tenants, the possibility of bankruptcy must be considered. Legal actions are expensive and ponderous where actions to recover rent are undertaken.

Tenants may fail to perform repairing and insuring obligations. They may cause physical damage to or stigmatize a property. They may alienate adjoining owners or other tenants.

These prospects lend a risk to property which is near-unique. Perhaps the closest parallel is the risk of investing in ordinary shares which derives from bad management policies; it is much reduced, if it can be paralleled at all, in government securities and bank deposits.

2   *Sector risk* is the chance that sectoral price movements affect the subject investment. Such a risk is certainly present in the ordinary share market,

where the choice of sector may be vital. Electricals may underperform industrials and chemicals; within that sector, microelectronics may underperform household goods.

A property's sector risk is more sharply focused than this. Given the 'lumpiness' of property investment, where large sums of money may be tied up in one investment, property is particularly prone to sector and regional risk.

Performance differences occur between sectors and regions caused by changes in the rents and capitalization rates. For example, although shop average yields fell between 1977 and 1985, industrial yields rose by nearly 200 basis points (the ICHP average industrial yield was 8.5 per cent in 1977 and 10.2 per cent in May 1985).

The average industrial yield shows a greater variation by region. The south-east industrial average yield was 8.8 per cent in 1977 and by 1985 had returned to the same figure. The industrial yield in the north was also 8.8 per cent in 1977, but had risen to 11.9 per cent by 1985 (May) and rents had remained static since 1980, with corresponding real declines in value.

An industrial property in the north, bought in 1977 and having performed as the index, with the yield increase of 8.8 per cent to 11.9 per cent, would show an 8-year average annual return of just 1.47 per cent between May 1977 and 1985. A property in the south-east would have an annual average return of 10.4 per cent over the same period.

This combination of rental growth or decline and capitalization rate change can cause significant short-term variations in total returns. For example, the Hillier Parker index of returns to City offices fell from 1,058 to 530 between November 1989 and May 1993. During the same period the industrial index rose from 1,284 to 1,395.

Overlaid upon this is international risk. UK funds have been seen to spread their property investments in recent decades through the UK, Europe and North America. Both the relative performance of property rental values and yields in these areas and exchange rate fluctuations contribute to a pronounced sector risk in individual property investment which cannot so easily be diversified away by exploiting the lower unit of investment which typifies other markets. (On the other side of the coin, depending upon the nature of the liabilities of the investor, international diversification can be an efficient reducer of risk in the portfolio context: see Wurtzebach and Baum (1993)).

3 *Structural risk* is the chance of high repair costs, high maintenance costs or refurbishment becoming necessary, and eventually rebuilding becoming necessary, either through structural failure or economic or functional

obsolescence. Such risks are not paralleled in other markets other than indirectly and even then in a highly diversified manner. (For example, there may be a structural risk attaching to the performance of ordinary shares in a heavy industry company with one old manufacturing plant, but this risk type would be much reduced in the case of a chain of retail shops, where many more units (if owned freehold) would diversify such risk and reduce its impact upon performance.)

Despite considerable recent output (Salway 1986; Baum 1991), much work remains to be completed in the general area of property depreciation and obsolescence (see page 231). It is not currently easy to generalize about the life of building types. It is, however, possible to say that freehold interests in prime shop units are much less prone to structural risk (often the buildings are old yet solidly constructed, having transcended the usual cycle of redevelopment; they are simple, ground floor cubes; and the responsibility for shop fronts, fittings and so on is transferred to the tenant) than are modern industrial units (where the nature of occupation, the nature of construction and technological impact upon industry reduce economic life). It is also clear that land is less likely to depreciate in normal circumstances so that property investments with a proportionately larger land value are less prone to obsolescence and hence to structural risk. Office buildings in the City of London (for example) are less prone to structural risk than similar buildings in Houston where land values are less protected by physical boundaries and planning restrictions, and are in any event lower due to the relative eminence of the City of London as a financial centre.

Other structural risks may be passed on to tenants through full repairing and insuring leases, but the ultimate responsibility for obsolescence and fundamental defects rests with the property owner who consequently shoulders a risk unique to this form of investment.

4 *Legislation risk* is the chance of changes in case law and statute law which directly affect investment returns. Certain property investors have suffered in this respect in past decades by the introduction and extension of the Rent Acts, the Leasehold Reform Act, VAT, the Town and Country Planning Act and others (see Baum and Sams 1991). As one man's meat is another man's poison, so the concept of 'shifting value' identified in the Uthwatt Report (1942) probably resulted in balancing gains for others. For example, the rental values of residential properties outside the Rent Acts increased as protected tenancy rents became artificially depressed. More generally, legislation risk can have an upside as well as a downside. The introduction of Sunday trading, for example, doubtless increased the relative value of out of town shopping outlets.

Property is therefore especially prone to legislation risk. Equities are not exempt from this: health and safety regulations can have a massive impact upon drug companies, for example. Nonetheless, the experience of some residential landlords upon extension of the Rent Acts and the introduction of the Leasehold Reform Act 1967, while probably of limited impact, sharply focused property investment as a high legislation risk sector.

5 *Taxation risk* is related to the above category, and describes the chance of imposition of new taxes upon the investment type or of alterations in current taxes. Property can be uniquely prone to taxation risk. Prior to massive institutional investment, it was possible to generalize that the person in the street was much less likely (aside from home ownership) to be a property investor than a stock market investor; that is still true in terms of direct investment. Property is easily identified as a taxation target and is not electorally disastrous, as long as home ownership is avoided. This fact in itself explains the tax incentives given to single house ownership (capital gains tax exemption, tax relief on mortgage interest, the now-abolished partial tax relief on insurance premiums for policies used in endowment mortgages) in a context of relative disincentive for private property investment. (In the USA, tax allowances and particularly beneficial depreciation schedules coupled with syndication of ownership interests and a free rental market in all sectors made it much easier to invest in property outside the family home prior to the 1986 tax reforms; and only in 1985 was tax relief on multiple property ownership abolished in Australia.) Taxes upon UK property investments apparently affect only the corporate sector and the wealthy. (Many institutional funds are tax exempt.)

Local authority rates are constantly under the public eye and are unlikely to vary greatly; however, while they tax occupation rather than ownership, it is clear that rate increases cause rent (and return) reductions. The introduction of rate free (for 10 years) enterprise zones, for example, increased property values within the zones (albeit at the expense of immediately surrounding areas: see, for example, MacGregor *et al*. (1985)); and the introduction of the Uniform Business Rate and the rating revaluation in 1990 had an impact on relative values.

More importantly, new taxes such as development land tax, introduced in 1976, can have an enormous impact upon return. The introduction of capital gains tax in 1965 had a great redistributive effect; the indexation of capital gains tax in 1982 has reduced this impact. The effect of VAT on rents was forecast to be significant although its actual impact has not appeared to be as much as predicted.

Various income tax reliefs for particular categories of property investment – woodlands, for example, or industrial buildings – are constantly in
danger of adjustment or abolition. Taxation risk for property is a major
factor which is less likely to attack the alternative markets.

6 *Planning risk* is the risk that central or local government planning policies (in the broadest sense, including transport policy, regional policy,
power policy and so on) impinge negatively or positively upon property
investment values. At the regional level, policies of redistribution (such as
the siting of government departments in depressed areas) will have broad
effects; at the local level, proposals for such traffic improvements as the
M25 and the Channel Tunnel had an immediate impact upon values. At the
individual level, particular planning decisions have an enormous impact
upon value. The downside corollary is a speculative purchase of land with
development potential which eventually settles upon someone else's land,
and it is of course downside risk that equates with most investors' perception of risk as an investment quality.

The effect of planning is so enormous that further elucidation is probably
unnecessary. Let it suffice to say that its effects upon other sectors of the
investment market are less pronounced.

7 *Legal risk* is the chance that the title to an investment is unsatisfactory
or that it is discovered that a right exists over the subject land which affects
its value. It is the risk that a rent review notice is missed; or, conversely,
that a request for an excessive rent is not challenged in time by a tenant.
These possibilities are generally unique to property. Each will be someone's
loss balanced by someone's gain; to all, they represent risks.

In contrast with the above risk classifications, designed for application
to property and within which there are direct and indirect applications to
alternative markets, finance theory applies three broad categories of risk to
investment. Reilly (1985) summarizes these as follows:

1 *business risk*   is the uncertainty of income flows caused by the nature of
   the firm's business;

2 *financial risk*   is the uncertainty introduced by the method of financing
   an investment;

3 *liquidity risk*   is the uncertainty introduced by the secondary market for
   an investment – how long will it take to convert the investment into cash,
   and what price will be received?

Applying these classifications to property is approached by imagining each property investment as an individual business. Business risk is then a derived risk which is reduced enormously by fixed rents in leases or between rent reviews and by upward only rent reviews. Liquidity risk has the meaning stated above. Financial risk affects property which is acquired by using some borrowed funds, and is the corollary of a geared purchase. While all investments are sensitive to some extent to interest rate fluctuations, it can be seen that property which is highly geared (as it often is) carries with it a high financial risk.

In summary, property is subject to many risks, several of which are unique to this sector. General risk classifications which are applied to the alternatives show property to be prone to all general categories but relatively protected from business risk by leasing practice. These general classifications are of very limited value in explaining property risks, and the fuller examination which preceded this classification may be of considerably more value. This depends, however, on the definition of risk.

Money or real risk?

Risk may be analysed in terms of money income (what is the possibility of variations in the actual income and capital returns from the expected?) or in terms of real income (what is the possibility of variations in the real value of actual and capital returns from the expected?). The choice is a significant one and depends greatly upon the liabilities of the investor. A predictive comparison of property with (for example) fixed interest gilts is simpler on the former basis, while a comparison with index-linked gilts is simpler when predicated on the latter basis.

The money risk of fixed interest gilts if held to redemption is almost nil, founded on the prospect of government default. There is some money risk if a sale before redemption is possible. Real risk is, on the other hand, quite high due to the fixed money income produced and the possibility of variations in the real value of money.

The money risk of equities is higher, as dividends and share prices vary. Real risk should intuitively be less than for fixed interest gilts due to a broad correlation between inflation and dividends and between dividends and share prices, although empirical evidence may be found to dispute this.

The money risk of index-linked gilts is considerable, even if held to redemption, due to uncertainties regarding future inflation levels; while the real risk is very low, created only by lagging of the inflation linking (see Chapter 1). If a sale before redemption is a possibility, additional real risk is experienced as a result of future inflation expectations, themselves subject to change, being reflected in price and altering the inflation-linked nature of the return (see Example 2.1).

■ EXAMPLE 2.1

Assume a suitable target rate for a purchase of index-linked gilts is 13 per cent. In 1995 a 5-year index-linked gilt, coupon 3 per cent, has been issued with interest paid annually in arrears at a price of £100. Inflation between 1995 and 1998, when the gilt was resold, ran at 5 per cent per annum. Inflation between the resale date and redemption was expected to run at 10 per cent per annum.

The income is given as £100 × c, where c is the coupon, increasing at a rate of $1 + g$, where g is the compound inflation rate from issue to year of income. In years 1996, 1997 and 1998, the annual income is as follows:

1996	£100 × 0.03 × 1.05	= £3.15
1997	£100 × 0.03 × $(1.05)^2$	= £3.31
1998	£100 × 0.03 × $(1.05)^3$	= £3.47

In years 1999 and 2000 it is expected to be as follows:

1999	£100 × 0.03 × $(1.05)^3$ × 1.10	= £3.82
2000	£100 × 0.03 × $(1.05)^3$ × $(1.10)^2$	= £4.20

The resale price is given by £100$(1 + d_1)(1 + d_2)(1 + d_3)(1 + d_4)(1 + d_5)$. This is £100$(1 + 0.05)(1 + 0.05)(1 + 0.05)(1 + 0.10)(1 + 0.10)$ = £140.07. In 1998, an investor with a target rate of 13 per cent would pay a price given by

$$\frac{£3.82}{1.13} + \frac{£4.20}{(1.13)^2} + \frac{£140.07}{(1.13)^2} = £3.38 + £3.29 + £109.70$$

$$= £116.37.$$

For the 1995 purchaser, his return is the internal rate of return (IRR) (i) of the following income flow:

$$- £100 + \frac{£3.15}{1 + i} + \frac{£3.31}{(1 + i)^2} + \frac{£3.47}{(1 + i)^3} + \frac{£116.37}{(1 + i)^3}.$$

The IRR (i) is 8.33 per cent per annum; this is a real return not of 3 per cent per annum but of 3.17 per cent per annum. Were, alternatively, inflation expected at 2 per cent per annum after 1998, the IRR would become 3.40 per cent per annum; this is a real return not of 3 per cent per annum but of −4.4 per cent per annum.

The real risk of index-linked gilts therefore depends upon the timing of a sale prior to redemption and upon future expectations of inflation.

Bank deposits display almost negligible money risk but have considerable real risk produced largely by the propensity of the fixed capital return to be reduced in real value by inflation, and the imperfect and only very indirect linkage between interest rates and inflation.

The money risk of a property investment is, as we have already shown, potentially very high. It is probably higher than its real risk, which is reduced by a broad correlation between inflation and rental values and between rental values and capital values, so that property represents a medium-risk (in real terms) investment type, roughly on a par with equities (although property review patterns possibly argue in favour of the latter), riskier than index-linked gilts but less risky than fixed interest gilts (see Figure 2.1).

Real risk might be a preferable basis for investment comparison. But we are sure that, at present, property investment appraisals should be carried out in a manner which lends itself to investment comparison; and that comparison is most practicable by using money values in cash flow predictions. Consequently we err on the side of a money risk hierarchy for the rest of this book. In these terms, fixed interest bonds held to redemption are least risky; bank deposits are next; index-linked gilts are next; and property, with the levelling of return produced by leasing practice, and putting liquidity to one side, is exceeded only by equities in terms of money risk.

This, however, ignores our final debate over risk definitions.

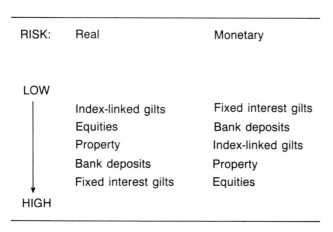

RISK:	Real	Monetary
LOW		
	Index-linked gilts	Fixed interest gilts
	Equities	Bank deposits
	Property	Index-linked gilts
	Bank deposits	Property
	Fixed interest gilts	Equities
HIGH		

Figure 2.1 A possible real and monetary risk hierarchy

Individual or portfolio risk?

Fraser (1985b) has produced evidence based on the Jones Lang Wootton (JLW) Property Index (quarterly) for his proposition that, whether measured in money or real terms, and whether measured in terms of downside risk or overall risk, property has, between 1977 and 1985, been the least risky investment category of the three major institutional investment vehicles (fixed interest gilts, equities and property). At the individual property level, this empirical evidence is impossible to reconcile with a priori reasoning. One would expect to be correct in a presumption that, in money terms at least, property is riskier than fixed interest gilts held to redemption.

There are two reasons for this apparent contradiction. First, Fraser's analysis examines period by period returns rather than yields to redemption. Second, Fraser's analysis relates to portfolios of property and gilts rather than the individual constituent assets. The JLW Property Index is constructed by forming a hypothetical portfolio of actual office, shop and industrial properties. Many of the risks which attach to individual property investment have been diversified away. For example, shifting value – if it exists – would naturally compensate falling value in one location by rising value in another, thus smoothing out variations.

Similarly, the extremely stable real value profile of the ICHP Rent Index from, for example, May 1982 to May 1985 masks considerable variations in the three broad sectors of offices, shops and industrials. Even within those categories there are many more inter-regional, inter-city and inter-property variations hidden away. Consequently, the use of indices containing a large number of properties, which may be outside the scope of a typical investor, will present a misleading riskless view of property as an asset.

Markowitz developed a basic portfolio model (Markowitz 1959) which showed how risk may be reduced within a portfolio by combining assets whose returns demonstrated less than perfect positive correlation.

(What follows is a simplistic and non-technical introduction to modern portfolio theory (MPT) and the capital asset pricing model (CAPM), predicated in terms of a single period expectations model. A simple numerical example on page 278 illustrates the principle. Readers who require a full discussion of MPT should refer to a standard finance text.)

Given that the typical investor is risk-averse, the combination of two or more investments whose returns fluctuate over time and in different conditions but in opposite directions can reduce risk without at the same time reducing return. Thus, if it can be shown that as industrial properties decline in value shops increase in value and vice versa, a two-asset property portfolio is superior to that of either individual asset. The investor de-values a risky asset; two risky assets in combination would be worth more than the sum of the two individual values.

Measuring risk by use of standard deviations (see Chapter 8) and return by internal rate of return or net present value of a time series of returns to that sector, it is possible to plot on a graph the risk—return combination of two equally priced and perfectly negatively correlated investments. Let us imagine that these are the shop and industrial investments referred to above.

Imagine that the shop (X) has an expected IRR of 14 per cent and a standard deviation of IRRs of 24 per cent; and that the industrial property (Y) has an expected IRR of 18 per cent and a standard deviation of IRRs of 52 per cent. Whether an investor would choose X or Y would depend upon his risk—return indifference: a risk-averse investor (A) would choose X; a risk-seeking investor (B) would choose Y (see Figure 2.2).

Let us further imagine that investments X and Y are infinitely divisible, and that the purchaser's available funds can be expended in any combination of X and Y from 100 per cent X to 100 per cent Y (this may be possible through unitization of property investments). Given their perfect negative correlation, a 50:50 combination will have nil risk; the return will be the average of the two IRRs, i.e. 16 per cent.

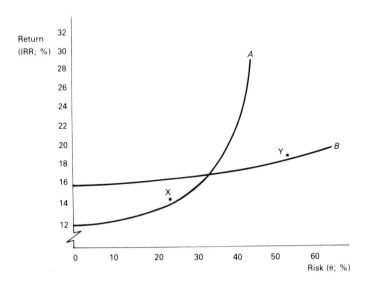

Figure 2.2 The risk—return trade-off

Figure 2.3 shows all possible combinations, joined in a continuous line. Note that investor A would choose 100 per cent X or any combination of X and Y up to a maximum amount of the risky asset Y given by the point 0. Investor B would choose 100 per cent Y or any combination of Y and X up to a maximum amount of the low-return asset X given by point P. Note that both A and B can narrow down their choice further. For either, less than 50 per cent of investment Y produces a two-investment portfolio which has a higher risk – for a lower return! This choice should be a portfolio combination between points V and 0. There is an efficient set of combinations shown by that part of the curve connecting points V and Y, known as the efficient frontier (see Figure 2.4). All other combinations can be disregarded.

We must now relax the simple assumption of a two-property portfolio. Given a much larger choice of property, equity and other risky investments, any two or more of which may be combined, a whole set of efficient frontiers may be constructed (see Figure 2.5).

It can be noted that all risk–return combinations of IJ are bettered by alternatives. In addition, certain parts of all other curves are bettered at some point. A new efficient frontier of portfolios may be constructed roughly along a line reconnecting points A and H (line AH).

It can also be noted that 100 per cent of the least risky asset A and 100 per cent of the highest return asset H are alternative positions on the

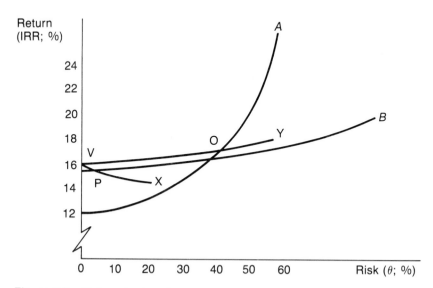

Figure 2.3 Risk and return in a two-asset portfolio

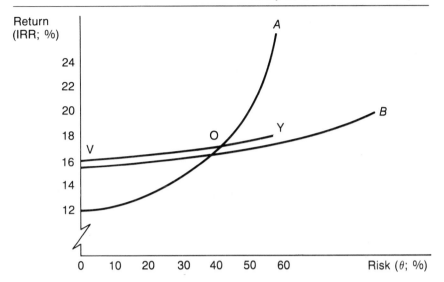

Figure 2.4 The efficient frontier

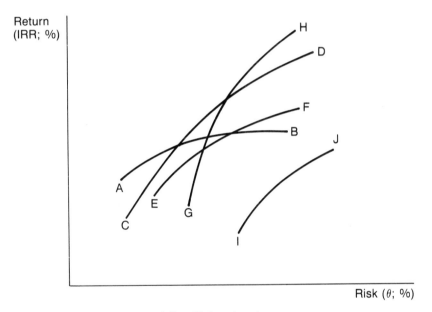

Figure 2.5 Multi-asset portfolio efficient frontiers

efficient frontier. In between there may be any number of combinations of two or more property (and equity) assets. The investor's choice will depend upon his risk–return indifference.

Any point along line AH is a risk–return trade-off. But some investments may be found which are risk free. For some investors, it may be preferable to invest wholly in risk free investments. What happens to the efficient frontier if risk free assets are combined with an efficient portfolio of risky investments? It can be shown that the standard deviation of a portfolio that combines a risk free asset and a portfolio of risky assets is the linear proportion of the standard deviation of the risky asset portfolio. In other words, given a standard deviation of 0 for a risk free investment, a 50:50 combination of that risk free investment with the risky portfolio will produce a risk of 50 per cent of the risky portfolio. A new linear efficient frontier may be constructed (see Figure 2.6). Assume the risk free return is 12.5 per cent.

It is clear from Figure 2.6 that one set of combinations (RV) dominates all other possibilities (including, for example, RS). Depending on the investor's risk return indifference, a point along this line should be selected. This (slightly modified) is known as the capital market line.

By definition, all portfolios on the capital market line are efficiently diversified. It is not possible to reduce risk for an increased or equal return even by adding further negatively correlated investments. The risk of this

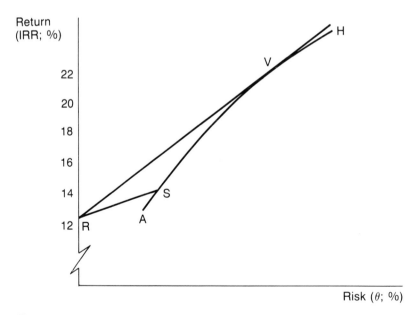

Figure 2.6 The efficient frontier with a risk free asset

portfolio is the risk of the whole market (systematic): there is no residual or non-market risk, and it is now the volatility of the market which produces risk for the portfolio.

Adding further investments will not affect the unsystematic risk of the portfolio, which has been diversified away. It may, however, have an effect upon its systematic risk. How volatile is a new investment in relation to the market portfolio? If it exaggerates the upturns and downturns in the port-folio, it is a risky asset and should only be purchased if the rate of return it promises is sufficiently high: that is, one that suggests that positive abnormal returns will be made.

β is the measure of volatility of an investment in relation to the market portfolio, that is, a portfolio comprising every known asset weighted in terms of market value. A β of 1.0 implies that as the market increases in value by 10 per cent, the expected value of the new investment increases by 10 per cent. A β of 2.0 implies that as the market increases in value by 10 per cent, the expected value of the new investment increases by 20 per cent. A β of 0.5 implies that as the market increases in value by 10 per cent, the expected value of the new investment increases by 5 per cent.

We have already discussed the possibility of investing in a (monetary) risk free asset — say fixed interest government bonds held to maturity. The rate of return on such an investment can be called the risk free rate (RFR).

The market portfolio is not risk free. It is free of unsystematic risk; there-fore, all it contains is systematic risk. The return on the whole market will vary in value over time in relation to the return on the risk free investment. The expected return on the market portfolio $(E(R_m))$ should therefore be higher than the risk free rate. It comprises the risk free rate plus an expected risk premium $(E(R_p))$.

$$E(R_m) = \text{RFR} + E(R_p)$$

or

$$E(R_m) = \text{RFR} + \beta[E(R_m) - \text{RFR}].$$

The return on a risky investment can be similarly derived. It should com-prise the risk free rate plus a risk premium which reflects the systematic risk of the investment relative to the market. Where an investment is twice as risky as the market, the expectation is that it should earn twice the risk premium. The measure of this relative riskiness is β. Thus the return on a risky investment a (R_a) is given by

$$R_a = \text{RFR} + \beta(R_p).$$

Empirical studies in the UK (for example, County NatWest 1992) have shown that R_p has in recent years been close to 2.5 per cent. Given a risk free rate (the return on short-term Treasury Bills or the redemption yield on short-dated government bonds, in either case with maturity matching the single period which forms the basis of the model) of around 7 per cent at the time of writing, the expected return on the market can be estimated.

$$R_m = 0.07 + 0.025$$
$$= 9.5\%.$$

The required return on risky investments can also be calculated. Let us assume (without necessarily recommending the use of CAPM in the property market: see Chapter 8, particularly pages 275–8) that a historic examination of the performance of property investments in relation to the whole stock or asset market has produced estimates of β for offices, shops and industrials. (Brown (1985) has attempted exactly this type of analysis.) Let us assume that the results are as follows:

Shops	$\beta = 0.3$
Offices	$\beta = 0.4$
Industrials	$\beta = 0.5$

(Note that all three categories are less risky than the market, a result which would support Fraser's examination based on the JLW Property Index described on page 40.) The expected or required returns are as follows:

Shops
$$R_S = \text{RFR} + \beta(R_p)$$
$$= 0.07 + 0.3(0.025)$$
$$= 7.7\%$$

Offices
$$R_O = \text{RFR} + \beta(R_p)$$
$$= 0.07 + 0.4(0.025)$$
$$= 8.0\%$$

Industrials
$$R_i = \text{RFR} + \beta(R_p)$$
$$= 0.07 + 0.5(0.025)$$
$$= 8.25\%$$

The implications of such an analysis for property investment appraisal are enormous. However, the theoretical basis of the CAPM is not accepted without question; its application to property is not necessarily settled; and tests for βs in the UK property market are rare and uncorroborated.

Despite these reservations, much can be learned about the behaviour of the property market from this theory. Seven sources of individual property investment risk were identified earlier in this chapter, and at a portfolio level it is clear that many are in the nature of unsystematic risks which can be diversified away by balanced portfolio construction.

1 *Tenant risk* − largely the risks of voids leading to nil rents − can be normalized by the purchase of a large number of properties. As the number of investments held increases, the chance of a total void (say 10 per cent) approaches the certainty of a partial 10 per cent void across the portfolio. As long as the expected cash flow reflects this prospect risk is now negligible.

2 *Sector risk* can be diversified away, to some extent, by its very nature. While it may not be possible to construct a property portfolio which mirrors the performance of national indices (see Brown 1985), balancing by type, by region and by city will result in considerable risk reduction.

3 *Planning risk* can be diversified away. We have already referred to shifting value: one planning refusal may be balanced by a permission elsewhere; a drift in values towards the south-east caused by the M25 and the Channel Tunnel can be normalized by holding property in both the north and the south.

4 *Legal risk* is similar and can be largely removed by diversification. As one bad title is suffered it may be that another legal right which is valuable but was not paid for is discovered.

5 *Taxation risk* can affect all property in the same (negative or positive) manner. The introduction of a new tax on property ownership is an example of how all property may be prone to a taxation risk which is itself systematic.

6 *Legislation risk* is similar. Imagine the effect on values of a new Law of Property Act which abolishes freehold ownership or nationalizes land. The 1993 Department of the Environment Consultation Paper which threatened to outlaw upward-only rent reviews was forecast to immediately reduce commercial and industrial property investment values by over 4 per cent, with a long-term reduction of over 10 per cent (Crosby *et al.* 1993). The risk is again systematic.

7 *Structural risk* is, in some respects, diversifiable. A spread of building types, construction materials and so on will convert the possibility of excessive loss into the certainty of a normal burden of repair and rebuilding. However, the impact of fashion upon building design may not be altogether unsystematic. While a balanced portfolio might reduce the risks of technological change and its impact upon industrial design, more basic changes in architectural practice may affect all properties in the same manner. For example, natural light may be found to be less efficient for all properties than a new type of artificial lighting. All buildings

would then become obsolete to a greater or lesser extent. New lift designs might have a similar, though less dramatic effect. And microtechnology might eventually change the pattern of property employment so drastically that all sectors of the market are prone to the same risk.

In conclusion, property as an investment is (like all investments) prone to both unsystematic and systematic risks. While the former may be diversified away, the latter cannot. The effect of balanced portfolio construction is thus to reduce but not abolish property investment risk. Is it possible to generalize about this? Is the high individual risk of property irrelevant: or is the lower portfolio risk the correct measure?

Much depends upon the behaviour of the typical investor in the particular sub-market under consideration. Does the investor practise a policy of diversification within the property market? Does he have sufficient funds to do this properly?

The answers to these questions can only be provided by reference to the particular. If the prime institutional investment market is the sub-market under consideration, then the answer to the first question is probably positive, but to what extent, and in how rational a manner, it may be difficult to judge. The answer to the second question is that it is extremely unlikely. Given the current minimum level of investment necessary to purchase prime investment property, few if any funds can diversify internationally, regionally, by city and by property type in order to diversify away tenant risk, sector risk, planning risk, legal risk and some structural risk. Even the largest insurance companies may not be in this position. The analyst's strategy must therefore be to identify the most likely purchaser, the relevant conception of risk and its effect upon the likely selling price or return to that purchaser. The vast majority of transactions in the UK property market involve purchasers and vendors who are not able to avoid unsystematic risk. For this reason we do not propose to proceed with portfolio analysis as the basis for the major part of this text. We shall however, use the theory again (in Chapter 8) in an illustrative example.

INITIAL YIELD ANALYSIS AND CONSTRUCTION

Early in this chapter we explained the use of the initial yield as the popular measure of the quality of an investment. Because the initial income level of an investment is usually known or can be predicted with some certainty it can be compared with price to produce a readily understood yield measure shown below:

$$\text{initial yield} = \frac{\text{current income}}{\text{price}}.$$

It should now be recognized that a series of features which affect the quality of the investment affect the initial yield level through the operation of market demand and the price determination process. As market conceptions of any or all of income and capital growth, liquidity, operating expenses, psychic income and risk change for the better, the effect upon price will be positive. Given no change in current income, which is determined largely irrespective of these considerations, the effect must be upon initial yield.

The initial yield is therefore a highly complex measure of the quality of an investment. In theorizing what the level of initial yield should be for an investment, a process of yield construction may be undertaken.

Irving Fisher's classic work on interest (Fisher 1930) and work by Meiron Gordon in the 1950s (Gordon 1958) established the basis for yield construction.

Following Fisher, required total returns can be broken down into rewards for three factors: time preference, or impatience (i); expected inflation (d); and risk (r). A rate can be constructed from these inputs so that the required return $I = (1 + i)(1 + d)(1 + r) - 1$.

Simplifying this, a risk-free rate can be constructed from i and d, and the rate on risk free investments such as short-term Treasury Bills combines rewards for these two factors, so that

$$\text{RFR} = (1 + i)(1 + d) - 1$$

and

$$I \quad = (1 + \text{RFR})(1 + r) - 1.$$

(Note that an approximation is given by $I = \text{RFR} + r$. This is the format adopted in the illustration of yield construction below.)

Following Gordon, the initial return k available on an investment can be related to the required total return I simply in terms of the net income growth g which is anticipated, so that

$$k = I - g.$$

Combining Fisher and Gordon, the following equation can be constructed:

$$k = \text{RFR} + r - g.$$

This is the basis for a process of yield construction, but some further development is necessary, especially for property as an unusual asset class. It is unusual because it depreciates over time, both as the result of physical deterioration and as the result of obsolescence (Baum 1991). Given that in the above equation income growth is a market expectation referring to movement in an index, an extra reward is required to compensate for depreciation (d). Hence, following Baum (1988),

$$k = \text{RFR} + r - g + d.$$

Hence the first step in a process of yield construction for a property investment is to find a risk free (or neutral) rate obtainable elsewhere in the investment market. What return is available from investments which are free of income and capital growth in money terms, absolutely liquid, free of operating expenses, devoid of psychic income and money risk free?

Of the alternatives presented in Chapter 1, the closest proxy for the risk free rate is the redemption yield on fixed interest gilts (but see pages 9–12 for qualifications to this). The cash flow is certain, removing growth and risk; the investment is liquid; it has little prestige or hobby spin-offs, and it is cheap to manage. In Chapter 1 we showed how the effective IRR (redemption yield) of a hypothetical Exchequer $12\frac{1}{4}\%$ 1999 gilt could be calculated as 7.58/7.5 per cent. This will serve as our risk free rate. (Arguably, the index-linked gilt yield is a closer approximation to a risk free rate for investors who are concerned with real returns.)

The initial yield on our property investment (let us assume a prime shop) can be constructed by a normative process as follows. The risk free rate is adjusted in a series of stages to account for the factors which affect shop properties. (All figures used have no logical or empirical foundation: they are for illustration only.)

A risk adjustment (a risk premium r) may first be applied. Given that the gilt is risk free, and (whether viewed in an individual or portfolio sense) that the shop investment is risky, and illiquid, assume $r = 4$ per cent. Adding 0.5 per cent for operating expenses, the required initial yield increases to 12 per cent.

Rental growth prospects for the market have a reducing effect on initial yield. Assume that the consensus long-term forecast is for nominal rental growth of 4 per cent per annum.

The expected depreciation rate for a prime shop is probably very low due to high site values and the tenant's tendency to regularly re-fit the premises. Assuming a rate of nil, the result is a required initial yield of 8 per cent.

neutral/risk free yield	risk and illiquidity	operating expenses	growth	initial yield
7.5%	4.0%	0.5%	−4.0%	8.0%

A positive process of yield analysis, using market information to observe what actually happens in practice, would show that in 1993, 5 per cent would be a much more likely initial yield for a prime shop. The risk free rate was not dissimilar to the hypothetical example illustrated above. One of several conclusions may be drawn.

1 If the adjustments used reflect the preferences of an individual investor, he should not purchase the investment at the market price.
2 The market price and initial yield suggest that successful bidders for the property are less pessimistic about risk, and illiquidity, or are more optimistic about net growth, or a combination of both factors is in operation. For example, if a portfolio risk measure is used and a small (2 per cent) risk premium is viewed as necessary, illiquidity is not a problem due to intended infrequency of trading and the growth prospects are considered to be 1 per cent per annum better, the construction (normative) process can be equated with the analytical (positive) process as follows:

neutral/risk free yield	risk and illiquidity	operating expenses	growth	initial yield
7.5%	2.0%	0.5%	−5.0%	5.0%

Alternatively, assuming much greater optimism regarding growth, the process might become

neutral/risk free yield	risk and illiquidity	operating expenses	growth	initial yield
7.5%	4.0%	0.5%	−7.0%	5.0%

In the early 1980s the low level of initial yields for shop investments was severely questioned, and most analyses centred on the excessive rental growth expectation that appeared to push initial yields so low. More attention is now being paid to the premium component of the equation, with the downside risk of property investments now the dominant factor and the tenant's covenant, length of lease and presence of upward only rent reviews having emerged as the important factors. Cash flow is as important as growth prospects in the appraisal of property investments.

Whatever the lessons to be learned from such a process, two clear conclusions can be drawn.

1 In the pricing process (estimation of the most likely selling price, market valuation) the estimation of adjustments in the normative process of yield construction is difficult, and in practice has been neglected in favour of the positive process of yield analysis. Part 2 of this book shows how yield analysis has been used, and how the technique performs in the current property investment market.
2 In the estimation of worth to an individual investor the yield construction process is more promising. The opportunity exists to agree adjustments with the client, but the quantum of adjustment is difficult to judge and the result is sensitive to changes.

Appraisal by initial yield analysis (empiricism) is the market standard. That is not to say that it provides a satisfactory methodology. The implications of initial yield (implicit) appraisals are considered in Part 2.

COMPARING INVESTMENT OPPORTUNITIES: NET PRESENT VALUE AND INTERNAL RATE OF RETURN

Valuation involves the estimation of worth to an individual. Given the price of the investment, it can be expressed in either of two ways: first, as a net present value (NPV) of the cash flow over the price; second, as an (internal) rate of return.

In this section we compare three investments to illustrate these means of comparison and to round off Part 1 of this book by completing the process of investment comparison.

Each investment is to be held for 5 years. The price is known in each case. The NPV and IRR of each is to be estimated.

Investment A is a stock. It is priced at £5. The last dividend, just paid, was £0.50. Let g_1 be the expected growth in dividend in year 1 plus 1, g_2 be the expected growth in dividend in year 2 plus 1, g_3 be the expected growth in dividend in year 3 plus 1, g_4 be the expected growth in dividend in year 4 plus 1, and let g_5 be the expected growth in dividend in year 5 plus 1. Let d_1 be the dividend in year 1, d_2 be the dividend in year 2, d_3 be the dividend in year 3, d_4 be the dividend in year 4, d_5 be the dividend in year 5 and k_5 be the expected dividend yield at the end of year 5. The expected cash flow is as given in Table 2.2.

Investment B is a property. It is priced at £5 million. The rental value, just agreed under a new lease, is £500,000. Let g_1 be the expected net growth

Table 2.2

Year	Income (£)	Capital (£)	Total (£)
0		− 5.00	− 5.00
1	$0.5g_1$		$0.5g_1$
2	d_1g_2		d_1g_2
3	d_2g_3		d_2g_3
4	d_3g_4		d_3g_4
5	d_4g_5	d_5/k_5	$(d_4g_5)(d_5/k_5)$

in rental value in year 1 plus 1, g_2 be the expected net growth in rental value in year 2 plus 1, g_3 be the expected net growth in rental value in year 3 plus 1, g_4 be the expected net growth in rental value in year 4 plus 1, and let g_5 be the expected net growth in rental value in year 5 plus 1. Let k_5 be the expected yield at the end of year 5. The expected cash flow is as given in Table 2.3.

Investment C is a bond. It is priced at £80. The coupon is £5. Redemption in 5 years' time is, at par, £100. The expected cash flow is as given in Table 2.4.

One immediate conclusion can be drawn from these cash flows. No risk attaches to the cash flow in investment C, because both income and capital flows are known with certainty.

More risk attaches to investment B. The income over 5 years is known with certainty, but the capital value in year 5 is subject to the values of g_1, g_2, g_3, g_4, g_5 and k_5.

The greatest risk attaches to investment A. Neither the income stream nor the capital value is known with certainty; both are subject to future income growth and the future dividend yield.

So bonds are less risky in nominal terms than property; and property is less risky than stocks.

What is the value of each investment?

Table 2.3

Year	Income (£)	Capital (£)	Total (£)
0		− 5 million	− 5 million
1	500,000		500,000
2	500,000		500,000
3	500,000		500,000
4	500,000		500,000
5	500,000	$500{,}000.g_1.g_2.g_3.g_4.g_5/k_5$	$500{,}000 + 500{,}000.g_1.g_2.g_3.g_4.g_5/k_5$

Table 2.4

Year	Income (£)	Capital (£)	Total (£)
0		− 80	− 80
1	5		5
2	5		5
3	5		5
4	5		5
5	5	100	105

The value of the gilt can be estimated without further inputs.

The NPV is the summated present value of all cash inflows less the summated present value of all cash outlows. To calculate the NPV requires the estimation of the correct discount rate or required return, I, given in the simplified Fisher equation above as RFR + r.

The (internal) rate of return is that discount rate which equates the present values of all inflows and the present values of all outflows.

The discount rate appropriate to gilts is the risk free rate. Assuming investment C is a gilt, the NPV must be nil, and the IRR is the risk free rate for the purposes of our other valuations.

NPV and IRR routines are standard on financial calculators and spreadsheet programs. For a fuller description of the calculation method underlying these routines see Baum and Mackmin (1989).

The IRR for investment C is 10.32 per cent. This establishes a risk free rate for the valuation of the other assets.

To value investment B, what risk premium is appropriate? Following the above text, the property is certainly riskier in nominal terms than the gilt; a 4 per cent risk margin may be appropriate for a retail property. The appropriate discount rate is then 14.32 per cent.

Next, what future value should be assumed? Let us assume no depreciation and growth at 7 per cent per annum. Finally, let us assume that yields do not change and that the current initial yield of 10 per cent will apply in 5 years' time.

The resale value will then be [£500,000 × (1 + 0.07)^5]/0.10, or £701,276/0.10 = £7.01 million.

At a discount rate of 14.32 per cent, the NPV is £37,454, meaning that the investment is marginally attractive in comparison with the gilt, the return more than compensating for the risk. At a price of £5,037,454 the property would be fairly priced; its value is the current price plus the NPV.

The IRR is 14.52 per cent, again showing that the investment is attractive in comparison with the gilt.

To value investment A, what risk premium is appropriate? Investment A is riskier than investment B because more uncertainty attaches to the cash flow. Assume 6 per cent is appropriate, producing a discount rate of 16.32 per cent.

What dividend growth should be assumed? Let us assume 8 per cent per annum, producing a dividend stream as follows: in year 1, $£0.5 \times 1.08 = 0.54$; in year 2, $£0.5 \times (1.08)^2 = £0.58$; in year 3, $£0.5 \times (1.08)^3 = £0.63$; in year 4, $£0.5 \times (1.08)^4 = £0.68$; in year 5, $£0.5 \times (1.08)^5 = £0.73$.

What will the future dividend yield be? Currently, it is 10 per cent; assume it falls to 8 per cent. The resale value would then be $£0.73/0.08 = £9.18$.

At a discount rate of 16.32 per cent, the NPV is £1.31, meaning that the investment is attractive in comparison with the gilt, the return more than compensating for the risk. At a price of £6.31 the stock would be fairly priced; its value is the current price plus the NPV. If £5m were expended on 1 million shares, the NPV would be £1,310,000, a greater surplus than the property would show.

The IRR is 22.87 per cent, again showing that the investment is attractive in comparison with the gilt, and also comfortably the most attractive of the three.

This type of analysis is developed in more detail in Part 4. The reasons for the divergence between this type of valuation process and the conventional valuation technique are the subject of Part 2.

Part two

CONVENTIONAL MARKET VALUATION MODELS

3

The evolution of conventional appraisal techniques

INTRODUCTION

The basis of accepted techniques for the appraisal of property investments evolves from the attitudes and perceptions of those who carry out the appraisals and those who own and occupy the properties being appraised. The influences on them range from the concepts and techniques taught to them in the formative years of their careers to the market conditions which apply at the time of the valuation and their perceptions of future changes in those conditions.

They will also be influenced by the role of the appraisal. In the UK, value has come to mean exchange value or market value; valuation is used in place of pricing; and it is only relatively recently that other types of value – and valuation – have been discussed in detail. Part 2 of this book deals exclusively with the assessment of market value, or pricing (assessing the likely sale price of the investment).

The conventional techniques for assessing market value have evolved over a significant time period and have been adapted and amended as circumstances change. Although Trott (1980: 1) suggested that 'for many decades the conventional methods of investment valuation were accepted as logical, practical and seemingly immutable', this can be shown to be untrue: techniques can be seen to bend and change after an extensive time delay for reflection and analysis.

It is virtually impossible to understand the detail of valuation methods without an examination of how these methods evolved and without considering the context within which the changes took place.

This chapter traces the evolution of the conventional market valuation models. It will be argued within this text that the reverse yield gap which first appeared in the late 1950s heralded a significant change in the perception of all investors, a change which amended the basis of the conventional valuation model from an investment cash flow approach to a property comparison approach. The chapter will use 1960 as a convenient watershed, reviewing the development of the models up to 1960 and investigating the context of this evolution (the perceptions of investors and valuers up to that date).

The changed perceptions of investors and the valuers' response will then be examined for the period after 1960. This will enable an analysis of current practice to be undertaken in Chapter 4.

THE HISTORICAL DEVELOPMENT OF VALUATION TECHNIQUES PRIOR TO 1960

In the first edition of this text, a detailed examination of how valuation techniques evolved during the twentieth century was undertaken. This examination was based upon primary research into the behaviour of property values in central Nottingham, a major urban centre in the UK (Crosby 1985), and a review of the basic textbooks of the era.

The conclusions of this analysis were that the model evolved through various stages caused by valuers' attempts to adapt for changing economic scenarios and/or perceptions of those circumstances. We do not intend to repeat the detail of that analysis in this edition, but we set out a resumee of the results.

At the most basic level the valuation of the three main interests in a property (the rack rented freehold, the reversionary freehold and the leasehold) can be set out as follows.

■ EXAMPLE 3.1: RACK RENTED FREEHOLD

Net rent passing and estimated rental value (ERV) £21,000 per annum; the all risks yield is estimated to be 6.25 per cent.

ERV	£21,000	
YP perp. at 6.25%	16.0000	
Valuation		£336,000

■ EXAMPLE 3.2: REVERSIONARY FREEHOLD

As Example 3.1 but the rent passing is £10,000 per annum and there are 2 years to go to the end of the lease.

Rent passing	£10,000		
YP 2 years at 6.25%	1.8270		
		£18,270	
Reversion to ERV	£21,000		
YP perp. at 6.25%	16.0000		
PV 2 years at 6.25%	0.8858		
		£297,633	
Valuation			£315,903

■ EXAMPLE 3.3: LEASEHOLD

The leasehold interest in Example 3.2.

Rent received (ERV)	£21,000	
Less rent paid	£10,000	
Profit rent	£11,000	
YP 2 years at 6.25%	1.8270	
Valuation		£20,097

The appraisal technique illustrated in Example 3.3 is very simple. The value of the reversionary freehold and leasehold interests are 'such that the sum of the two is always equal to the total value of the freehold in perpetuity' (Norris 1884).

(It is interesting to note that in 1981, Sykes (1981) developed his rational model along the same lines by determining the value of the leasehold interest as being the value of the freehold in perpetuity less the value of the reversionary freehold interest. This was not, by then, conventional practice.)

This basic model was adapted and refined during the first part of the twentieth century. Although the conventional approach to the rack rented freehold remains largely unchanged, the reversionary freehold and leasehold valuations have developed (some would suggest regressed). These changes are set out below.

Reversionary freeholds

Before 1960, the major change to the model illustrated in Example 3.2 was in respect of yield choice. In the early textbooks of the twentieth century, examples showed that the yield to capitalize the term was taken at a lower rate than the yield on the reversion. Although analysis of actual valuations carried out during the inter-war period did not confirm this approach, after the Second World War it became normal practice to adopt a lower term yield. Lawrence and May (1943) set out the thinking of the time.

> The £100 income, being less than the property is really worth, is very well secured and may reasonably be capitalized at a lower rate per cent than would be appropriate in dealing with the full annual value of the premises.
>
> (Lawrence and May 1943: 9)

This statement implies that the change in yield was a reduction in the term yield (rather than an increase in the reversionary yield) on account of the extra security of the term (lower default risk). The reduction was generally of 1–2 per cent. The following example appeared in Smith (1933).

■ EXAMPLE 3.4: REVERSIONARY FREEHOLD

'A freehold house is let on lease, which will expire in 20 years' time, at a ground rent of £10 per annum. The net annual value is £100 per annum. Value the ground rent at 4% and the reversion at 5%' (Smith 1933: 86).

Ground rent	£10	
YP 20 years at 4%	13.5903	
		£136
Reversion to ERV	£100	
YP perp. at 5%	20.0000	
PV 20 years at 5%	0.3769	
		£754
Valuation		£890

Prior to 1960, another development to the reversionary valuation model, the horizontally sliced layer model, was just beginning to emerge. However, as its major influence was felt post-1960, discussion of this model is undertaken later in this chapter. By 1960, the standard method used by valuers was the vertically sliced term and reversion model using lower yields on the term than the reversion.

Leaseholds

The leasehold model was the subject of far greater change in this period. These changes included increasing the capitalization rate due to a perception that a leasehold was a riskier or less attractive interest than a freehold, the introduction of dual rate concepts and the movement towards tax adjustment.

The concept of dual rate was being actively discussed in texts at the beginning and in the first half of this century (for example, Davies 1908; Smith 1933). Practice was slower to follow. These texts suggested that external reinvestment to provide a replacement of capital at the end of the term could only take place at lower rates than the capitalization rate of the leasehold interest. As practice was generally ignoring dual rate as an approach, these authors suggested that the alternative route was to value single rate using a higher yield based on comparable evidence of leasehold sales. As the whole point of the dual rate concept was to make up for the lack of leasehold comparables (see later), this was an extremely dubious piece of logic.

Davies (1908) and Smith (1933) included examples of leaseholds using both single rate and dual rate solutions. Smith also introduced the concept of tax on the sinking fund accumulations and on the portion of income going into the sinking fund but commented that 'it is often found in practice that purchasers seem to take no account of it' (Smith 1933: 123).

Our investigation of practice indicates that valuations in the 1930s were undertaken using single rate capitalization, but after the war a dual rate untaxed method was used. The yields adopted were approximately 1–2 per cent higher than for freehold capitalization rates. Sinking fund rates were around 2.5–3 per cent.

Lawrence and May (1943) set out valuations of the freehold, head leasehold and sub-leasehold interests in the same property.

■ EXAMPLE 3.5: FREEHOLD REVERSION, HEAD LEASEHOLD, SUB-
LEASEHOLD INTERESTS

A corner shop and dwelling house in a good shopping centre in the town. The freehold is let on a 99 years' lease expiring in 36 years' time at a ground rent of £10 per annum.

The head lessee let the shop 16 years ago on a 21 year (full) repairing lease at a rent of £100 per annum. The premises are now worth a rent of £180 per annum on a (full) repairing lease.

(Lawrence and May 1943: 304–5)

(a) Freeholder

Ground rent	£10		
YP 36 years at 4%	18.9083		
		£189	
Reversion to ERV	£180		
YP perp. at 5.5%	18.1818		
PV 36 years at 5.5%	0.1455		
		£476	
Valuation			£665

(b) Head leaseholder

Rent received	£100		
less Ground rent	£10		
Profit rent	£90		
YP 5 years at 6%/3%	4.0265		
		£362	
Reversion to ERV	£180		
less Ground rent	£10		
Profit rent	£170		
YP 31 years at 7%/3%	11.1112		
PV 5 years at 7%	0.7130		
		£1,345	
Valuation			£1,707

(c) Sub-leaseholder

ERV	£180	
less Rent paid	£100	
Profit rent	£80	
YP 5 years at 8%/3%	3.7264	
Valuation		£298

By the beginning of the 1960s the taxation implications of leaseholds were being incorporated into leaseholds (expecially short leaseholds) and a very similar example to the one above in Lawrence *et al.* (1962) included the sub-lessee's interest valued using the tax adjusted dual rate YP. A profit rent of £400 per annum lasting for 10 years was capitalized using a YP for 10 years at 9.5 per cent and 2.5 per cent adjusted for tax at 7/9d in the pound (approximately 33p). By then Parry's tables had incorporated tax adjustments. (It is evident that a very significant step towards getting any new method accepted is to make it as accessible as possible to the user.)

This is how valuation techniques evolved during the first part of the twentieth century. The next section outlines the context of that evolution.

EXPECTATIONS OF INVESTORS, 1910–60

The expectations of investors in different types of investment medium can be analysed on the basis of market indicators and knowledge of the past. We use a number of indicators to help this analysis. These are the rate of inflation or the reducing purchasing power of the pound; the yields acceptable in capital markets; and indices on Nottingham shop rents (in the abscence of any national property market indicators before the 1960s). Table 3.1 sets out the information used for the following analysis.

The yield on conventional undated gilts between 1910 and 1960 ranged between a yearly average of 2.6 per cent and 5.4 per cent. The average yield was 3.75 per cent between 1910 and 1950 and 3.9 per cent between 1910 and 1960.

Inflation ran at an average of 3.05 per cent per annum between 1910 and 1960. Up to 1950 the average was 2.79 per cent per annum. On a year to year basis the income from gilts showed a 1 per cent real return up to 1950. Between 1950 and 1960 the inflation rate was over 4 per cent per annum and the yield on gilts steadily rose from 3.5 per cent in 1950 to 5.4 per cent in 1960 to re-establish a real return. A rise in gilt yields in times of inflation may have been expected but the volatility of the inflation rate is in marked contrast to the stability of gilt yields. The average 5-yearly prices index growth is set against the average gilt yield in the same period in Figure 3.1.

The figure illustrates two points. The first is that investors in gilts did not seem to mind that in some years the value of their income was reduced to a negative real return. The second point is the variability of inflation. The second point may help to explain the first. Investors probably thought that prices were equally likely to go down as go up. Although long-term analysis shows an upward trend (1910–60: 3.05 per cent per annum), investors could point to a number of disturbances in the period such as the two World Wars and the Depression of the early 1930s. They could also point to the fact that the negative inflation rate occurred in the most stable time and (given stability) they would expect the same thing to happen. From 1945–6 onwards

Table 3.1 Nottingham city centre retail property: rents, inflation and initial yields, 1910–60

Years	Prime rent		Average rent index		Retail price index	Prime initial yields	Gilts
	1910 = 100	1946 = 100	1910 = 100	1946 = 100	1913 = 100		
1910	100.0	43.3	100.0	38.2	94	5.0	3.1
1911	96.9		96.0		95	5.0	3.2
1912	95.4		92.9		98	5.0	3.3
1913	95.4		91.6		100	4.5	3.4
1914	95.4		91.6		101	6.5	3.3
1915	95.4		91.6		121	–	3.8
1916	95.4		91.6		143	–	4.3
1917	96.9		94.6		173	–	4.6
1918	99.2		99.3		199	6.75	4.4
1919	101.5		104.4		211	5.0	4.6
1920	104.6		109.8		244	5.0	5.3
1921	106.9		114.8		222	4.5	5.2
1922	109.2		120.5		179	5.5	4.4
1923	111.5		125.6		171	6.0	4.3
1924	118.5		132.5		172	6.25	4.4
1925	123.1		138.7		173	6.0	4.4
1926	127.7		148.8		169	5.5	4.6
1927	133.8		157.6		164	5.0	4.6
1928	140.0		168.4		163	4.0	4.5
1929	147.7		180.1		161	5.0	4.6
1930	153.8		198.7		155	6.0	4.5
1931	135.4		159.9		145	9.0	4.4
1932	135.4		158.9		141	8.0	3.7
1933	135.4		158.2		137	6.5	3.4
1934	135.4		160.3		138	6.5	3.1
1935	135.4		161.9		140	6.0	2.9
1936	135.4		166.7		144	6.0	2.9
1937	143.8		177.8		152	5.5	3.3
1938	152.3		187.2		153	5.0	3.4
1939	146.2		181.5		158	5.0	3.7
1940	140.0		172.1		179	7.5	3.4
1941	140.0		170.0		197	–	3.1
1942	140.0		170.0		210	–	3.0
1943	140.0		170.0		217	–	3.1
1944	140.0		170.4		222	7.0	3.1
1945	161.5		192.8		226	6.0	2.9
1946	230.8	100	262.0	100	236	5.0	2.6
1947		105.6		108.9	249	4.5	2.8
1948		110.2		116.0	268	4.4	3.2
1949		111.9		124.1	275	4.5	3.3
1950		114.1		131.4	283	4.5	3.5
1951		116.7		138.0	311	4.5	3.8
1952		123.3		146.3	338	5.0	3.2
1953		139.8		160.9	349	5.5	4.1
1954		158.6		170.0	355	5.25	3.8
1955		179.8		198.3	371	5.0	4.2
1956		200.0		224.5	389	5.5	4.7
1957		212.0		253.7	404	5.5	5.0
1958		222.6		276.5	416	5.5	5.0
1959		233.4		293.3	418	6.0	4.8
1960		242.7		308.3	422	6.0	6.4

Sources: Prime rent, average rent index and prime initial yields data compiled by Crosby from data obtained from a number of sources. The main source is Harlow Shelton & Co., Chartered Surveyors, Nottingham. Retail price index data from National Income Expenditure and Output of the UK 1865–1965 (for reference, see Crosby 1985). Gilts data from Abstract of British Historical Statistics and 2nd Abstract of British Historical Statistics (2½% Consols, undated stock, gross redemption yields) (for reference, see Crosby 1985).

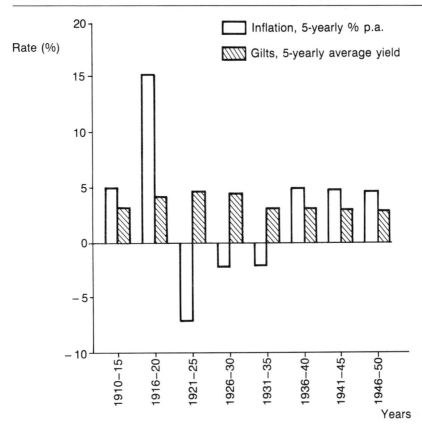

Figure 3.1 Comparison of yields on gilts with retail price index, 1910–50
Source: Table 3.1

they may well have been expecting the same conditions of 1920–9 (a reducing cost of living).

The evidence of rising gilt yields in the 1950s suggests that investors' perceptions changed and they began to realize that inflation might be endemic. The majority of the market had responded to these changed perceptions by 1960–1. The property market had different indicators, but perhaps the same reasons for not reacting positively to economic indicators until after 1960. The movement in rents, as indicated by shop rental values between 1910 and 1960 in the Nottingham City Centre, also shows a series of cycles with an overall trend upwards. In the war periods of 1914–18 and 1939–45 shop rentals declined, and they also declined sharply in the Depression of the 1930s. Between these disturbances shop rentals grew. In the period 1918–30 rental values doubled while the cost of living was reduced by approximately 25 per cent. The average rent index 5-yearly changes between 1910 and 1950 are shown in Figure 3.2.

The effect of the very high increases in rent during 1945–50 may have heightened alarm in that a repetition of 1920–30 may have been part of investors' perceptions. Even though the average growth rate between 1910 and 1950 was 3.13 per cent per annum, the investor's past experience did not give confidence that this would continue. The period 1910–30 is a similar image to 1930–50, and this supports the view of a possible expectation of rental falls within the decade 1950–60. After all, the level of knowledge of both valuer and investor was limited. No rental evidence in the form of indices was published and only past experience of periods of growth and decline could be utilized. The upward trend may not have been as well perceived as the fluctuations.

Comments within valuation reports by surveyors confirm this reluctance to accept a continuing upward trend in inflation and rental values. In 1944 the expectation of some inflation after the war was present. For example,

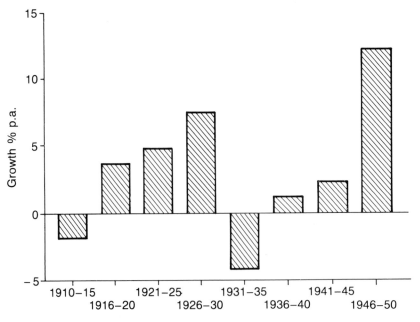

Figure 3.2 Nottingham rent index change, 1910–50
Source: Table 3.1

in one report:

> We feel it is difficult to forecast the possible trend in rents when the war is over but if a certain degree of inflation is likely to be present – as seems possible – it would be prudent to ask a higher rent for each succeeding period of seven years.

The expectation of future inflation after the war may have been a result of the continuance of inflation after the First World War in 1918 up to 1920 prior to the reduction in 1921.

However, a valuation report of 1959 contained the following:

> but this depends on the future trend of rental values. Since the war this has been upward, but it is difficult to see this trend continuing ...

Even after 14 years of price rises and rental increases, the reluctance to accept that this might continue is still apparent. The increase in rents from 1945 to 1950 was 12.2 per cent per annum; from 1950 to 1955, 8.6 per cent per annum; and from 1955 to 1960, 9.2 per cent per annum, a 15-year average of 10 per cent per annum.

The change in rental values of shops on a number of specific streets in Nottingham illustrates what actually happened. Long Row rose from £3.00 Zone A in 1946 to £7.50 in 1961. Albert Street was estimated at £2.00 Zone A in 1946 and £6.00 in 1961. Clumber Street increased from £1.50 Zone A to £4.25 over the same period. In thirty-seven different locations across Nottingham city centre only two rent points (both on Lower Parliament Street) did not show at least a doubling of rental value. The suburban centres of Nottingham grew by an average of 7.8 per cent per annum between 1946 and 1961, with the average Zone A of £0.36 rising by over three times to £1.11 (Crosby 1985).

The rental evidence illustrates a period of constant growth in shop rents around 10 per cent per annum between 1945 and 1960 while prices increased at an average of 4.25 per cent per annum.

An examination of gilt yields between 1945 and 1960 shows the yield from gilt-edged stock ($2\frac{1}{2}$% Consols) going through a period of transition. Between 1946 and 1960 the yield on gilts rose from 2.6 per cent to 5.4 per cent. At the same time the initial yield on prime shops was the same in 1947 as it was in 1960. The yield gap reduced from 2.7 per cent in 1947 to 0.1 per cent in 1960 (Figure 3.3).

This changing relationship between gilt and shop yields indicated the start of the reverse yield gap between fixed income and growth investments which was maintained until 1993 when it was temporarily extinguished for all

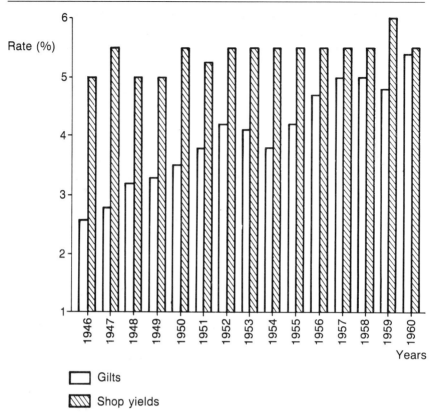

Figure 3.3   Prime shop initial yields and gilts, 1946–60
Source: Table 3.1

but prime shop property. The yield on UK ordinary shares was $4\frac{1}{2}$ per cent in 1947 and 5 per cent in 1960 (Senior 1975). As the average yield on gilts was 3.75 per cent between 1910 and 1950, and the yields on gilts in 1950 was 3.5 per cent, it seems probable that inflation was not seen as a problem in the investment market at that point. The yield on gilts only exceeded one standard deviation from the 1910–50 mean in 1956 (4.7 per cent) so it further seems probable that the market as a whole reacted to inflation, and its effect on real incomes, in the second half of the 1950s. The leaders of the herd can be assumed to have reacted before that.

It might be thought that property investors and valuers would not have to react in the same way as property could be a growth investment and could have the ability to react to a decline in the value of money by increasing the nominal income level. Even though the investment market had seen that growth potential was equally important as security (by 1959–60 riskier UK share yields were initially about the same as risk free gilts), yields on property did not rise to maintain a risk differential with gilts. There are two possible reasons for this:

1 valuers and property investors were equally aware of economic changes and perceived that property was a growth investment which did not warrant a yield higher than gilts (growth potential offsetting lower security);
2 valuers and property investors had missed both points – they were unaware of the concept of value, had ceased to look beyond property for value comparisons and still did not perceive property as a growth investment.

Evidence shows that the latter more closely represents the reality. Rent review patterns, for example, are an instructive source.

Property need not be a growth investment. The valuer and investor can structure leases in such a way that the income from property is fixed under a lease for many years (as has happened by accident in the early 1990s with over-rented properties). Lease lengths can be for any number of years as determined by owners and tenants. Regarding this historical time period, some published comment exists regarding the length of lease and the advent and extent of rent reviews within leases, but it is contradictory.

To clarify the situation, we carried out an analysis of lease lengths and review patterns on shop properties. Lease details were extracted from prime shops regardless of UK location. The data was banded for time periods of around 5 years from 1945 onwards (Figure 3.4).

The evidence suggests very little change in perception during the 1950s. Landlords were willing to grant tenants long leases without rent reviews throughout the period and therefore appeared to have very little faith in continuing rental growth. The security of income offered by good covenant tenants was perceived to outweigh any opportunities of participating in rental growth. This conclusion ignores any resistance to change from tenants. However, our previous comment regarding landlords' fear of a collapse of growth, coupled with a lack of perception of change, is more probable, as evidenced by a number of landlords still granting leases such as one in Eastwood, Nottinghamshire, where the tenant was given a 21-year lease from 1956 with an option to renew for a further 21 years at the same rent (basically a 42-year lease with no rent reviews, and the tenant having the option to go in the middle of the term).

Further evidence of perceptions can be taken from the yield table formed by Senior (1975) regarding the level of yields on ground rents. Ground rents let on very long leases, often 99 years, were the property market's nearest

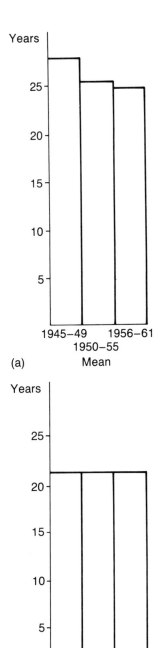

(a)   Mean

(b)   Mode

Figure 3.4 Prime shop property, UK, 1945–61: lease and/or rent
review periods: (a) mean; (b) mode
Source: Crosby 1984, 1985

equivalent to an undated gilt-edged stock. The income was secure as often the property rental value exceeded the ground rent many times over and the reversion was so far off as to be of very little value. The comparison of gilt yields and ground rents as determined by Senior is illustrated in Table 3.2.

The yields on ground rents with more than 60 years unexpired remained constant at 4–5 per cent while the yield on gilts rose. Assuming a yield of 4.5 per cent, the yield gap started at +1.75 per cent in 1947 and was reversed by 1960 at −0.75 per cent, a relative shift of 2 per cent over 13 years. If gilts were representative of the safest risk free form of investment then investors in 1960 could have received a higher return with lower risk from gilts and would have been ill-advised to buy ground rents.

The evidence of yields from the investment market suggests that the realization that inflation was following a long-term upward trend was formed in the 1950s and by 1956 gilt yields approached 5 per cent (or 1 per cent above the average for the period 1910–50). By 1960 the initial yield on UK equities was lower than that on UK gilts, which suggests that by then the majority of investors were prepared to pay less for certain income than they were for growth potential. The evidence also suggests that property investors were slow to react and the evidence of yields on ground rents and rent review patterns confirms that property investors had not perceived any major changes in the economy within which they operated.

Given this lack of perception, the behaviour of investors over the period

Table 3.2 Gilt and ground rent yields (%)

Year	Gilts	Ground rents (60 years unexpired)	Differential
1947	$2\frac{3}{4}$	4/5	$1\frac{1}{4}/2\frac{1}{4}$
1948	$3\frac{1}{4}$	4/5	$\frac{3}{4}/1\frac{3}{4}$
1949	$3\frac{1}{2}$	4/5	$\frac{1}{2}/1\frac{1}{2}$
1950	$4\frac{1}{2}$	4/5	$-\frac{1}{2}/\frac{1}{2}$
1951	4	4/5	0/1
1952	$4\frac{1}{4}$	–	–
1953	4	–	–
1954	$3\frac{3}{4}$	4/5	$\frac{1}{4}/1\frac{1}{4}$
1955	$4\frac{1}{4}$	4/5	$-\frac{1}{4}/\frac{3}{4}$
1956	$4\frac{3}{4}$	4/5	$-\frac{3}{4}/\frac{1}{4}$
1957	5	4/5	−1/0
1958	5	4/5	−1/0
1959	5	4/5	−1/0
1960	$5\frac{1}{4}$	4/5	$-1\frac{1}{4}/\frac{1}{4}$

Source: Senior 1975

can now be reconciled with the valuation model adopted to determine whether the model was based on a defensible logic.

THE RATIONALE OF THE APPRAISAL MODELS

Fully let freehold

The valuation of a rack rented freehold shop property in (say) 1950 would have been undertaken on the basis of a capitalization of the rent at the appropriate yield. For example, the prime shop yield in Nottingham was estimated to be 4.5 per cent at that time (see Table 3.1). Assuming a rent of £4,000 per annum, the calculation based on direct comparable analysis would be as shown in Example 3.6.

■ EXAMPLE 3.6

ERV	£4,000	
YP perp. at 4.5%	22.2222	
Valuation		£88,889

The landlord would expect the rent to be fixed for 21 years at least, possibly 35 or 42 years, if the tenant represented a very good covenant. The valuation has a logical basis if viewed in the light of the following propositions.

1 Property is more risky and less liquid than fixed interest government securities ($2\frac{1}{2}$% Consols) (see Chapter 2), which yielded around $3\frac{1}{2}$ per cent to redemption at that time.
2 There is no assumption of an upward trend in rents. The likelihood of a fall in rents is just as possible as an increase and therefore the object of fixing a rent for as long as possible is seen as a positive advantage to minimize the risk of a fall in income. The upward movement of rent is not necessary as the initial yield is already 1 per cent above the yield on fixed interest stock.

These assumptions are consistent with the previous analysis of investors' perceptions prior to the movement towards the reverse yield gap which took place later in the decade. The valuation is a conveniently presented discounted cash flow valuation.

Assume that the rent is fixed for 21 years (and that the market would expect another 21-year lease to be granted at the end of the current lease)

Table 3.3

Years	Rent £	YP 21 at 4.5%	PV at 4.5%	Present value (£)
1–21	4,000	13.4047	1.0000	53,619
22–42	4,000	13.4047	0.3968	21,275
43–63	4,000	13.4047	0.1574	8,442
64–84	4,000	13.4047	0.0625	3,350
85–105	4,000	13.4047	0.0248	1,329
106–126	4,000	13.4047	0.0098	527
127–147	4,000	13.4047	0.0039	209
148–168	4,000	13.4047	0.0015	83
169–189	4,000	13.4047	0.0006	33
190–perp.	4,000	22.222*	0.0002	213
*YP perp. at $4\frac{1}{2}$%				£88,880[a]

Note: [a]Error due to rounding, conventional valuation and discounted cash flow both give £88,889.

and that rental values are not expected to show a long-term upward or downward trend. Remember that gilts yield $3\frac{1}{2}$ per cent. A discounted cash flow valuation with a 1 per cent risk premium would be as shown in Table 3.3.

Reversionary Freehold

The normal technique for a 1950 valuation of a term income with a reversion to a new lease in the future would be as shown in Example 3.7.

■ EXAMPLE 3.7

A shop property is let on a 21-year lease, with 6 years unexpired in 1950. The rent under the lease is in the region of 50 per cent of the rental value in 1950 (Nottingham average index 1910 = 100, 1935 = 161.9, 1950 = 344.3). Assuming the same rental value of £4,000 per annum in 1950, the rent under the lease is taken at £2,000 per annum.

The approach at that time would be a capitalization of the reversion at a yield higher than the term. Our previous discussion leads to a conclusion that the term yield is a 1 per cent reduction rather than the reversion yield being a 1 per cent addition. Adopting this approach the term yield would be at 3.5 per cent with the reversion at 4.5 per cent.

Current rent	£2,000		
YP 6 years at 3.5%	5.3286		
		£10,657	
Reversion to ERV	£4,000 pa		
YP perp. at 4.5%	22.2222		
PV 6 years at 4.5%	0.7679		
		£68,257	
Valuation			£78,914

The following comments should be noted.

1   The term yield is now level with the yield on gilt-edged stock. The term rent is seen as secure, the tenant occupying property worth twice as much as his rent payment. The income is fixed under a contract and the risk of default or fluctuation is minimal. Whether the term is as risk free as the gilt is open to question but a yield of 3.5 per cent is arguably the correct yield for the very best property, which would additionally presume a letting to an impeccable tenant.

2   The rent on reversion is estimated to be the rental value at the time of the valuation. Having regard to the perceptions of investors this would have represented a valuer's best estimate of what the actual rent would be. There is no implication of growth within the capitalization rate and the valuer had no reason to suspect a definite increase any more than the review taking place in a trough, such as happened after 1930. The reversion would have taken place in 1956, 11 years after the war ended, and a sustained period of rental growth had only been evidenced longer than 11 years once since 1910 (in 1918–30). The more recent history of depression, recovery, war, recovery, was a shorter term cycle (3 years down, 6 years up, 6 years depressed, 6 years up) up to 1950.

3   The rent on reversion would have been assumed to be fixed on a long lease of either 21, 35 or 42 years in order to stabilize any possibility of fluctuating returns.

4   The yield for the capitalization of the reversion would have been selected on the basis of comparisons with similar or fully let property investments and represented a level of return that would be sufficient if it was the internal rate of return from the investment. Again, this is a discounted cash flow valuation. The margin above gilts represented the extra risks

attached to property and had no inherent growth implied within it. The investor's willingness to accept a lease with no rent reviews is a testimony to that fact.

Given these assumptions and perceptions, the approach represents a logical, defensible, technique to both the capitalization and prediction of income flow. The valuation assumes a fixed rent to reversion, a reversion to a rental level consistent with the valuer's estimate of future rental level, and a sustaining of this level into the distant future. This income profile is consistent with expectations (see Figure 3.5).

Leaseholds

The approach to leasehold investment valuation is based on the same expectations regarding maintenance of rental values and the fixing of rents on long review patterns.

The approach has been less consistent since the turn of the century than the approach to the freehold investment valuation, but by 1950 the use of dual rate tables was accepted. The use of tax adjustments was well documented, and would become the normal approach after 1960.

The valuation of the leasehold interest in the previous property illustrates the process (rental value £4,000 per annum, rent paid £2,000 per annum, unexpired term 6 years).

ERV	£4,000 pa
Rent paid	£2,000 pa
Profit rent	£2,000 pa
YP 6 years at 5.5%	
and 2½% adj.	
tax at 40%	3.1654
Valuation	£6,331

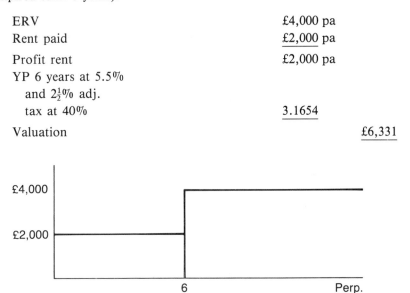

Figure 3.5 Income profile of Example 3.7

Note the following.

1 The profit rent remains at the same level as existing and expires in 6 years' time. With perceptions of fluctuating rental values rather than continually rising values the leaseholder could be expected to sublet the property for the whole of the remaining term with no reviews. The net income would therefore remain constant.

2 The interest expires in 6 years' time and upon expiry the lessee has no further interest in the property, and therefore no value. It is an investment which terminates, and all the return is in the form of income. The investor must recoup the capital out of income while a freeholder owns the interest in perpetuity and the expectations are that this will mean that the value of the asset can be maintained. In order to compare the investment in a leasehold interest with a freehold the leasehold investment must be made perpetual. The dual rate approach was evolved to make this comparison, with a tax adjustment justified by the fact that, for the tax-paying investor, the sinking fund would be derived from a taxed profit rent.

3 Having made the investment comparable with a freehold and in the absence of rental growth expectations the only question remaining is whether a leasehold is more risky than a freehold. The perceptions were that it was, so a higher return was used. In practice the valuer would look for other leasehold comparisons in accordance with his training (to look for similar comparisons). In the event of absence of such comparisons, a margin was adopted over and above the freehold yield for similar property on the basis that the technique had made the spendable income of the leasehold comparable with the income from the freehold. In textbook examples 1 per cent higher was a normal margin.

4 The sinking fund rates adopted were justified because sinking funds were available at yield levels in the order of 2/3 per cent net of tax.

5 The sinking fund element of net income was not treated differently from the rest of the income for income tax purposes so a tax adjustment was also logical.

The major conclusion from the foregoing analysis is that, in the context of the future expectations of investors and valuers, conventional techniques had a logical and defensible basis in 1950 and by analogy at other times prior to a change in investors' perceptions which occurred in the later 1950s. Whether these valuation models continued to be defensible after the change in perception will be considered in the next section.

THE REVERSE YIELD GAP AND ITS IMPLICATIONS

The level of prices continued to rise during the 1960s and averaged 4.03 per cent per annum between 1960 and 1970 (see Figure 3.6). The yield on gilts had already started to rise in the last half of the 1950s and continued to do so during the 1960s. By 1970 the yield on consols stood at 9 per cent (see Figure 3.7). The average gilt yield over the period was 6.77 per cent which was above the average inflation rate of 4 per cent per annum. A major realignment had taken place and the level of interest rates was again higher than the inflation rate giving investors a real return. By the end of the 1960s the rising level of inflation (6.27 per cent) was matched by a rise in gilt yields to maintain a differential of between 2 and 3 per cent. In the 1950s this differential had not been present. The average yield on gilts was 3.9 per cent between 1950 and 1955 while inflation was at 5.6 per cent per annum, a negative real return. From 1956 onwards the yield on gilts responded upwards and this response can be seen to continue in the 1960s.

The emergence of the reverse yield gap between gilts and UK equities in 1960 confirms the change in investment perceptions and the importance now attached to the real value of returns. The continuing presence of this gap in the 1960s (by 1970 the reverse yield gap was 4 per cent) shows the

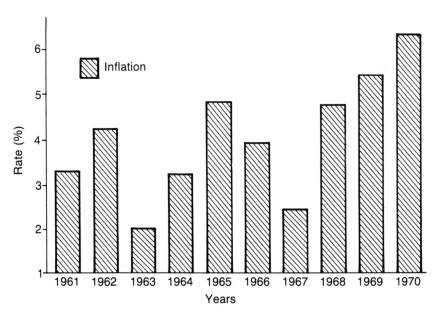

Figure 3.6 Annual growth of retail prices, 1961–70
Source: CSO 1983

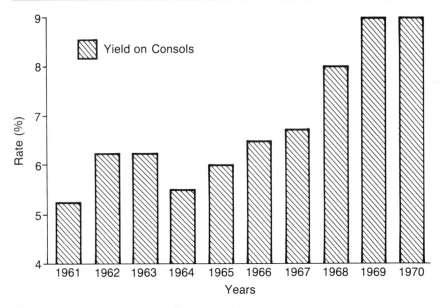

Figure 3.7   Average yield on Consols, 1961–70

long-term acceptance of the attractions of purchasing growth investments in times of inflation.

THE PROPERTY MARKET RESPONSE

The property market response is summarized in three indicators: the yield on property investments, rental levels and lease terms.

Yields

The majority of sources show an upward drift in all risks yields in the latter part of the decade (see Table 3.4). According to Senior, the most dramatic move in property yields came in ground rents with more than 60 years unexpired. These yields were reported as 4–5 per cent in 1960 but by 1970 were at 12 per cent (see Table 3.5).

Rents

Shop rental values also show an increase in the decade. The Nottingham average index rose by 8.9 per cent per annum and the prime index rose by 7.8 per cent per annum. The Michael Laurie analysis of commercial

Table 3.4 Prime and average shop yields, 1960–70

Year	MLP/EIU average	Senior prime	Senior secondary	Nottingham prime
1960		5.5	7.0	6.0
1961		5.5	7.0	5.5
1962		5.5	7.0	5.5
1963	6.5	5.5	7.0	5.5
1964	6.25	5.5	7.0	5.5
1965	6.75	6.0	7/8.0	5.0
1966	6.50	6.0	7.0	5.5
1967	6.37	6.5	7.5	6.0
1968	7.25	7.0	7.5	6.5
1969	7.30	7.0	7/8.0	5.0
1970	7.70	7.5	8.0	5.5

Sources: Senior 1975; Crosby 1985; Enever 1977

property values shows an average increase of 13.0 per cent per annum between 1962 and 1970. The 8.92 per cent per annum increase in Nottingham rents represents a real increase of 4.72 per cent per annum. It may seem anomalous for the yield on shops to rise in the second half of the 1960s when rents are increasing so strongly.

The yield on ground rents may offer the reason for the anomaly. Investors in property did not seem to realize the devaluing effects of inflation until after 1960. The gap between gilt and ground rent yields stood at 1.75 per cent in 1961. A change is apparent in 1964–5, which reversed the relationship of the previous 8 years in which ground rent yields had been

Table 3.5 Ground rents and gilt yields, 1960–9

Year	Yield (%)	Gilts	Gap
1960	4/5.0	5.25	0.75
1961	4/5.0	6.25	1.75
1962	5.0	6.25	1.25
1963	5.0	6.0	1.00
1964	6.0	5.5	−0.50
1965	8.0	6.0	−3.00
1966	10.0	6.5	−3.50
1967	12.0	6.75	−5.25
1968	12.0	8.00	−4.00
1969	12.0	9.00	−3.00

Source: Senior 1975

lower than gilts. It has already been established that while gilt markets showed signs of changing perceptions in 1956, there is no sign of a change in property market perceptions until 1963−4.

The movement in shop yields during the latter half of the 1960s may have been as a result of this change in perception. As ground rents were looked on with increasing suspicion, investors were now looking for participation in growth potential and, although shop rents were increasing at very high real growth rates, the ability to participate in growth had been seen to be very poor up to 1960, witnessed by typical rent revision terms.

The Review Period

The normal review or lease term up to 1960 was 21 years. An analysis of the review patterns of prime shop property in the 1960s shows the beginnings of change as regular reviews were introduced into prime shop leases in this period. In the period 1945−61 only 4.9 per cent of leases analysed had rent reviews within the lease term and the normal lease term was 21 years. In the period 1962−70 rent reviews were included in 62 per cent of leases. Between 1962 and 1965, 21 years remained as the normal review/lease term but the average fell from 25 years to 20 years. Between 1966 and 1970, the normal review term was 7 or 14 years and the average term was 13 years. Again, dramatic change came in the late, rather than the early, 1960s.

An analysis of lease particulars in the East Midlands region for prime shop property in 1962−3 shows that the average lease/review term was 17 years with a mode of 21 years. By 1967−8 the normal review pattern had fallen to 7 years with an average of 12 years. In contrast the normal lease term for secondary property was 7 years at both times (Crosby 1985). This analysis supports the conclusion that growth potential, and the ability to participate in it, was a major factor in the upward shift in yields in the mid to late 1960s. Investors had realized that growth was a very important consideration but few apart from the most recent of leases enabled participation in that growth.

Summary

The above analysis appears to suggest that the property market's response to changes in the economic criteria of investors lagged behind the general investment market's response by up to 10 years. By the early 1970s the response had been made. The average review pattern for prime shop yields in the period 1971−5 was 7 years and the mode 5 years. Prime shop lease terms in the East Midlands in 1972–3 were on either 5 or 7 year reviews with an average of 6 years. Prime shop yields fell from a peak of 7.5 per cent in 1970 to around a low of 4.5 per cent in 1972 and early 1973. Investors' and valuers' expectations and perceptions had changed during the decade and, coupled with a number of other factors, this would lead to the valuation techniques debate of the 1970s and 1980s.

These other factors included the rise of the financial institutions as major owners of property investments, bringing with them their advisors such as stockbrokers, analysts and actuaries, and the beginning of a critical awareness among the academic community led by Wood (1972) and Greaves (1972b).

In 1976, stockbrokers Greenwell and Co. criticized both valuers' reliance on direct comparison when so little of the stock of property investments was traded each year, and also criticized traditional techniques for masking the assumptions behind a valuation (Greenwell and Co. 1976). The same company noted the lack of an index of average yields in the property market (now remedied) and criticized prime yield indices as 'discredited indicators of value' questioning, by implication, conventional all risks yield valuation techniques. The Economist Intelligence Unit suggested in 1981 that 'those who claim that there is room for improvement in valuation techniques have established their case' (Daniels 1981).

Greer (1979) has neatly summarized the pressures which encourage perpetuation of outdated techniques in property investment appraisal.

> Both professional and academic literature reflects a deep vein of dissatisfaction with traditional approaches to the problem of risk in real estate investment analysis. A veritable flood of articles have appeared in recent years seeking to introduce techniques which have long been commonplace in other fields. Unfortunately, little of this path-breaking work has found its way into practice or into introductory textbooks or courses.
>
> Each generation of real estate analysts educates its own successor. Training and professional certification are largely controlled by trade groups, which in turn are governed by successful practitioners who were educated by their professional predecessors. As a consequence of this 'intellectual inbreeding', real estate analysts employ methods and techniques which represent the state of the art in other fields a generation ago. Old, less-effective tools of analysis tend to be perpetuated in spite of the ready availability of something better.
>
> This explains, but does not excuse, the prevalence of outmoded technology in real estate analysis. Intellectual cross-fertilization from corporate finance and the decision sciences in general can enable real estate

analysts to cast off the stigma of obsolescence and compete more effectively with professionals from such other fields as public accounting and management consulting who are experiencing increasing success in invading the traditional turf of appraisers and feasibility analysts.

The criticisms of the conventional approaches stem from the changes and processes detailed above, but generally relate to a change in the expectation of investors.

EXPECTATIONS OF INVESTORS, 1960 ONWARDS

The pre-1960 perceptions of investors had justified all risks yield valuation techniques based on the following assumptions.

1 It is assumed there is no growth in future rental over present rental values.
2 It is assumed that rents are fixed on long leases without review.
3 The capitalization rate (on a level, equivalent yield basis) is the internal rate of return expected from the investment.
4 An approximate 2 per cent yield differential between prime shops and gilts reflected the disadvantages of property investment.

It therefore represented a true cash flow technique at the target rate of return. Since the inception of the reverse yield gap and the acceptance of rent reviews, a number of these assumptions have been disturbed.

1 The assumption of growth in the future is the essence of the reverse yield gap. The quantification of this implication is examined in Chapter 5.
2 The practice of fixing rents on long leases without review changed and analysis shows that by 1980 the normal review pattern was 5 years. Changes in value level can now be incorporated frequently.
3 The capitalization rate depends on the preconceived level of growth in the future. The rate does not necessarily represent an expected internal rate of return over the life of the investment and, for prime property investments, it has implied growth in every year since 1960 with the exception (in some sub-markets) of 1992–3.
4 The internal rate of return expected is not known and is the subject of later discussion. However, most commentators refer to a 2 per cent margin above the internal rate of return on gilts to cover the disadvantages of property investment (see Chapter 2).

The impact of these changes is illustrated by the valuation of the

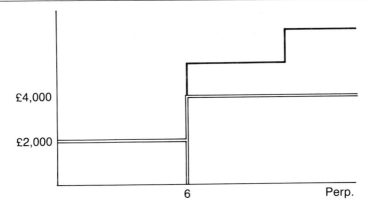

Figure 3.8 Expected future income profile – post reverse yield gap

reversionary freehold (Example 3.7). It would show a different expected future income profile (see Figure 3.8) in 1970 than in 1950.

Note that:

1 taking the yield on gilts to be around 10 per cent, the yield required from the property is now higher, say 12/13 per cent;
2 the rent on reversion is expected to be higher than the current rental value now;
3 rent reviews are expected in the new lease so regular upward revisions at 5-yearly intervals should be incorporated.

Current techniques employ a reversion to the current rental value and then capitalize in perpetuity. If the implication of the reverse yield gap is accepted then the level of income expected is not explicit in these valuations and the capitalization rate is the product of the purchaser's expectation: within the capitalization rate growth is implied so it is no longer a target rate of return.

On the surface, it would appear strange that techniques have not changed since the 1960s given the changes in investors' perceptions. Although the logical base of the conventional model appears to have collapsed it is still in almost universal use in the UK for the market valuation role. The current practice of valuation is examined in the next chapter.

4

The current conventional market valuation model

INTRODUCTION

This chapter critically examines current UK practice for the valuation of investment properties. The previous edition of this text was written during a period of sustained growth in property values and concentrated upon valuation in a rising market. The circumstances are now very different and this edition is written in the middle of a recession which has seen substantial falls in property values in both real and nominal terms.

In addition to the changes in the market place, the information base of this analysis has been substantially increased. This is the result of research undertaken by the authors into the practice of valuing reversionary free-holds (Crosby 1991) which, when added to the work on leaseholds (Baum 1986), gives a comprehensive view of market valuation methods.

This research reveals a profession which adopts a variety of approaches to its work. Nonetheless, comparable information provides a foundation for all market valuation methods. We have illustrated that, prior to the first appearance of the reverse yield gap before 1960, the conventional market valuation model was effectively an explicit discounted cash flow approach whereby the expected future cash flow was discounted at a required return (see Chapter 2).

After the appearance of the reverse yield gap the model became a comparison model based upon an all risks yield which represented a unit of comparison, no longer the required return. As the valuation model understated the prospective income flow by ignoring any future growth in rental value, the yield compensated by being set at a level which was lower than the target rate of return. The gap between the all risks yield and the required rate of return represented the expected or implied rental growth rate hidden within the valuation. This is directly analogous to Gordon's explanation of the reverse yield gap between stocks and bonds (see Chapter 2).

In effect, the model ceased to be an investment approach and became a comparable approach based upon the all risks yield. This chapter assesses the model as a pricing technique which attempts to make the best use of market comparables; it has no place in analysis of price and the measurement of investment worth.

It is clear that the best pricing technique, i.e. an accurate one, must be based on the best evidence of market price derived from other transactions in the same sub-market. The model's efficiency in its use and adaptation of market evidence is therefore the main criterion to be adopted in assessing its quality. This test is now applied by examining the conventional (pricing) valuation solutions to standard valuation problems.

THE FULLY LET FREEHOLD

Of all three categories of property investment, the fully let freehold is least prone to variation and hence to inaccurate valuation. As the model comprises simply the rent passing (which is also the estimated rental value (ERV)) divided by the all risks yield and as there are no differences in application of the model by different practitioners, the chances of different valuers coming up with different valuations based upon the same information base are small. However, the valuation relies upon the strength of the comparable; and comparables may be sparse in a slack market dominated by reversionary freeholds. The quantity and quality of comparable transactions is the key to all comparable valuations; in fully let freeholds methodological factors are less important.

However, when comparables cannot be applied directly, all adaptations are intuitive. For example, if a reversionary freehold comparable shows an equivalent yield of 6 per cent (see the next section), how should this information be applied to a fully let property? What if the comparable is let on 5-year reviews but the subject property is let on 3-year reviews? As the model is based upon rent and yield, only the yield can be adjusted to cope with differences between subject and comparable (hence the name, the all risks yield).

THE REVERSIONARY FREEHOLD

Three conventional techniques for valuing reversionary freeholds are recognized. These are the term and reversion, the equivalent yield and the layer (or hardcore) approaches. The basic texts on valuation tend to suggest that the term and reversion approach is the most commonly used method and the other two are lesser used variations. Our research indicates that this is not now true and that horizontally sliced layer and equivalent yield approaches dominate practice in the larger firms and financial institutions.

The major findings of our research into the practice of reversionary freehold valuation in the UK were that, although the majority of valuers questioned still used term and reversion usually or always (60 per cent), they tended to be valuers who were not specialists in the investment valuation field. They worked for provincial private practices and local authorities and did few valuations of this sort each year. They tended to rely upon traditional training which continued to support the term and reversion method.

Horizontally sliced layer and equivalent yield methods are adopted mainly by valuers in London and the larger metropolitan areas specializing in this type of work. In terms of number of valuations undertaken by each method, the survey found an even spread between the three approaches. The message from practice is clear. The term and reversion method is not the staple diet of specialist investment valuers (Crosby 1991).

In order to compare the three approaches, a single example is now used.

■ EXAMPLE 4.1

Value a good quality freehold office investment let at a net fixed rent of £150,000 per annum with the final 6 years of a historic lease still to run. The net estimated rental value of the building is £300,000 per annum. An identical building next door has recently been let on 5-yearly reviews at its estimated rental value and subsequently sold for £5,000,00.

Analysis

$$\text{capitalization rate } (k) = \frac{£300,000}{£5,000,000} = 6 \text{ per cent.}$$

If the valuation had been of a fully let property, the capitalization rate could have been applied directly. If perfect comparables exist, arguments over technique are redundant and direct capital comparisons are all that is required. However, the subject property is a reversionary property and an adjustment technique is required in order to reconcile imperfect comparables.

Term and Reversion

Term rent	£150,000	
YP 6 years at 5%	5.0757	
		£761,350
Reversion to ERV	£300,000	
YP perp. at 6%	16.6667	
PV 6 years at 6%	0.7050	
		£3,524,800
Valuation		£4,286,160

Analysis

Initial yield $= \dfrac{£150,000}{£4,286,160} = 3.50\%$

Reversionary yield $= \dfrac{£300,000}{£4,286,160} = 7.00\%$

Equivalent yield $= 5.97\%$

Notes

1 The term yield is derived from the fully let comparable and then adjusted down to represent the security of the term income. This security is supposed to come from the fact that the default risk is less as the tenant is less likely to leave the premises while paying less than ERV.
2 The capitalization rate of the reversion is based upon the fact that the property becomes fully let in 6 years time and the comparison is a fully let property, therefore the yield can be applied directly.
3 An alternative application of the technique adopts the same differential between the term and reversion yield but instead of adopting $k - 1$ for the term and k for the reversion it adopts yields which straddle the capitalization rate, that is, $k - 0.5$ on the term and $k + 0.5$ on the reversion. The reason for this is explained below.

Criticisms

1 The term represents a fixed income for the next 6 years. The capitalization rate represents a growth implicit yield, therefore if the yield choice within the valuation is going to distinguish between the different parts of

the valuation (term and reversion), it should take account of the fixed income nature by applying a yield appropriate to a 'safe' income in default terms but an extremely 'unsafe' income in real terms.

2 The term yield is often reduced by the 'normal' amount of 1 per cent but it is not always an advantage to have a lower value term. In a rising market where rent review settlements lag behind open market lettings, it may be an advantage to lose a tenant and obtain a higher rent from a better quality tenant. In a falling market, covenant of the tenant becomes crucial to value and rules of thumb regarding the value of a secure tenant again appear simplistic.

3 A reversionary property may not have the same qualities as the fully let property. The capitalization rate of 6 per cent implies growth which is realizable every 5 years. Theoretically, the growth potential of reversionary properties (let with unexpired terms which are less than the normal review pattern) is greater than for the fully let property, therefore the combined effect of valuing the reversion at the fully let all risks yield and the term at 1 per cent less creates a 'correct' valuation. However, the market does not perceive reversions in this light and it is rare for a reversionary property to be valued at an equivalent or average yield which is lower than the all risks yield of the fully let property. The market tends to adopt a philosophy that discounts the reversionary property value due to the fact that the ERV has been obtained when fully let but is only an estimate in the reversionary valuation. This uncertainty regarding the ERV estimate creates additional risk in the reversionary valuation and the value is therefore discounted as indicated in note (3) above.

4 There is a problem with the yield choice on the reversion in that the 6 per cent yield implies rental growth which is participated in every 5 years. The PV relates to the behaviour of the ERV in the 6-year waiting period. The ERV grows continually and therefore the reversion should be deferred at a lower yield to imply a better growth potential. This point is illustrated in Chapter 6.

The final result is a valuation that is logically incorrect and practically difficult to understand. It must be incomprehensible to most observers as it isolates one aspect of the investment (security of term income) while keeping all others hidden within the yield. It is, of course, a product of an age which has long since departed and the traditional application of the method should be laid to rest immediately.

However, it does perform one useful purpose that the applications which have replaced it find very difficult to perform. That is the valuation of properties let on long fixed terms without rent review prior to the final reversion. If our example had an unexpired term of 16 years rather than six, the valuation could be approached by a term and reversion method, but adopting a high yield on the term to reflect the fixed income. This yield could be based on fixed income government securities adjusted for the additional risks of property investment but tempered by the prospect of obtaining a known quantity of rent for a long term secured on the existing tenant or an assignee (this yield could be more than gilts but less than an equated yield for a rack rented property).

Layer

The horizontally sliced layer technique came into constant use in the 1970s in response to the rent freeze. In the research into practice, the age profile of valuers using layer methods indicated a bulge in the age group who entered practice in the early 1970s.

However, in the 1960s, capital gains tax legislation led to the initial use of layer techniques when valuers sought a method which could identify the prospective capital gain element of the reversionary situation. From that work evolved a technique which could be used to 'calculate' the top slice yield. Although we set this out in the first edition of this text, we noted its obsolescence and we have consigned the 'modified layer' approach to the scrap heap as it has no relevance to modern practice. Its only use is to approximately reconcile the capital value of a reversionary property valued by term and reversion to the layer valuation and we see no purpose in doing that.

Term rent	£150,000	
YP perp. at 6%	16.6667	
		£2,500,000
Reversion to ERV	£300,000	
Less bottom slice	£150,000	
Top slice	£150,000	
YP perp. at 7%	14.2857	
PV 6 years at 7%	0.6663	
		£1,427,876
Valuation		£3,927,876

Analysis

Initial yield$\quad$ = £150,000$\quad$ = 3.82%

$\qquad\qquad\quad$ £3,927,876

Reversionary yield = £300,000$\quad$ = 7.64%

$\qquad\qquad\qquad$ £3,927,876

Equivalent yield$\quad$ = 6.44%

Notes

1 The bottom slice income is perceived to extend into perpetuity on the basis that there is little likelihood of the rent ever falling below the passing rent because of the combined effect of upwards only rent reviews and perceived rental growth prospects.

2 The top slice is much more risky. It is based upon an estimate of ERV about which it is difficult to be precise. In addition, because of the top slice nature of the increase, an error in the ERV estimate would create a correspondingly greater error in the value of the top slice. For example, had the ERV only been £270,000 per annum (a 10 per cent error), the top slice rental would have been £120,000 per annum rather than £150,000 per annum (a 20 per cent fall). The geared nature of the increase is therefore very sensitive to errors of estimates and is therefore the risky part of the valuation.

3 The layer technique more closely aligns with the perceptions of the modern valuer and is therefore more easily adapted for specific circumstances. If the valuer feels that the ERV estimate is very suspect then the valuer can amend the top slice yield by more than 1 per cent (in practice 2 per cent is often used).

Criticisms

1 It is difficult to accept the arbitrary split of the income into two parts as the risk of non-receipt attaches to the whole income.

2 The application of the layer method uses a growth implicit yield on the bottom slice which is fixed in nominal terms. As all the growth is in the top slice, and the top slice is highly geared, it might be expected to adopt a high fixed income yield on the bottom slice and a very low yield on the top slice to imply a very highly geared growth potential. The valuation is unstable and suffers from the same problems as the term and reversion approach outlined in criticism (4) regarding the same yield on PV as on YP, but magnified because of the gearing problem.

3 The choice of the yield split between top and bottom slices is very arbitrary and cannot be undertaken other than intuitively.

4 It is almost impossible to intuitively increase the yield on both top and bottom slices for a property which is let on a long fixed term before reversion. In the survey of practice, valuers using this method (and equivalent yield) ditched it in favour of term and reversion for that problem.

Although mathematically and conceptually fraught with problems, the layer technique does have two major advantages for practice, and they are the concentrations on the important variable of ERV and the lack of downside risk caused by upwards only rent reviews (assuming long unexpired terms and good covenants).

Equivalent yield

Equivalent yield differs from the other two approaches in that it does not differentiate between the yields on top and bottom slice or term and reversion. As it applies the same yield to both parts of the income flow, it does not matter whether a horizontally or vertically sliced approach is adopted. In the practice survey, horizontally sliced equivalent yield was more prevalent than its vertically sliced alternative.

Term rent	£150,000		
YP perp. at 6.5%	15.3846		
		£2,307,692	
Reversion to ERV	£300,000		
Less bottom slice	£150,000		
Top slice	£150,000		
YP perp. at 6.5%	15.3846		
PV 6 years at 6.5%	0.6853		
		£1,581,540	
Valuation			£3,889,232

Analysis

$$\text{Initial yield} = \frac{£150,000}{£3,889,232} = 3.86\%$$

$$\text{Reversionary yield} = \frac{£300,000}{£3,889,232} = 7.71\%$$

Equivalent yield = 6.50%

Notes

1 The equivalent yield is sometimes called the equated yield without growth and represents the internal rate of return of the cash flow assuming a reversion to no more than current rental value. Future rental value growth is still excluded.

2 The equivalent yield method is supposed to be particularly useful in the analysis of transactions. Another reversionary transaction can be analysed by determining the IRR of the conventional cash flow, which can then be applied to the subject property with suitable adjustments for differences between the comparable and subject property.

3 Criticisms of the two previous models based upon mathematical problems and arbitrary adjustments of the two yields within the valuation are eliminated as there is only one yield.

4 Criticisms of the other two models based upon the choice of a growth implicit yield on the term (or bottom slice) are also eliminated. The single capitalization rate is the true all risks yield of the investment. It represents the growth potential of the investment as a whole and the other risks applied to the property as a whole (not to parts of the income profile).

5 Practitioners tend to adopt slightly higher equivalent yields than capitalization rates on fully let properties due to the discussion in note (3) and criticism (4) of the term and reversion approach. The extent of this increase (we have used 0.5 per cent) is arbitrary.

Criticisms

1 Being a true all risks yield technique, the valuer is left to intuitively adjust for every difference between the subject and comparable property. These differences are not just for physical and locational differences, they are also for differences in the tenure (fully let to reversionary freehold) and, if both comparable and subject property are reversionary, for differences in unexpired term and ratio of rent passing to ERV (see Chapter 6).

2 The model is only as good as the comparables on which it is based. As indicated in the previous paragraph, a perfect comparable for a reversionary property is one which has the same locational qualities, is physically similar and also has the same unexpired term and the same rent passing to ERV ratio. As the subject and comparable property diverge, the quality of the valuation diminishes. This is not exceptional to the equivalent yield model. But if the subject property has a long fixed term, there is a wide intuitive leap necessary to adapt the yield. In this case, as for layer, valuers often revert back to the term and reversion approach using a high yield on the term to reflect the lack of growth potential.

Conclusions

The criticisms of conventional approaches for market valuation are based on two criteria.

1 *Rationality.*   There is little evidence to suggest that there is any logic to the models as currently used if logic is defined as the model which most fits the perceptions of the owners of property investments. Even in the midst of the recession of 1992–3, prime property yields imply a long-term growth rate in rental values. Valuing fixed elements of the cash flow at growth implicit yields and assuming reversions are always to no more than current ERV, are so obviously devoid of reality that it is no wonder they have come under so much attack since 1960.

2 *Comparables.*   As there is no longer a rational basis for these models, the reason they have survived is because of the perceived role of the valuation in fixing price levels. Comparison with identical or similar assets has long been accepted as the best basis for assessing likely selling price. The argument boils down to which conventional technique makes the best use of comparables; and is there a better way of utilizing comparable information? All comparable techniques are only as accurate as the quality and quantity of comparable information. However, the equivalent yield model is totally objective in its analysis of transactions in that it calculates the IRR of the current cash flow assuming a reversion to current ERV only. It does not subjectively amend term or bottom slice yields as compared with reversion or top slice yields. By removing these arbitrary adjustments to yields, it is the only true all risks yield approach. The equivalent yield is a measure of the qualities of the comparable and needs to be adjusted for the differences inherent in the lease structure of the subject property and for any other differences. All differences are encompassed within the yield and this is the only thing that can be changed.

As should be expected in cases of irrationality, problems arise when comparable and subject properties start to differ and one or other of them becomes abnormal. In the property market of the 1990s some of these abnormal problems have become the norm and the inadequacies of the techniques set out in this chapter have become more obvious. Leaseholds and over-rented properties (two examples of less standard valuation problems) are examined below.

LEASEHOLDS

As with freeholds, a single example is used to illustrate the conventional approach to leaseholds.

■   EXAMPLE 4.2

A leasehold interest has 20 years to run, subject to a fixed head rent of £100,000 per annum. The current rental value is £200,000 per annum, subject to 5-yearly reviews. Market evidence suggests a freehold capitalization rate k of 6 per cent for this type of property.

Much criticized, the tax-adjusted dual rate valuation appears to remain in limited use. The tax exemption of the pension fund has prompted unadjusted dual rate valuations. Single rate valuations have also been suggested (see, for example, Enever 1981). These three approaches will be taken as the available conventional techniques.

The three share a common feature leading to a problem requiring immediate consideration. The remunerative or capitalization rate k is traditionally settled by reference to the all-risks yields obtained by purchasers of freehold investments in similar property with a small upward adjustment to account for the so-called extra risk of leasehold investment. This may be said to be the result of several inter-related factors: the top slice nature of a leasehold, making the profit rent considerably more sensitive to changes in full rental value than is the net freehold income; the dual contractual burden suffered by the leaseholder; the risk of a dilapidations expense inherited from previous leaseholders; and others.

The adjustment to k is often accepted as plus 1 per cent or 2 per cent over the freehold remunerative rate, which would lead in this case to a remunerative rate of 7 per cent or 8 per cent.

The logic of such adjustment is not questioned here (see Chapter 7). Investors are generally said to be risk-averse (see Chapter 2): so greater volatility in the net income, even if equal chances were applied to increases and decreases, would be seen as a factor justifying a higher yield.

However, the quantum of the adjustment is in the hands of the valuer. In the usual case, where market evidence is slight or imperfect, a considerable burden settles itself upon the valuer's intuition. This problem will be borne in mind for later reference: but for the purposes of the examples a remunerative rate of 6 per cent is used to isolate other errors and to reduce variations in an area where the valuer's inspiration is in danger of influencing his logic.

Dual rate, tax-adjusted

Rent received	£200,000 pa	
less Rent paid	£100,000 pa	
Profit rent	£100,000 pa	
YP 20 years at 6%		
+ 3% tax 40p	8.1950	
Valuation		£819,500

Analysis

Yield = 6% × £819,500 = £49,170

Sinking fund (gross) = £100,000 − £49,170

       = £50,830

Sinking fund (net) = £50,830 (0.6)

       = £30,498

× A £1 pa, 20 years		
at 3%	26.8704	
Capital recouped		£819,500

Notes

1 As noted above, the 6 per cent capitalization or remunerative rate would normally be derived from sales of comparable freehold properties and adjusted upwards to account for extra risk.

2 The accumulative rate of 3 per cent is supposed to represent the net-of-tax return available on a guaranteed sinking fund policy taken out with an assurance company, being absolutely safe. The sinking fund is designed to replace the initial capital outlay on what is a wasting asset. The historical organization of the profession demanded that a property-wide means of comparison evolved: while leaseholds might best be compared with redeemable stock, reality required that they be comparable with property investments, specifically freeholds. The wasting nature of the asset had, then, to be countered by the replacement of capital over the period of the lease so that an interest similar to a freehold can be shown to exist, provided the right steps are taken, and the right price is paid.

3 The tax adjustment of 40 per cent counters the fact that any tax-paying purchaser of the investment would lose a portion of his profit rent in tax. While the effect on the remunerative rate or yield is not regarded as important (all, or most, investment opportunities are quoted on a gross-of-tax basis) its effect on the sinking fund payment is vital. Without adjustment, the sinking fund would become inadequate as a result of

income tax reducing the whole profit rent. As it has to accurately recoup capital, a 'grossing up' factor is applied to cancel out the effect of tax (see, for example, Baum and Mackmin 1989): this grossing-up factor (in this case $1/(1 - 0.4)$) is the tax adjustment.

4 A 'true net' valuation (using a net profit rent, a net remunerative rate and no tax adjustment) would produce an identical result.

Criticisms

1 Why use such a low accumulative rate? Bank deposits or building society accounts have earned considerably more in almost every year since 1960 and yet are regarded as safe. It is true that they do not provide a guaranteed accumulation: but there is probably an equal risk of increases and decreases in the rates offered. Even risk-averse investors would be unlikely to discount the yield they would accept on guaranteed accumulations by as much as is necessary to produce 3 per cent. Borrowers would certainly not set up 3 per cent sinking funds when the cost of the capital they have employed to purchase the interest could be four times as great.

2 Why adjust for tax at 40 per cent? Valuations are usually estimates of market value. Hence, the purchaser's tax rate is unlikely to be known and a guess, or average, has to be made. Forty per cent may be a realistic average where the small-scale investor is interested: but this ignores the common case where a tax exempt fund is likely to buy, or where a company paying corporation tax is likely to purchase, either for occupation or investment. The considerable interest of gross funds in this market may be explained by the use of tax-adjusted valuations leading to low asking prices, and resulting in high equated yields for the purchasers.

3 As noted in the RICS research report (Trott 1980), the combination of three variables (remunerative rate, accumulation rate, tax rate) in the tax-adjusted dual rate valuation makes a full analysis of transactions hazardous. Different values for the three variables may combine to produce the same years' purchase figure.

4 Other criticisms may be made: as, to a certain extent, these are common to all conventional techniques, they will be dealt with later.

These criticisms may be countered by an approach which is often used to reflect the interest of the gross funds and slightly more realistic accumulative rates.

Dual, rate unadjusted for tax

Rent received	£200,000 pa
Less rent paid	£100,000 pa
Profit rent	£100,000 pa
YP 20 years at 6% + 4%	10.6858
Valuation	£1,068,580

Analysis

Yield = 6% × £1,068,580 = £64,115

Sinking fund = £100,000 − £64,115

= £35,885

× A £1 pa, 20 years
   at 4%   29.7781

£1,068,593

Notes

1 A slightly higher net accumulative rate is used here to allow what might be seen as more realistic valuations to be made. It was significant that the 1978 (10th) of Parry's Valuation Tables included dual rate tables with 4 per cent accumulative rates for the first time. It is interesting to note, however, that, if this technique is designed for the gross fund, the gross rate of sinking fund accumulation – 4 per cent – is actually lower than the equivalent rate in the previous example (3 per cent net at 40 per cent tax is equal to 5 per cent gross).

2 A tax adjustment is superfluous in this case as the income of a gross fund is not reduced by tax. If this, however, represented a market valuation, any bidding taxpayer would have to accept a very low yield in order to compete while allowing for recoupment of capital.

Criticisms

1 It is easily proven that a single rate years' purchase figure allows for recoupment of capital at the remunerative rate (see, for example, Baum and Mackmin 1989). The justification for a dual rate approach is the argument that, *if a sinking fund were actually taken out in practice*, there would be no reason for the accumulative rate offered by an assurance company coinciding with the remunerative rate attainable upon purchasing the investment, thus necessitating a dual rate approach.

But are sinking funds actually taken out in practice? There are sound reasons for concluding that few investors would arrange for recoupment of capital in this way.

(i) *Occupiers* can usually be regarded as long-term (more than the profit rent period) tenants. The initial capital outlay, probably an overdraft, or regarded as an investment of cash 'in the business', is recouped out of profits, which (hopefully) outlive the profit rent. A perpetual income may in many cases be the result, in which case a sinking fund is inappropriate.

(ii) *Investors* are likely to be holders of a number of property interests. In such a case, recoupment of capital from a wasting asset like a leasehold is unlikely to be by means of a sinking fund: it can be by investing profit rents in similar investments. It is possible to show (see Baum 1982) that an increasing income and portfolio is likely to grow from a small portfolio of leaseholds by continuous reinvestment. Note the behaviour of building societies, effectively mass purchasers of limited term property incomes by way of mortgage loans. Repayments are turned over immediately to become fresh loans: and all repayment calculations are carried out on a single rate basis. The requirement to invest in a similar investment can also be questioned: the investor will be happy to invest in any investment with the correct/risk return characteristics.

(iii) *Borrowers* in either category will have a cost of capital well in excess of the 3 or 4 per cent accumulative rate. Consequently, no purchaser would set up a sinking fund to recoup capital at low accumulative rate when, as an alternative, they could reduce a debt costing much more.

2 It has been well illustrated (Fraser 1977) that, while the concept of the sinking fund in leasehold valuations is designed as an attempt to reconcile the differences between the freehold and the wasting leasehold asset, the recoupment of capital in times of inflation becomes inadequate. Freeholds are (if depreciation is set aside) likely to increase in capital and rental value over time. If the sinking fund replaces the initial capital cost of the leasehold, then the leasehold fails to keep pace with the freehold, and the rationale of the dual rate concept is not put into practice.

Various methods of adjusting the sinking fund to cope with inflation have been suggested by writers including Fraser, Greaves and Rose. Their approaches are fully documented in the RICS report (Trott 1980), which concludes that 'index-linked annual sinking funds ... are not practical and (their use in valuation should) be discouraged'. It appears that such methods approximate to the introduction of valuation programs for calculators when the market is adopting computers. In times of inflation, the sinking fund is obsolete, and methods designed to streamline the dual rate valuation are doomed to extinction.

3 The fundamental mathematical error which is inherent in all dual rate valuations of varying profits rent is also well documented (see Trott 1980; Harker 1983; Bowcock 1983a; and Baum and Mackmin 1989). The double sinking fund, annual equivalent and sinking fund approaches, and Pannell's method (for comparisons, see Baum and Mackmin 1989: ch. 5) deal with the problem with varying degrees of success; the final sentence of the previous paragraph applies here also.

Single rate

Rent received	£200,000 pa	
Less rent paid	£100,000 pa	
Profit rent	£100,000 pa	
YP 20 years at 6%	11.4699	
Valuation		£1,146,990

Analysis
Yield = 6% × £1,146,990 = £68,820
Sinking fund = £100,000 − £68,820
= £31,180
× A £1 pa, 20 years
at 6%   36.7856

£1,146,975

Notes

1 As demonstrated by the analysis, the single rate valuation allows for the recoupment of capital at the remunerative rate. Whether such a rate could be earned in practice is not necessarily important for the reasons stated within criticism (1) of the dual rate unadjusted for tax approach (see also Colam 1983).

2 However, recoupment of capital would have to be out of taxed income, as profit rents are subject to income tax and reinvestment in any medium would only be possible with the after-tax income. Hence a net of tax valuation is necessary. The example used is a net of tax valuation for a gross fund: if the potential purchaser is a taxpayer competing with taxpayers, then a tax adjustment will be needed. In such a case the net profit rent

should be capitalized by a years' purchase factor at a net-of-tax yield, otherwise a dual rate valuation will be the result.

3 All foregoing criticisms appear to be met. The accumulative rate is no longer critically low; the problem of average tax adjustment can be avoided by investigating the market; there is no artificial assumption that a sinking fund is actually taken out, as reinvestment is at the remunerative rate, thereby obviating the problems of recoupment in times of inflation; and there is no mathematical error when valuing varying profit rents at a single rate of interest (but see Bowcock 1983a). Unfortunately, more fundamental problems present themselves in the valuation of freeholds.

Conclusions

Leasehold investment valuations are relatively rare compared with the more common freehold. However, the complexity of the leasehold problem is far greater than for freeholds and the margin for error is much greater.

The basic approach is the same as for freeholds. The prospective cash flow of the leasehold investment is set out on the assumption that rents are reviewed up to current rental levels, but future increases in rental value are ignored. The cash flow is capitalized at the all risks yield, found by comparison.

In the preceding critique, it is concluded that the dual rate approach should be laid to rest and single rate valuations would be a preferred alternative.

However, a fundamental problem remains. This is examined in detail in Chapter 6 and is summarized below.

All conventional approaches to leasehold valuations, whether single rate or dual rate, rely on a comparison technique. The perfect comparison, in addition to physical and locational qualities, would be leasehold, of the same unexpired lease term, with the same reversionary date and the same ratio of rent to ERV.

It is impossible to envisage such a catalogue of similar qualities. The market's solution is therefore to use freehold comparables because they are more plentiful. But freeholds are not the same; in fact, apart from both being properties, they could not be more dissimilar. In an effort to compensate for some of these differences, valuers using conventional techniques are encouraged to add a risk margin to the freehold all risks yield. Using the all risks yield from a freehold, which incorporates an implicit expectation of future growth in rental values, a depreciation rate and a risk premium (see Chapter 2), as the value measure for a shorter term and differently structured cash flow, is so simplistic that valuations carried out by that method are, in our opinion, virtually useless.

We are not alone in this view. The realization of the inadequacy of the conventional approach has led many valuers to adopt growth explicit approaches (see Chapter 6) or to base conventional valuation yields on comparisons derived from outside of the property market.

OVER-RENTED PROPERTIES

So far we have looked at the conventional approach to pricing valuations of properties let at either their ERV or at rents less than ERV. Since 1990, the UK has experienced a deep recession and rental values have fallen in nominal terms in many locations, especially those which showed the major growth in the 1980s boom. This includes the City of London and the southeast region of the UK. According to IPD (1992), by May 1992 70 per cent of Central London offices were over-rented and by an average of over 35 per cent. The degree of over-renting increased over the following year to May 1993. Given a low inflation and low growth outlook for the UK economy (and the fact that over 60 per cent (by value) of the IPD database was let on leases with over 15 years unexpired, the vast majority on upwards only rent reviews (Crosby *et al.* 1993)), valuers are likely to have to deal with over-renting for a long time to come.

Given the major concentration of institutional property in the most badly affected locations, the valuation of over-rented properties has already become a normal occurrence for the major firms and financial institutions and the application of the investment method has been the subject of intense scrutiny. It has not stood up to the scrutiny very well and we set out the conventional approach and its limitations below.

■ EXAMPLE 4.3

A Central London office building is to be valued in June 1992. It was let on a 20-year FRI lease in March 1990 with 5-year reviews at a passing rent of £2 million per annum. The estimated rental value has now fallen to £1 million per annum. The fully let rack rented capitalization rate is estimated to be 8 per cent. Gilts yielding approximately 10 per cent.

Valuers in practice started to approach the challenge of over-rented properties by 'top-slicing' the portion of the contractual rent they considered to be in excess of the current rental value. They capitalized the core income as if the property was fully let at the appropriate all risks yield. They then capitalized the top-slice income for the unexpired term of the lease at a rate which reflected the fact that it was a fixed income supported by the upwards only rent reviews and that it was dependent on the tenant's ability to continue to pay the rent. The approach is shown diagrammatically in Figure 4.1.

Core income		
ERV	£1,000,000	
YP perp. at 8% (ARY)	12.5000	
		12,500,000
Top-slice		
Passing rent	£2,000,000	
ERV	£1,000,000	
Overage	£1,000,000	
YP 17.75 years at 13%	6.8135	
		6,813,459
Valuation		£19,313,459

This approach is logical to valuers because, given that the layer method is standard, they are used to layering a rising income between the passing rent and the ERV. With an over-rented property, valuers are merely reversing the layers. In this approach, valuers are capitalizing the top-slice income for the whole period for which the tenant is contracted to pay the higher rent.

Some valuers considered that a sinking fund should be applied to the top-slice income because it is a wasting asset. Our views on dual rate valuations are clearly set out above and there is no justification for adopting a dual rate solution to this problem.

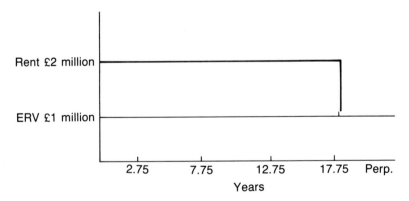

Figure 4.1   Over-rented property income profile

There are two main problems with the conventional approach.

1 If the all risks yield implies long-term rental growth (which is the case with a yield of 8 per cent), then the ERV may rise to exceed the passing rent before the lease expires. Therefore, it may be incorrect to capitalize the top-slice income for the whole of the unexpired term.
2 Capitalizing the top-slice ignores the rental growth implied by the all risks yield so that part of the overage is double counted.

To compensate for the fact that the overage might be eliminated before the end of the lease, the term of the overage can be taken to the first review only (2.75 years). However, the overage is unlikely to be eliminated by the next review; and the only realistic or rational approach is to forecast the review at which the overage is eliminated. This can be done by either considering the implied rental growth within current capitalization rates or by making an explicit forecast of rental growth over the short and medium term.

Valuers advocating and using conventional techniques have resisted the challenge of models which incorporate rental growth for the past 30 years. In the case of over-rented properties, there appears to be no choice.

Even if the necessity to forecast the point at which the rent will be reviewed to more than the current rent is accepted, the core and top-slice method will still not be a defensible approach. This is illustrated below. If it is assumed that the rent will rise above £2 million per annum by the review in 12.75 years' time (2005), the valuation will be as follows.

Core income			
ERV	£1,000,000		
YP perp. at 8% (ARY)	12.5000		
		12,500,000	
Top-slice			
Passing rent	£2,000,000		
Less ERV	£1,000,000		
Overage	£1,000,000		
YP 12.75 years at 13%	6.0731		
		6,073,085	
Valuation			£18,573,085

The valuation is lower than the previous solution by 4 per cent. However, this is still an over-valuation because there is double counting of the notional rent increases at the reviews in 1995 and 2000 (those included by the use of 8 per cent on the bottom slice). This is illustrated in Figure 4.2, where the shading represents that part of the income flow which is effectively valued twice.

To overcome this problem, valuers must now explicitly consider growth. The best solution to this problem would be to shelve the popular layer method and to adopt a term and reversion approach. Having anticipated when the overage is eliminated, the term of 12.75 years could be valued at a risk free rate subject to a risk premium to reflect weakness in the covenant of the tenant, with the reversion valued as usual at the all risks yield.

Term rent	£2,000,000		
YP 12.75 years at 13%	6.0731		
		£12,146,170	
Reversion to ERV	£1,000,000		
YP perp. at 8%	12.5000		
PV 12.75 years at 8%	0.3748		
		£4,685,513	
Valuation			£16,831,683

This valuation remains subject to a single remaining error in the way that the reversion is discounted in a term and reversion valuation. This is referred to above on pages 89–91 and is further discussed in Chapter 5.

There is a simple alternative to adopting either a core and top slice or a term and reversion approach to the over-rented problem. Many valuers have reverted to an initial yield approach on the basis that, in many markets, the core data of rack rented capitalization rate and rack rental

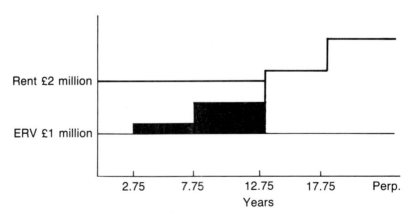

Figure 4.2 Double counting of overage

value are impossible to gauge. In the Central London office market, for example, all new lettings are subject to rental inducements and almost all older lettings are over-rented. There is virtually no direct evidence of 'real' rents or all risks yields. Properties let on long leases with no prospect of a rent increase before the lease expires have become fixed cash flows secured on the covenant of the tenant, and have little to do with conventional property risks. The initial yield can be based upon the gilt yield with a margin for illiquidity and default risk, or have reference to the level of return on debenture stock secured on the tenant company.

Properties let on shorter leases have to pay more regard to the property risks inherent in the reversion, making an initial yield approach hazardous in the extreme.

CONCLUSIONS

Conventional techniques have been under attack for over 20 years. Around 1960, they changed from discounted cash flows at required rates of return to comparison techniques using yield as the unit of comparison. Investment rationality ceased to be a criterion and objectivity and accuracy in the use of transaction evidence became the key to their acceptance.

Few problems have been seen in the valuation of fully let properties, where comparables can be directly applied. Problems only emerge in thin markets as with all comparable approaches.

For reversionary freeholds, however, the method has more problems as lease structure has an influence on the quality of the comparable. If plenty of comparables with similar lease structures exist, the method produces solutions which are reasonably based in accuracy, if not rationality. However, as the quality of comparables diminishes, the lack of rationality leads to valuations which are not soundly based and leave too much to the intuition of the valuer. These problems become extreme as the differences between the comparable and the subject property get wider and the conventional techniques have increasing difficulty with unusual lease structures.

The market of the early 1990s has made a large number of properties unusual. It is ironic that the true limitations of the conventional techniques have been exposed by falls in rental value even though it was the new perception of growth in the 1960s which precipitated the debate. Over-rented properties therefore represent a very significant valuation problem, but have served a very valuable purpose in making the valuation profession increasingly aware of the limitations of the tools of their trade.

Conventional leasehold valuation has always been the most discredited aspect of conventional valuation methodology. Not only are there a multitude of detailed criticisms, there are a number of fundamental flaws which the conventional model cannot compensate for. A comparison technique relies upon the quality and quantity of comparables. There is not sufficient quantity in the leasehold market, and, even if there were, quality would be unlikely to exist due to the individuality of each interest based upon complex lease arrangements. The recessionary market of the early 1990s has only reinforced the view that conventional valuation techniques remain a challenge to the integrity of a thinking profession.

A new approach to market valuation is needed now. The alternatives to the conventional approaches are set out in the next chapter.

Part three

CONTEMPORARY MARKET VALUATION MODELS

5

Contemporary growth explicit
valuation models

INTRODUCTION

During the 1970s numerous techniques were suggested as alternatives to the conventional growth implicit approach for the valuation of property investments. Conspicuously missing from the debate was an examination of the function the models were supposed to perform. This changed in the 1980s: see Chapter 1.

In assessing any technique, it is essential to establish its purpose or objective. In this part of the book we concentrate on the pricing process.

In estimating market price, the most important observation is the behaviour of the market place. In order to carry out a successful valuation, the valuer must collect the same information as is available to the rest of the market and attempt to interpret it in the same way. The core of the pricing process is the interpretation of transaction evidence.

If the market relies upon conventional techniques to interpret market evidence, then it is to be expected that these techniques will influence price in the short term. At present, a debate is being held regarding the accuracy of valuations as measured against sale prices (Drivers Jonas/IPD 1988; Venmore Rowland and Lizieri 1991; Brown 1992). This debate has revolved around the statistical methods being used to measure the data.

However, an equally interesting and as yet unresearched strand to this debate is the valuation process itself, and how pricing valuations influence subsequent sale prices.

The conclusion of this debate may well indicate that techniques influence short-term fluctuations in prices. It would then be a nonsense to suggest that the pricing valuation model should mimic the behaviour of the market, as it is effectively a part of that market.

In any event, irrational pricing models will ultimately fail. Fundamental market changes will take place, influenced by sheer economic rationality, and pricing valuations will in certain circumstances fail to indicate sale prices in the short term. Prices paid for short leaseholds in the early 1980s and over-rented freeholds in the early 1990s are both examples of the pricing process failing to keep in step with rationality and with the prices achieved in the market.

We have seen in Chapter 3 how valuation models are not static and the history of valuation technique indicates a constant re-alignment to changing economic and other circumstances. The current demise of the conventional leasehold model and the questioning of the relevance of the reversionary freehold model for over-rented properties indicates that change is still taking place.

In this part of the book we shall set out and test alternative approaches to the market valuation of freehold and leasehold investments. The basis of the pricing valuation is the analysis of transactions; the basis of a rational pricing model, as set out in Chapter 2, is

$$k = \text{RFR} + r - g + d$$

where k is the initial yield, RFR is the risk free rate, r is the risk premium, g is the expected rate of rental growth and d is the expected depreciation. RFR and r together make up a required rate of return; g and d together produce net expected rental growth. The required return and net rental growth form the foundation of a fuller analysis of transactions.

ANALYSIS OF TRANSACTIONS

Implied rental growth rate analysis

Let us assume a fully let prime property investment has just been bought at a capitalization rate of 5 per cent. In a conventional valuation this capitalization rate of 5 per cent would be applied to the subject property, adjusted slightly according to the differences between subject property and comparable.

But the investor did not buy the expectation of a fixed income into perpetuity and the subsequent total return of 5 per cent per annum. The investor expected rents to be reviewed in an upward direction. From these rent increases (and related capital value increases) comes an increase in the total return. Five per cent is not an acceptable level of total return. What is the required return?

The required rate of return

The investor would have regard to returns available from other investments in the same risk class as property. If we assume for the moment that we are taking a portfolio view of property, the required or target rate of return should be based upon the rate of return for a risk free asset plus a premium for the added risk and illiquidity associated with investing in property.

In nominal terms, government dated gilts give a risk free return over a range of different time periods. The income and capital repayments are at a known level (if the investment is held to redemption) and default risk is at a minimum. The returns are subject to inflation risk, which creates problems for investors with real liabilities, but we shall use dated gilts as a surrogate for the risk free rate of return, and assume that the current level of gilt yields is around 11 per cent.

The next stage is to estimate the risk premium. Property is undoubtably riskier in nominal terms than gilts, because the cash flow is less certain (see Chapter 2). We have assumed a 2 per cent premium for the purposes of this exercise.

The level and timing of rental growth

The other major input into the model is the expected level and timing of rental growth. If a purchaser accepts a particular initial yield for an investment, the yield implies that a particular level of rental growth will be necessary to provide the required rate of return. Alternatively, if a level of rental growth is assumed, the investor's prospective rate of return (IRR, see Chapter 2) can be calculated. An assumption of one major input leads to the calculation of the other.

The time at which the rental growth can be realized is also relevant. The implied rental growth rate can be found from the assumption of a target rate of return only if the rent review pattern of the transaction property is known or assumed. The result represents the long-term average rate of rental growth expected by the market. It is an interpretation of the expectations of the investor and the amount of growth necessary to make the purchase reasonable.

The limitations of these assumptions are investigated in Chapter 6.

Calculation of implied rental growth rate

■ EXAMPLE 5.1

A freehold shop property has just been let on a 25-year lease with 5-year rent reviews at a net rent of £200,000 per annum and subsequently sold for £4,000,000.

$$\text{Capitalization rate } (k) = \frac{£200,000}{£4,000,000} = 0.05 = 5\%$$

Assumed target rate of return (e) $\qquad = 13\%$
Timing of rent reviews (t) $\qquad = 5$ years
Implied annual rental value growth rate (g)

There are a number of formulae which can be used to work out the implied constant annual rental value growth rate. They all reconcile as they are based upon identical assumptions (and therefore limitations) and two approaches are set out below.

1   The basis of the calculation is to set up an equation where the equated yield is made up of the capitalization rate plus the annual sinking fund to replace the capital gain at the equated yield over the review period. If the original sum is £1 the capital gain is equal to

$$(1 + g)^t - 1$$

The annual sinking fund formula incorporating e and the review term t is

$$\frac{e}{(1 + e)^t - 1}$$

The formula is therefore

$$e = k + \frac{e}{(1 + e)^t - 1} \times [(1 + g)^t - 1]$$

Rearranging,

$$k = e - \frac{e}{(1 + e)^t - 1} \times [(1 + g)^t - 1]$$

Let p be the rental growth over the review period t and SF be the annual sinking fund to replace £1 over the review period at e. Then $k = e - (\text{SF} \times p)$. g may then be derived from p, as $1 + p = (1 + g)^t$.

We can now find the implied rental growth rate to get a 5 per cent initial return up to a 13 per cent total return based upon 5-yearly rent revisions:

$$k = e - (SF \times p)$$

$$0.05 = 0.13 - \frac{e}{(1+e)^t - 1} \times p$$

$$0.05 = 0.13 - 0.1543p$$

$$p = \frac{0.13 - 0.08}{0.1543}$$

$$p = 0.51847 \qquad (51.85\% \text{ increase in rental value every five years})$$

$$1 + p = (1 + g)^t$$

$$1.51847 = (1 + g)^5$$

$$g = [(1.51847)^{1/5}] - 1$$

$$g = 0.0871 \qquad (8.71\% \text{ pa})$$

2   A second formula is based on a discounted cash flow (DCF) net present value approach to the problem. The required rate of return or target rate is the equated yield. The outlay is the capital value $1/k$; the inflows represent the value of the term income until the first review; the property is then assumed to be sold at the first review. The rental value on review is capitalized at the same capitalization rate as represented by the current purchase and the capital value obtained is then entered as an inflow at the first review. The equation for an income of £1 is

$$\frac{1}{k} = \frac{1 - (1+e)^{-t}}{e} + (1+g)^t \times \frac{1}{k(1+e)^t}$$

The formula can be rewritten in conventional UK valuation format to enable a valuer to solve implied growth rate calculations with the aid of familiar formulae or a set of valuation tables.

$$(1 + g)^t = \frac{\text{YP perp. at } k - \text{YP } t \text{ years at } e}{\text{YP perp. at } k \times \text{PV } t \text{ years at } e}$$

$$(1 + g)^5 = \frac{\text{YP perp. at } 5\% - \text{YP 5 years at } 13\%}{\text{YP perp. at } 5\% \times \text{PV 5 years at } 13\%}$$

$$= \frac{20 - 3.5172}{20 \times 0.54276} = \frac{16.4828}{10.855} = 1.5185$$

$$g \qquad = (1.5185)^{1/5} - 1 = 0.0871 = 8.71\% \text{ pa}$$

The solutions reconcile and indicate that the rent must increase by a factor of 1.5185 against the previous rent at each review in the future if the required return from the property is to be achieved, excluding other considerations. This simple model enables us to develop an explicit discounted cash flow market valuation method.

DISCOUNTED CASH FLOW VALUATION MODELS

Introduction

In simple terms, the major criticism of conventional appraisal models as applied to the post reverse yield gap property market is the implicit nature of the capitalization rate employed and its failure to perform as a target rate or expected internal rate of return as it had performed prior to the appearance of the reverse yield gap. A DCF appraisal model which is explicit regarding the anticipated cash flow can now be developed employing a discount rate which represents the investor's target rate.

DCF appraisals in this format, but recommended for analysis rather than market valuation, were first suggested by Marshall who termed his model 'equated yield analysis' (Marshall 1976). This was to draw attention to the internal rate of return/redemption yield nature of the discount rate employed (increasingly termed 'equated yield' in the property market, to distinguish from the all risks yield or growth implicit capitalization rate used in conventional appraisals).

However, an immediate problem must be faced. The perpetual nature of a freehold property investment implies an infinitely long cash flow projection. While the discounting process will reduce the value of future tranches of income, eventually to a nominal amount, by which point the projection may cease, the process may remain inconveniently lengthy. This may be a minor problem in computation, but remains a considerable problem in presentation. What is needed, therefore, is a method of shortening the process.

Several alternatives will be considered. These include a shortened cash flow model: a DCF by formula approach; the 'rational' model; and a real value hybrid.

An explicit cash flow model

A means of shortening the cash flow projection naturally presents itself when the behaviour of most investors in the market is considered. While property may in most cases continue to be considered as a long-term investment, investment holding periods will not typically be perpetual. It may be quite possible to envisage a resale at some future point; often, a natural point of sale represents itself. The behaviour of the investment market confirms that a natural resale point will be coincidental with a reversion or rent review; the assumption of resale at such a point will permit the termination of cash flow projections, replacing future cash flows by the resale price.

Marshall's equated yield analysis format included termination of the cash flow after 30 years for a fully let freehold. Up to that point rental growth expectations cause the rental flow to be increased at each expected review date in the future. The yield used to discount the cash flows is the target rate; all growth potential is explicit. Capital growth is also explicit, by courtesy of the resale assumption. At the resale point Marshall recommended capitalization of the then rental value at the equated yield.

By implication, this ignores any growth potential in the investment after the 30-year period. This may be a convenient and realistic allowance for depreciation. However, the use of risk-adjusted equated yields already assumes risk of depreciation, consequently, we must reject capitalization at the resale point at the equated yield. Implied rental growth analysis is based on a presumption of perpetual growth in a freehold: this must be reflected in the resale price projection. The resale price is therefore arrived at by capitalization of the then rental value at a rate which implies future growth; the implied rate of growth is derived from the current market capitalization rate; so the same rate should be used at the point of resale.

Thus valuation by a shortened explicit cash flow model requires four major inputs:

1 equated yield e;
2 market capitalization rate k;
3 rent review period t; and
4 from e, k and t, implied growth g can be calculated.

■ EXAMPLE 5.2

Value the freehold interest in a shop property to be let on a 25-year lease with 5-year reviews at its current net rental value of £100,000 per annum. Use an equated yield of 13 per cent; market capitalization rates are around 5 per cent. Assume a holding period of 30 years. Implied rental growth is

8.712 per cent from the previous analysis. Figure 5.1 gives the income pro-file and Table 5.1 presents the valuation for this example.

A different holding period does not change the result. Assume a sale after 15 years. Table 5.2 presents the new valuation.

Note that both valuations reconcile with the conventional valuation:

$$\frac{ERV}{k} = \frac{£100,000}{0.05} = £2,000,000$$

As stated in Chapter 4, the fully let freehold (of all investment types) is least prone to inaccurate valuation by the implicit conventional technique. The advantage offered by a DCF valuation in the above format is not that (as long as growth forecasts are linked to the market by an implied rental

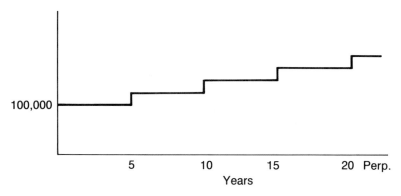

Figure 5.1 Income profile of Example 5.2

Table 5.1 Valuation for Example 5.2, assuming a holding period of 30 years

Years	Current ERV £ pa	A £1 at 8.712%	Forecast income (£)	YP 5 years at 13%	PV at 13%	Present value (£)
0–5	100,000	1.0000	100,000	3.5172	1.0000	351,720
6–10	100,000	1.5184	151,840	3.5172	0.5428	289,870
11–15	100,000	2.3056	230,560	3.5172	0.2946	238,890
16–20	100,000	3.5009	350,090	3.5172	0.1599	196,880
21–25	100,000	5.3156	531,580	3.5172	0.0868	162,260
26–30	100,000	8.0716	807,160	3.5172	0.0471	133,720
30	100,000	12.2562	1,225,620	20.0000[a]	0.0256	626,660
						2,000,000

Note: [a]YP perp. at 5%.

Table 5.2 Valuation for Example 5.2, assuming a sale after 15 years

Years	Current ERV £ pa	A £1 at 8.712%	Projected income (£)	YP 5 years at 13%	PV at 13%	Present value (£)
0–5	100,000	1.0000	100,000	3.5172	1.0000	351,720
6–10	100,000	1.5184	151,840	3.5172	0.5428	289,870
11–15	100,000	2.3056	230,560	3.5172	0.2946	238,890
15	100,000	3.5009	350,090	20.0000[a]	0.1599	1,119,520
						2,000,000

Note: [a]YP perp. at 5%.

growth formula) a more accurate valuation will result, but that:

1 more information is provided for future analysis purposes;
2 the yield used enables cross-investment comparisons; and
3 specific problems affecting the cash flow of the investment can be incorporated.

The fact that conventional and modern approaches reconcile is proof of the assertion that contemporary market valuations are based upon transactions and not forecasts. The perpetual capitalization rate of the comparison was broken down into the required return or equated yield, the review pattern and the growth rate. If the property income is then projected forward at that growth rate, reviewed every 5 years and discounted at the equated yield, the solution will be the same as that produced by a simple capitalization in perpetuity at 5 per cent. As the comparable was identical to the subject property a direct capital comparison could be made. The comparable had a rent that was double the subject property, so the valuation must be half as much, £2,000,000 against £4,000,000.

The long version of the DCF can be shortened by assuming a resale at the capitalization rate. If, however, the capitalization rate for the property needs to be adjusted (e.g. if the property was let on 3-year reviews while the 5 per cent capitalization rate derived from comparables is based on 5-yearly reviews) the calculation can be shortened by use of DCF formulae (a summation of the perpetual geometric progression).

Discounted cash flow by formula

The capital value of an income flow is the summation of the discounted value of each block of income. If it is assumed that the rents grow every 5 years at a constant rate and the discount rate also remains constant, the income flow represents a geometric progression. An examination of the solution for the explicit cash flow indicates that the YP 5 years at 13 per cent is included in the capitalization of each block of income. In addition, every 5 years, the previous rent increases by $(1 + g)^5$ and each block is discounted by $(1 + e)^{-n}$ where n equals five more years than the previous block. The common ratio is therefore

$$\frac{(1 + g)^t}{(1 + e)^t}$$

and the formula summates to

$$\text{YP } n \text{ years} = \text{YP } t \text{ years at } e \times \frac{1 - (1 + g)^n/(1 + e)^n}{1 - (1 + g)^t/(1 + e)^t}$$

where income is £1 per annum, the total term is n years, the term of review is t years, the equated yield is e per cent and the growth rate is g per cent per annum.

This formula represents the summation of the DCF model to create a multiplier for use with the current rental value. A fuller explanation of the mathematics involved in creating formulae is included later in this chapter when real value models are considered. The solution to the example is as follows.

■ EXAMPLE 5.3

Details as Example 5.2. ERV £100,000 per annum; $e = 13$ per cent; $g = 8.712$ per cent; $t = 5$ years; $n = $ perpetuity. As $n = $ perpetuity,

$$\text{YP perp.} = \text{YP 5 years at } 13\% \times \frac{1 - (1.08712)^n/(1.13)^n}{1 - (1.08712)^t/(1.13)^t}$$

and

$$1 - \frac{(1.08712)^n}{(1.13)^n} = 1 - 0 = 1$$

So

$$\text{YP perp.} = 3.5172 \times \frac{1}{0.17587} = 20$$

YP perp. $= 20.00$: $k = 5$ per cent. The solution is:

ERV	£100,000 pa	
YP whole term	20.00	
Valuation		£2,000,000

Thus both shortened DCF and DCF by formula valuations are straight-forward and reconcile with conventional techniques in the case of the fully let freehold. This is not, however, necessarily true of reversionary freeholds or of leaseholds (see Chapters 6 and 7).

The rational model

A third variation on the shortened DCF approach is the rational model of Sykes (1981), the basis of which Greaves had already established (1972a). The basis of the model mirrors the approach of Norris (1884) and is best illustrated using a reversionary freehold. The capitalization of a rack rented property let on a normal review pattern is undertaken at the appropriate capitalization rate k found from market analysis. This capitalization rate is a surrogate for an increasing rental value (at each review date) discounted at the opportunity cost of capital (risk adjusted), i.e. the equated yield. The capitalization of a current rent fixed under a lease is at the equated yield, although this is shown as a capitalization in perpetuity of the current rent less the value of the current rent after reversion. The model unfortunately becomes cumbersome in its application to more complex reversionary free-holds and leaseholds.

The rational model, in the simple case of a reversionary freehold, can be simplified to two parts:

1 the fixed initial income before reversion; and
2 the resale price at the date of reversion.

Following the rationale so far established it is clear that a fixed rent should be capitalized at the required target rate or equated yield; and the resale price should be the predicted inflated price deferred over the period to reversion at the equated yield. In this format it is identical to our presen-tation of the equated yield valuation with a holding period determined not artificially but by the first reversion or review. The model suffers because no concise device for the YP of a terminable rising income has been estab-lished, although Greaves presented such a device in 1972 (Greaves 1972b, 1985). If, for example, an income of £1 per annum was expected to last for 20 years and to be reviewed at 5-yearly intervals, the valuation approach would be to capitalize the £1 per annum in perpetuity and then deduct the resale price at year 20. This creates problems in all but the most elementary of appraisals and attempts to suggest solutions to various applications (Sykes and McIntosh 1982; McIntosh 1983) have only served to highlight these problems, which are well documented. Any reader wishing to inves-tigate this model further should refer to Bowcock (1983b), Baum (1984a),

Baum and Yu (1985), Crosby (1985), Greaves (1985), Fraser (1985a) and Crosby (1986) (all consolidated in Crosby (1987)).

As a result of the criticisms made by these authors we pay no further attention to this work as published although we recognize its contribution to a wholly desirable progress towards DCF-based appraisals.

An alternative to equated yield, DCF or rational models − all of which are expressions of the same explicit cash flow projection and capitalization process − is the real value model of Wood (1972), which can be amended and reconciled with the equated yield approach (Mason 1978; Crosby 1983).

REAL VALUE MODELS

Real value theory

The real value model was formed by Wood as part of his Ph.D. research (Wood 1972) and was subsequently published (Wood 1973). It has gained little acceptance in its published form and was dismissed by the RICS research project interim report: 'It is considered that Dr Wood's "real value" approach is too complex for most practitioners to use in their day to day work' (Trott 1980).

No indication is given regarding whether this relates to the valuation or analysis role.

The real value approach of Wood starts from the simplifying premise that an income can be reviewed at each rent payment date to a new rental which matches inflation over the intervening period. The investor has as a result an inflation proof investment. A rent paid annually in arrears, however, would always be worth less than an inflation proof rent and would decline in real value over each year, while the inflation proof rent would have a static real value profile into perpetuity.

The rate of return required on such an income is the interest rate required for giving up the capital, taking into account all risks attached to the investment but excluding any extra return for the effects of future inflation. Wood termed this real return the inflation risk free yield (IRFY).

Fisher (1930) broke this down into a reward for three factors (see page 49); time preference or impatience i, expected inflation d and risk r. Wood's IRFY is a combination of i and r such that $IRFY = (1 + i)(1 + r) - 1$.

The valuation of a fixed income should not be carried out on the same basis. The rate of return must reflect the fact that on each rent payment date the same sum of money would be paid, regardless of the fact that, if inflation was present, the purchasing power of the last payment would be less than the previous payment. This inflation prone income would not have the ability to retain its purchasing power and the real value of the income would decline. The investor would require not only a real return to match his inflation proofed counterpart, but also an added return to make up for the decline in purchasing power (that is, $(1 + i)(1 + d)(1 + r) - 1$).

The yield differential between fixed interest and index-linked gilts illustrates the difference between an inflation prone yield and an inflation risk free yield (i).

The valuation of an inflation proofed income would be undertaken at the IRFY (i). If the income was receivable in one year's time, the valuation would be

$$\text{PV £1 in 1 year at } i = \frac{1}{1 + i}$$

The valuation of an inflation prone income receivable at the end of the

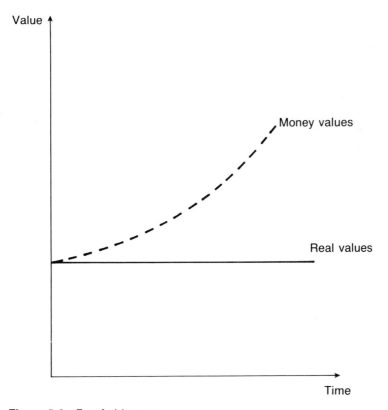

Figure 5.2 Proofed income

year would be at a higher rate of return. The IRFY would be supplemented by the inflation rate: the two incomes differ only insofar as in one case the income can amend itself for inflation, while the fixed income cannot (see Figure 5.2).

The real return is adjusted for the inflation rate d, and the fixed income is discounted in the usual way:

$$\text{PV £1 in 1 year at } (1+i)(1+d)(1+r) = \frac{1}{(1+i)(1+d)(1+r)}$$

Assuming inflation and growth are the same, the different profiles of the equated yield and real value approaches can be compared for an inflation proofed and a more normal property income, subject to a periodic review.

The periodically reviewed income compounds downwards in real terms until a review where the purchasing power is returned. In money terms the rent is reviewed to a higher level and can be used to purchase goods which have also increased in value. In money terms the income is increased to $1+d$ at the review while it remains static between reviews. In real terms the income is static at each review, but between reviews the income declines by $1+d$. See Figure 5.3.

In valuation terms, the term rent between reviews is capitalized as follows:

$$\text{income} \times \frac{1}{1+d} = \text{real value of year 1 rent}$$

This rent has now been adjusted for inflation and is equivalent to an inflation proofed rent, and can now be discounted at the IRFY (i):

$$\text{income} \times \frac{1}{1+d} \times \frac{1}{1+i} = \text{income} \times \frac{1}{(1+d)(1+i)}$$

$$\text{valuation of a proofed income} = \frac{1}{1+i}$$

$$\text{valuation of a prone income} = \frac{1}{(1+d)(1+i)}$$

The determination of yields for the proofed and prone incomes are then incorporated into the valuation of a periodic rental flow. Assuming 't' is the rent review term and 'n' the whole term (assume perpetuity for a freehold), the valuation can be built up in blocks of the review pattern term.

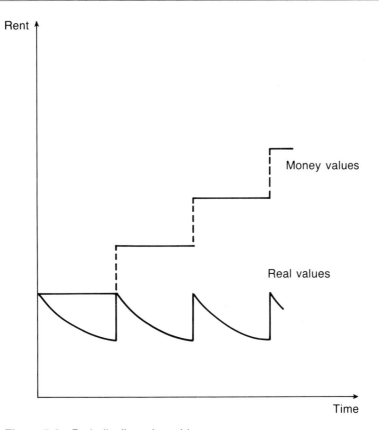

Figure 5.3   Periodically-reviewed income

The present value of £1 per annum formula is

$$\frac{1 - PV}{\text{interest rate}}$$

This can be substituted for the PV £1-formula when the rent is to remain static in money terms, but declining in real value. When the rent is assumed static even though it is declining in real terms the yield is adjusted as for the PV of £1.

Thus, PV of £1 pa at i adjusted for $d = \dfrac{1 - (1/(1 + i)(1 + d))}{(1 + i)(1 + d) - 1}$

The rent is assumed to remain static at review in real terms and the capital value of each block is discounted at the IRFY. The valuation of a periodically reviewed rent is undertaken by constructing a series and summating to obtain the real value formula of Wood for the YP of a rising income.

1st t years rent	$£R$ pa
$\times$ YP t years (prone)	$\dfrac{1 - (1/(1 + i)(1 + d)^t)}{(1 + i)(1 + d) - 1}$
2nd t years rent	$£R$ pa
$\times$ YP t years (prone)	As above
$\times$ PV t years (proofed)	$\dfrac{1}{(1 + i)^t}$
3rd t years rent	$£R$ pa
$\times$ YP t years (prone)	As above
$\times$ PV $2t$ years (proofed)	$\dfrac{1}{(1 + i)^t}$
Up to and including last t years rent	$£R$ pa
$\times$ YP t years (prone)	As before
$\times$ PV $n - t$ years (proofed)	$\dfrac{1}{(1 + i)^{n-t}}$

Summating this progression leads to a YP formula as follows:

$$\text{YP of whole term } (n) = \text{YP } t \text{ years (prone)} \times \frac{1 - (1 + i)^{-n}}{1 - (1 + i)^{-t}}$$

The valuation of a rising income can be undertaken using the above formula. The valuer needs to determine i, d, t and n. Trott (1980) comments:

The method has suffered from its complexity. A valuation technique, if it is to be accepted by the profession, must be easily understood and easy to use. Its theoretical soundness must be matched by a practical application. Unlike the later, and theoretically similar, equated yield analysis, Dr Wood's method is difficult to use. For instance, to obtain the years' purchase in perpetuity from Wood's tables the valuer must know: (i) the inflation risk free yield (i), (ii) the inflation risk rate per cent (d) and (iii) the rent review period (t).

These criticisms can be countered. Index-linked investments could provide suitable measures of comparative real returns. The typical rent review period is something all valuers are aware of. The analysis of future inflation rates would be the necessary subject of research; the distinction between real and inflationary growth would become a consideration.

As an analysis model, the extra inputs necessary can be subjectively assessed. However, the static real value assumption could usefully be dropped in favour of separate assessments of inflation and rental growth. Using the model for valuations, it would be necessary to make assumptions about expected inflation rates to assess implied real growth or falls in rental value. The model instigated by Wood therefore appears to have more use in the determination of real returns, as opposed to fixed income returns, for comparative investment appraisal. The real value model is better equipped in this respect than the equated yield approach.

While most investment portfolio performance measurement concentrates on the use of total returns rather than real returns for comparison purposes (property performance measurement is no exception), this is changing with the growing influence of index-linked investments. The evaluation of real returns and real and inflationary growth or loss is increasingly demanded, and in this context Wood's real value model may yet be shown to be of greater significance.

Although the criticisms of complexity when compared with equated yield models for investment appraisal seem unfounded, difficulties in application to market valuation are apparent. These difficulties can be overcome by simplifying the real value model and adapting it to the same basis as the equated yield model. The advantages of this move will be examined after some amendments are made and after the resulting model has been reconciled with the equated yield models.

A real value/equated yield hybrid

The main discrepancy between real value theory and equated yield techniques is the definition of growth. The equated yield models define the growth in rents in money terms as g while the real value theory discounts the fixed income by a yield made up of real return (IRFY) and inflation d. If a static real value profile is assumed then d and g are the same: the level of rental growth g is equal to the level of inflation d. In these circumstances the two models can be reconciled by substituting g for d in the real value formula. The equated yield model requires a choice of equated yield e while the real value model relies on a choice of inflation risk free yield i.

Real value theory suggests that a fixed income and a totally reviewable income can be distinguished by the rate of inflation, the fixed income being worse by the inflation rate compounded downwards. The difference between the two types of income could be viewed as being the rental growth that the reviewable income can exploit; or the rate of rental growth forgone by the fixed income recipient. The effect of this view would be to discount the fixed income by an additional factor of g or to increase the reviewable income by a factor of g. These two alternatives represent the two different methods. The additional discount by g represents the basis of approach for a real value hybrid; the increase in the reviewable rent by g has already been seen to be the basis of the equated yield technique.

The real value hybrid starts from the basis of discounting a proofed income at a real return (IRFY).

The valuation of a proofed income of £1 at the end of one year is given by

$$£1 \times PV\ £1 \text{ in 1 year at } i = \frac{1}{1 + i}$$

The valuation of a fixed income of £1 at the end of one year is again undertaken on the basis that it is declining in real value by the rate of rental growth. The rent can be discounted at g before being discounted at i or the discount rate can be made up of both i and g.
Either

$$£1 \times \frac{1}{1 + g} \times PV\ £1 \text{ in 1 year at } i = \frac{1}{1 + g} \times \frac{1}{1 + i}$$

or

$$£1 \times PV\ £1 \text{ in 1 year at } i\ (\text{adj.}g) = \frac{1}{(1 + g)(1 + i)}$$

The reconciliation of the real value and equated yield models can now be undertaken. The equated yield model requires a choice of e, while the real value model requires a choice of i. They both use g. The real value model does not require the selection of i. Consider the valuation of a fixed income of £1 for one year by both techniques.

Method (a): equated yield

$$£1 \times PV \text{ of £1 in 1 year at } e = \frac{1}{1 + e}$$

Method (b): real value

$$£1 \times PV \text{ of } £1 \text{ in } 1 \text{ year at } i \text{ (adj.} g) = \frac{1}{(1 + i)(1 + g)}$$

On the assumption that the same valuation should be found by either method, the inflation prone capital value of £1 is

$$\frac{1}{1 + e} \text{ or } \frac{1}{(1 + i)(1 + g)}$$

Therefore,

$$\frac{1}{1 + e} = \frac{1}{(1 + i)(1 + g)}$$

Solving the equation gives

(i) $i = \dfrac{1 + e}{1 + g} - 1$

(ii) $g = \dfrac{1 + e}{1 + i} - 1$

(iii) $e = (1 + i)(1 + g) - 1$

This mathematical relationship has already been noted in Chapter 1 (see page 12) in the context of fixed income and index-linked gilts.

To reconcile the methods, the equated yield approach requires a choice of e and g. The real value approach requires i, but i can be a product of e and g. So, given e and g, i can be calculated. The reverse is true (e from i and g) but as the widest acceptance of contemporary techniques has been for methods based on an assumption of e, the former is taken as a basis for the application of the model. If future trends move the emphasis to the selection of real returns for property investment the real value model can change to the latter basis.

The valuation, by both techniques, of a proofed income of £1 for 1 year illustrates the reconciliation. The equated yield technique increases the rent by rental growth before discounting at the equated yield. The real value approach assumes a reinstatement of the rent at the end of the year, and discounts the real value of the rent at a real return.

Method (a): equated yield

$$£1 \times (1 + g) \times PV \; £1 \text{ in } 1 \text{ year at } e = \frac{1 + g}{1 + e}$$

Method (b): real value

$$£1 \times PV \ £1 \text{ in 1 year at } i = \frac{1}{1+i}$$

To reconcile, the assumption of the same valuation by both methods is taken:

$$\frac{1+g}{1+e} = \frac{1}{1+i}$$

This equation solves exactly as in the previous example.

The criticisms of Dr Wood's approach made by Trott concerned the choice of inputs. The valuer must know:

1 the inflation risk free yield;
2 the inflation risk rate percentage;
3 the rent review period.

The discrepancy between Wood's inflation risk rate and rental growth has been countered in the real value hybrid. Any new approach based on explicit future value changes must either assume or know the review pattern; and the inflation risk free yield can be calculated from the equated yield and growth. The real value hybrid, therefore, enables the same inputs that are required for the equated yield model to be used and cannot therefore be dismissed on Trott's grounds.

Based on the above assumptions the model can be formulated. Using Example 5.3 (equated yield 13 per cent, rental growth 8.712 per cent per annum, reviews every 5 years) the capital value of the right to receive an estimated rental value of £100,000 per annum with the above inputs can be determined.

The valuation of the first 5 years must be the rent at an inflation prone yield $((1 + i)(1 + d)(1 + r) - 1)$. This can be represented by the equated yield.

Year 1–5	ERV	£100,000 pa
	YP 5 years at 13%	3.5172
Valuation		£351,720

(This part of the valuation is the same as in the equated yield approach.)

The rent review is not treated as an increase in rent, but as a reinstatement of the real value of the rent. In real terms the rent will be returned to its existing value of £100,000 per annum; but it will still be fixed for the next 5 years, and as it is inflation prone it is valued at the equated yield.

Year 6–10	ERV	£100,000 pa
	YP 5 years at 13%	3.5172
Valuation		£351,720

The progression can be built up to form an infinite number of capital values of £351,720 for each 5-year block, at the start of each block. Figure 5.4 illustrates this.

To complete the valuation, the capital value of each block must be discounted to present values. The yield at which to discount can be selected by determining whether the capital value is prone or proofed. The block of income from years 6 to 10 has a capital value of £351,720 at the end of year 5. The purchasing power of that value must be ascertained. As the capital value has been assessed by capitalizing a rent in real terms, and not money terms, then the capital value is also in real terms. It is apparent that if rents rose by 8.71 per cent per annum then the rent on review would be £151,840 (the amount of £1 in 5 years at 8.712 per cent = 1.5184 from the formula $(1 + g)^5$), not £100,000. The capital value of the right to receive £151,840 per annum for years 6 to 10 (in year 5) would also be higher, at £534,060.

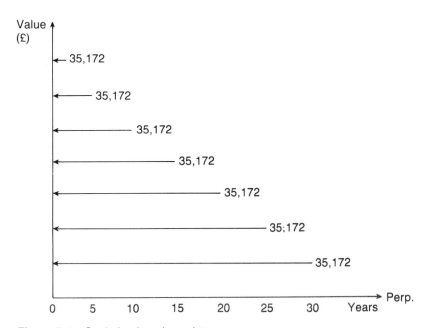

Figure 5.4   Capital values in real terms

The amount stated in the valuation (£351,720) represents the purchasing power of the right to receive the next 5 years' rent, not the actual money value (£534,060). The capital value of £351,720 is completely proofed against inflation and can rise continuously during the waiting period. It must therefore be discounted at an inflation risk free yield.

$$\text{IRFY } (i) = \frac{1+e}{1+g} - 1 = \frac{1.13}{1.08712} - 1 = 0.03944$$

$$= 3.944\%$$

The valuation of the interest is therefore a succession of rents of £100,000 per annum, capitalized every 5 years at an equated yield, and then discounted at the inflation risk free yield for the appropriate number of years.

Years 1–5	£100,000 pa	
YP 5 years at 13%	3.5172	
		£351,720
Years 6–10	£100,000 pa	
YP 5 years at 13%	3.5172	
PV 5 years at 3.944%	0.824	
		£289,870
Years 11–15	£100,000 pa	
YP 5 years at 13%	3.5172	
PV 10 years at 3.944%	0.679	
		£238,890

The above forms a geometric progression which can be summated into a formula.

The constants are rent and the YP 5 years at 13 per cent; the only change is the discount factor.

Assuming rent is £1, then capital value is the years' purchase. The last term will have a PV of the number of years less one term. Thus, the value of the last tranche is

$$\text{PV (whole term} - t \text{ years)} = \frac{1}{(1+i)^{n-t}}$$

The summation S is

$$(1) \quad S = \text{YP } t \text{ at } e \left[1 + \frac{1}{(1+i)^t} + \ldots + \frac{1}{(1+i)^{n-t}} \right]$$

Multiplying both sides by $1/(1+i)^t$,

(2) $\quad S\dfrac{1}{(1+i)^t} = \text{YP } t \text{ at } e\left[\dfrac{1}{(1+i)^{2t}} + \cdots + \dfrac{1}{(1+i)^n}\right]$

Subtracting (2) from (1) gives

$$S - S\dfrac{1}{(1+i)^t} = \text{YP } t \text{ at } e\left[1 - \dfrac{1}{(1+i)^n}\right]$$

$$S\left[1 - \dfrac{1}{(1+i)^t}\right] = \text{YP } t \text{ at } e\left[1 - \dfrac{1}{(1+i)^n}\right]$$

$$S = \text{YP } t \text{ at } e\left[\dfrac{1 - 1/(1+i)^n}{1 - 1/(1+i)^t}\right]$$

The advantage of the real value approach is that the latter term can be amended from

$$\dfrac{1 - 1/(1+i)^n}{1 - 1/(1+i)^t}$$

to

$$\dfrac{[1 - 1/(1+i)^n]/i}{[1 - 1/(1+i)^t]/i}$$

which constitutes

$$\dfrac{\text{YP } n \text{ at } i}{\text{YP } t \text{ at } i}$$

Including the first term, the formula becomes

$$\text{YP of the whole } (n) = \text{YP } t \text{ at } e \times \dfrac{\text{YP } n \text{ at } i}{\text{YP } t \text{ at } i}$$

To determine the capital value of the right to receive a rent of £100,000 per annum in perpetuity growing at 8.712 per cent per annum reviewable every 5 years (see Example 5.3), and to obtain an equated yield of 13 per cent, the valuation proceeds as follows:

Preliminary calculation

$$i = \dfrac{1+e}{1+g} - 1$$

$$i = \dfrac{1.13}{1.08712} - 1 = 0.3944 = 3.944\%$$

Valuation

ERV £100,000 pa

$$YP = YP \text{ 5 years at } 13\% \times \frac{YP \text{ perp. at } 3.944\%}{YP \text{ 5 years at } 3.944\%}$$

$$= 3.52 \times \frac{25.354}{4.459} \qquad\qquad = \underline{20.0000}$$

Valuation £2,000,000

The underlying assumptions have already been reconciled and the answer is consistent with previous results.

SUMMARY

Real value approaches have been heavily criticized and have not gained any acceptance within the property valuation profession. Yet the appraisal of property investment by comparison with expected real returns has no more problems associated with it, in theoretical terms, than comparative appraisal using fixed income returns, and lends itself to comparisons with both conventional and index-linked gilts. The use of a static real value profile is unrealistic, however, and inconsistent with market analysis to calculate growth rates, as expected inflation does not necessarily equal the market's expectation of rental growth. However, the split of growth into inflation and real elements makes analysis more difficult due to the multiplicity of variables. The real value hybrid model, on the other hand, equates growth and inflation so as to employ the same variables as other DCF techniques.

DCF by formula reconciles in all cases with the real value hybrid, as they are summations of identical geometric progressions. Consequently, in order to progress towards recommendations, only explicit DCF, short cut DCF and real value hybrid models are generally compared in the next two chapters by undertaking a range of practical problems in the valuation of freehold and leasehold investment properties.

6

Contemporary freehold market valuations

INTRODUCTION

In this chapter, we investigate the market valuation of freehold investments by both the growth explicit discounted cash flow (DCF) approach and the real value approach. In the second part of the chapter we compare the approach and solutions of the contemporary models with the conventional approach.

Before setting up a number of examples to illustrate the application of these models a short discussion is necessary to put the models in context.

First, the application to pricing or market valuation requires the valuations to be based upon transaction evidence. For the purposes of most of these examples, the same comparable will be used throughout. This comparable is assumed to be a fully let (rack rented) property which has just been let on a 5-year review pattern and sold to show a capitalization rate of 6 per cent.

Second, the analysis of the transaction requires an assumption of equated yield choice and we shall assume, as in the previous chapter, that the required return or equated yield is 13 per cent (derived from a risk free rate plus a risk premium). Later in this chapter we undertake a detailed critique of this subjective assumption.

Once that assumption has been made, the implied rental growth rate can be calculated. The analysis of the transaction is set out below.

$$(1 + g)^t = \frac{\text{YP perp. at } k - \text{YP } t \text{ years at } e}{\text{YP perp. at } k \times \text{PV } t \text{ years at } e}$$

$$(1 + g)^5 = \frac{\text{YP perp. at } 6\% - \text{YP } 5 \text{ years at } 13\%}{\text{YP perp. at } 6\% \times \text{PV } 5 \text{ years at } 13\%}$$

$$= \frac{16.6667 - 3.5172}{16.6667 \times 0.5428}$$

$$= \frac{13.1494}{9.0460} = 1.4536$$

$$g \quad = (1.4536)^{1/5} - 1 = 0.0776807 = 7.76807\% \text{ pa}$$

Third, as the models are being utilized to make the best use of the transaction evidence, where perfect comparables exist no technique is necessary. As the comparison is a fully let freehold on 5-year reviews, any valuation of a property let at its rack rental value, which is expected to grow with reviews every 5 years, does not require the application of any more complex model than the all risks yield approach.

The multiplier for a rack rented property let on 5-year reviews is 16.6667. This takes full account of the risk premium, the expected rental growth rate and the 5-year review pattern. Any DCF-based model using these inputs will produce the same result. Example 6.1 falls into this category.

Fourth, the models have been developed and will be applied using the usual market valuation assumption of income payable annually in arrears, even though the market collects rents (generally) quarterly in advance. Both conventional and contemporary models can be amended to quarterly in advance but, for the purposes of comparison, the contemporary models have been applied using the conventional basis.

The examples used to illustrate the application of the models are set out in Figure 6.1.

RACK RENTED FREEHOLDS

We investigate two different problems:

1 the valuation of property let subject to a review pattern where evidence of capitalization rates is available for the same review pattern (Example 6.1); and

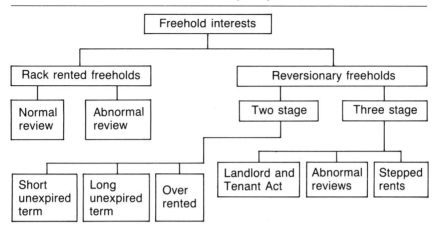

Figure 6.1 Examples used to illustrate model application

2 the valuation of property let subject to a review pattern where evidence is only available for property let on a different review pattern (Example 6.2).

■ EXAMPLE 6.1

Value the freehold interest in a property just let at its rental value of £200,000 per annum on a 5-year review pattern. Similar property also just let on a 5-year review pattern recently sold for a price based on a 6 per cent capitalization rate.

In both models no resort would need to be made to analysis for implied growth rate as a valuation direct to capitalization rate would be undertaken. If, however, the full analysis and valuation was undertaken, assuming $e = 13$ per cent and given that $k = 6$ per cent and $t = 5$ years, the analysis for implied growth gives an answer of 7.76807 per cent per annum.

Explicit discounted cash flow

Assume a 10-year holding period. $e = 13$ per cent, $t = 5$ years, $g = 7.76807$ and $k = 6$ per cent. The results are given in Table 6.1.

The projected rental increases are discounted at the equated yield until the deemed resale where the property is assumed to be sold at the capitalization rate for a fully let property (k). We already know that 6 per cent implies a growth rate of 7.76807 per cent per annum to achieve an equated yield at 13 per cent, so that in the simplest case of a rack rented freehold

Table 6.1

Year	Current rent pa (£)	A £1 5 years at 7.76807	Projected rent pa (£)	YP 5 years at 13%	PV at 13%	Present value (£)
1–5	200,000	1.0000	200,000	3.5172	1.0000	703,450
6–10	200,000	1.4536	290,720	3.5172	0.5428	555,000
10	200,000	2.1130	422,600	16.6667[a]	0.2946	2,074,890
						£3,333,340

Note: [a]YP perp. at 6%.

the explicit DCF is not necessary except to illustrate the assumptions behind the market capitalization rate.

Real value

$$i = \frac{1 + e}{1 + g} - 1 = \frac{1.13}{1.0776807} - 1$$

$$i = 0.0485481 = 4.85481\%$$

For a fully let freehold, the formula is

$$\text{YP of the whole income} = \text{YP } t \text{ at } e \times \frac{\text{YP perp. at } i}{\text{YP } t \text{ at } i}$$

and the calculation becomes

ERV   £200,000 pa

$$\frac{\text{YP 5 years at } 13\% \times \text{YP perp. at } 4.85481\%}{\text{YP 5 years at } 4.85481\%}$$

$$= \frac{3.5172 \times 20.5981}{4.3469} = \qquad\qquad \underline{16.6667}$$

Valuation   £3,333,340

In this case both methods reconcile to the conventional valuation based on a 6 per cent capitalization rate.

■ EXAMPLE 6.2

Value a rack rented freehold let on a different review pattern. Assume the same comparisons as before, but the subject property is let on a 3-year review pattern at £200,000 per annum.

The analysis for implied growth rate is as before: $g = 7.76807$ per cent per annum.

Explicit DCF

Assume a 9-year holding period. $e = 13$ per cent, $t = 3$ years, $g = 7.76807$ per cent and $k = 6$ per cent. Note, however, that k is the relevant capitalization rate where reviews are 5-yearly. Where reviews are 3-yearly, the potential for growth is enhanced and market capitalization rates would be forced down.

On 3-yearly reviews a new capitalization rate must be derived and this can be done by using the DCF formula developed in Chapter 5 or any other variation on the same theme, for example:

$$k = e - (\text{SF} \times p) \qquad \text{(see page 114)}$$

where k is the capitalization rate, e is the equated yield, SF is the annual sinking fund over rent review period t at e and P is the percentage rental growth over the review period t such that $p = (1 + g)^t - 1$ where g is the annual rental growth.

$$k = 0.13 - \frac{0.13}{(1.13)^3 - 1} \times [(1.0776807)^3 - 1]$$

$$= 0.13 - (0.295322 \times 0.251614)$$

$$= 0.13 - 0.073854$$

$$= 0.056146$$

$$= 5.6146\%$$

The results are given in Table 6.2.

The solution is nearly £23,000 higher than in Example 6.1, reflecting the advantage of 3-yearly reviews in a rising market.

To finish the calculation after only 9 years requires an accurate choice of capitalization rate. As this choice can be undertaken based on formula, the explicit DCF model for such a calculation is unnecessary but has the advantage of being explicit regarding the actual rental level in the future (in this case at years 3, 6 and 9). The same solution would be obtained by assessing

Table 6.2

Year	Current rent pa (£)	A £1 3 years at 7.76807%	Projected rent pa (£)	YP 3 years at 13%	PV at 13%	Present value (£)
1–3	200,000	1.0000	200,000	2.3612	1.0000	472,240
4–6	200,000	1.2516	250,320	2.3612	0.6931	409,630
7–9	200,000	1.5665	313,300	2.3612	0.4803	355,310
9	200,000	1.9607	392,140	17.8107[a]	0.3329	2,324,960
						£3,562,140

Note: [a]YP perp. at 5.6146%.

the capitalization rate at 5.6146 per cent and capitalizing the current estimated rental value at this rate.

ERV	£200,000 pa
YP perp. at 5.6146%	17.8107
Valuation	£3,562,140

Real value

The inputs into the model ($e = 13$ per cent, $g = 7.76807$ per cent per annum and $i = 4.85481$ per cent) are as calculated in Example 6.1. They are inserted into the 3 YP formula incorporating a change of review pattern from 5 years to 3 years.

ERV   £200,000 pa

$$\frac{\text{YP 3 years at } 13\% \times \text{YP perp. at } 4.85481\%}{\text{YP 3 years at } 4.85481\%}$$

$$\frac{2.3611526 \times 20.598128}{2.7306738} = \qquad 17.8107$$

Valuation   £3,562,140

The capitalization rate is also 5.6146 per cent (1/YP). All solutions reconcile.

TWO-STAGE REVERSIONARY FREEHOLDS

Short reversions

 EXAMPLE 6.3

Value the freehold interest in a shop property which is let on a lease with 4 years unexpired at £100,000 per annum. The estimated rental value is £200,000 per annum based on 5-year review patterns and a similar property, as before, has just been sold at a capitalization rate of 6 per cent. Assume the same *e* (13 per cent).

As before the following facts can be used: $e = 13$ per cent, $g = 7.76807$ per cent and $i = 4.85481$ per cent.

Explicit DCF

In line with investors' expectations of future growth, an explicit DCF approach would entail increasing the rent by the implied growth rate at each lease renewal or review and discounting the total income flow at an equated yield. The yield excludes any growth potential, which is already accounted for in the income flow, and should therefore be equivalent to the fixed income yield, that is, the equated yield. The results are given in Table 6.3.

Short-cut growth explicit discounted cash flow

So far we have been choosing arbitrary notional resale dates to illustrate the operation of the DCF technique. However, the two DCF solutions for fully let properties have been obtainable by either the use of the conventional

Table 6.3

Year	Current rent pa (£)	A £1 at 7.76807%	Projected rent pa (£)	YP at 13%	PV at 13%	Present value (£)
1–4	10,000	1.0000	10,000	2.9745	1.0000	29,745
5–9	20,000	1.3488	26,976	3.5172	0.6133	58,194
9	20,000	1.9607	39,214	16.6667*	0.3329	217,562
						£305,501

Note: [a]YP perp. at 6 per cent.

capitalization rate or by applying formulae when the capitalization rate was not known.

In market valuation, the objective is to be rational in interpreting one type of transaction for use with another. When dealing with a reversionary situation, the prospect of disimilarity between comparables and subject property increases and in Example 6.3 we have this disimilarity. The comparable gives us the YP multiplier for a rack rented property. In the short-cut DCF model this is assumed to give the resale value at the point of time that the property becomes rack rented on 5-year reviews (becomes the same as the comparable). From that point onwards, there is no need to discount the cash flows further into the future because we shall only, eventually, get the same answer as capitalizing in perpetuity at the capitalization rate (6 per cent).

On account of this, the DCF technique for market valuation has been short cut. The short-cut growth explicit DCF approach is undertaken by assuming that the investor receives a fixed income (the rent passing) from the property until the next rent review or lease renewal (whichever is sooner) plus a notional sale price based upon the rental value at that time capitalized at the all risks yield/capitalization rate. This cash flow is then discounted at the target rate of return. This would have the effect in Example 6.3 of reducing the notional resale date to 4 years time and so turning the reversionary valuation into a two-stage calculation, term and reversion.

The valuation becomes (set out in conventional format as the number of separate parts to the valuation has been reduced to 2):

Term rent	£100,000	
YP 4 years at 13%	2.9745	
		£297,450
Reversion to ERV	200,000	
A £1 4 years at 7.76807%	1.3488	
Inflated rental value	£269,770	
YP perp. at 6%	16.6667	
PV 4 years at 13%	0.6133	
		£2,757,560
Valuation		£3,055,010

In undertaking market valuations, there is very rarely a need to explicitly grow the cash flow beyond the date at which the full rental value on a normal review pattern is obtained. In all further freehold examples, we shall use the short-cut version of the growth explicit DCF model.

Real value

The 3 YP formula which forms the basis of the real value hybrid produces a 6 per cent capitalization rate which is more easily derived in this case from the market, and the reversion is capitalized at this rate. The term is capitalized at 13 per cent to take account of the fixed nature of the term income. The equated yield could be derived from $e = (1 + i)(1 + g) - 1$ but, as i was derived from e and g, 13 per cent (e) can be used directly.

Valuation			
Current rent	£100,000 pa		
YP 4 years at 13%	2.9745		
		£297,450	
Reversion to ERV	£200,000		
YP perp. at 6%	16.667		
PV 4 years at 4.85481%	0.8273		
		£2,757,560	
Valuation			£3,055,010

Note that all three results equate. However, the deferment of the reversion at 4.85481 per cent and the use of the current rental value on reversion differ from the DCF approach. A return to the original summation of the model in Chapter 5 will illustrate that real value and DCF models are doing the same thing in a different way. The real value approach views income profiles in real terms while the DCF model views the rental flows in absolute money terms. The reversion to a rental value of £200,000 per annum in the real value model is the expected real value of the rent on reversion while the rent of £269,770 per annum in the DCF model represents the actual amount of rent expected. To reconcile the two different figures would mean that a commodity which cost £200,000 now would be expected to cost £269,770 in 4 years' time.

The deferments are at two different yields. The real value approach recognizes the rent of £200,000 as having the ability to rise as rental values rise and can be expected to be worth more than an inflation prone sum. The deferment is at a growth implicit yield. The explicit DCF approach acknowledges the estimation of a rent in money terms in the future and discounts on the basis that the purchasing power of the estimated rent will decline as inflation increases in the 4-year waiting period.

The two approaches reconcile as follows. The term valuations are common; the reversions differ.

DCF: reversion $= \text{rent}(1 + g)^4 \times \dfrac{1}{(1 + e)^4}$

Real value: reversion $= \text{rent} \times \dfrac{1}{(1 + i)^4}$

As $1 + e = (1 + i)(1 + g)$, the DCF approach becomes

$$\text{rent } (1 + g)^4 \times \dfrac{1}{(1 + i)^4 (1 + g)^4}$$

which reduces to

$$\text{rent} \times \dfrac{1}{(1 + i)^4}$$

Short-cut DCF and the real value/equated yield hybrid model are therefore two different approaches to the same solution and the choice of model depends on ease of use rather than any criteria of accuracy. They give identical solutions to the problem.

Long reversions

In Chapter 4 we identified the problems which the conventional models have when the comparable lease structure and the subject property are very different. We also suggested that one such occasion was when the term of a reversionary valuation was very long.

Contemporary techniques have no problems with this situation. As they already recognize that the term value is fixed and is therefore prone to falls in value in real terms, they value the term at the appropriate required return (that is, they do not use a growth implicit yield to value the fixed income) regardless of the length of the term. Example 6.4 illustrates this point.

■ EXAMPLE 6.4

Value the freehold interest in a similar shop property to the one in Example 6.3. However, in this case, the lease has 24 years unexpired at a net rent of £100,000 per annum and the estimated current rental value is £200,000 per annum based on 5-yearly rent reviews. Assume the same facts as before: $e = 13$ per cent, $g = 7.76807$ per cent per annum, $i = 4.85481$ per cent and $k = 6$ per cent (based upon 5-year reviews).

Growth explicit DCF

Term rent	£100,000	
YP 24 years at 13%	7.2829	
		£728,288
Reversion to ERV	£200,000	
A £1 24 years at 7.76807%	6.0223	
Inflated rental value	£1,204,460	
YP perp. at 6%	16.6667	
PV 24 years at 13%	0.0532	
		£1,068,461
Valuation		£1,796,749

The valuation assumes a fixed income of £100,000 per annum for the next 24 years followed by a notional sale of the property for the rental value at the time (£1,204,460 per annum) capitalized at 6 per cent. The cash flow of £100,000 for 24 years plus the sale proceeds are discounted at the target rate of return, 13 per cent.

Real value

Term rent	£100,000	
YP 24 years at 13%	7.2829	
		£728,288
Reversion to ERV	£200,000	
YP perp. at 6%	16.6667	
PV 24 years at 4.85481%	0.3205	
		£1,068,461
Valuation		£1,796,749

As before, the two valuations reconcile at both term and reversion stages.

Over-rented properties

In Chapter 4, we identified the current problem facing practitioners in the UK concerning the valuation of properties let at more than their current rental value. This problem highlighted the difficulties in applying the conventional model to anything but the most simple of problems. The example used to describe the conventional approach was of a Central London office block which was 100 per cent over-rented. This example is used again to illustrate the DCF and real value solutions.

■ EXAMPLE 6.5

A Central London office building is to be valued in June 1992. It was let on a 20-year FRI lease in March 1990 with 5-year reviews at a passing rent of £2 million per annum. The estimated rental value has now fallen to £1 million per annum. Fully let capitalization rate estimated to be 8 per cent.

Figure 6.2 reproduces diagrammatically the problem faced by the valuer. The capitalization rate indicates that the rental value is expected to grow in the long term. However, as the rent is higher than the rental value, the valuer has to decide when the rental value will rise above the rent passing.

The rent is not expected to fall at any future review on account of the upward only rent reviews. Once the estimate of cross-over date is made, the valuation becomes a fixed term at the rent passing until the next review after the cross-over date, with a reversion to notional sale price at that review. If the cross-over date does not occur within the term of the lease, or before a break clause in the lease, the reversion date is the lease renewal date or the break clause date.

Growth explicit short-cut DCF

Analysis for implied growth in rents:

$$(1 + g)^t = \frac{\text{YP perp. at } k - \text{YP } t \text{ years at } e}{\text{YP perp. at } k \times \text{PV } t \text{ years at } e}$$

where g is the implied annual rental growth rate, t is the term of the rent review pattern of the rack rented property (5 years), k is the all risks yield

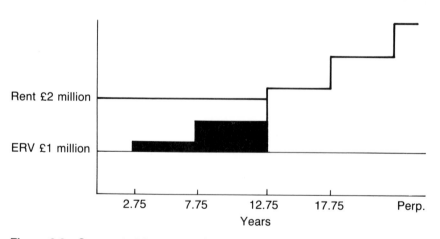

Figure 6.2 Over-rented income profile

of rack rented property (8 per cent) and e is the target rate of return/equated yield (13 per cent).

$$(1+g)^5 = \frac{\text{YP perp. at } 8\% - \text{YP 5 years at } 13\%}{\text{YP perp. at } 8\% \times \text{PV 5 years at } 13\%}$$

$$= \frac{12.5000 - 3.5172}{12.5000 \times 0.5427} = \frac{8.9827}{6.7844} = 1.3240$$

Implied growth $= (1.3240)^{1/5} - 1 = 5.7739$ per cent per annum

When does this suggest that the ERV will overtake the rent passing?

At first review	$£1,000,000 \times (1.057739)^{2.75}$	$= £1,166,920$ pa.
At second review	$£1,000,000 \times (1.057739)^{7.75}$	$= £1,545,018$ pa.
At third review	$£1,000,000 \times (1.057739)^{12.75}$	$= £2,045,625$ pa.

This suggests that rental growth will just overtake the rent passing by the third review in 12.75 years time, therefore it can be assumed that the reversion to a higher rent will take place in that year.

Rent passing	£2,000,000	
YP 12.75 years at 13%	6.0731	
		£12,146,171
Reversion to ERV	£1,000,000	
A £1 12.75 years at		
5.7739%	2.0456	
	£2,045,625	
YP perp. at 8%	12.5000	
PV 12.75 years at 13%	0.2105	
		£5,382,523
Valuation		£17,528,694

Real value

Calculate IFRY

$$i = \frac{1.13}{1.057739} - 1 = 6.8316\%$$

Rent passing	£2,000,000	
YP 12.75 years at 13%	6.0731	
		£12,146,171
Reversion to ERV	£1,000,000	
YP perp. at 8%	12.5000	
PV 12.75 years at		
6.8316%	0.4306	
		£5,382,523
Valuation		£17,528,694

It is possible for the valuer to intuitively decide that overage will still exist after a rent review, even though the use of a long-term average growth rate suggests that the overage has been extinguished. In our example the implied rental growth rate suggests that the overage is just eliminated in 12.75 years. If the valuer was not comfortable with that it would make little difference to the answer if the term was extended to the end of the lease. This is illustrated using the short-cut DCF only.

Rent passing	£2,000,000	
YP 17.75 years at 13%	6.8135	
		£13,626,917
Reversion to ERV	£1,000,000	
A £1 17.75 years at		
5.7739%	2.7084	
	£2,708,433	
YP perp. at 8%	12.5000	
PV 17.75 years at 13%	0.1143	
		£3,867,994
Valuation		£17,494,911

The difference in solution is minimal (less than £35,000 in £17 million). This departure from the implied rental growth rate is more likely to occur in less over-rented properties where the implied growth suggests the ERV overtakes the rent passing relatively quickly, at a time when the valuer expects a period of slower than average growth in the short term. However, this begins to raise some difficult questions. It must be remembered that the inputs to the model have been extracted from transaction evidence and, although small departures from the basis are defensible, disregarding the inputs totally would mean that the valuation had ceased to be a *market* valuation.

The valuations have been based upon the assumption that the ERV and the rack rented yield are readily available from comparables. These assumptions are theoretically comfortable but raise practical problems in a falling market. The real rental value in a falling market is masked by the giving of inducements and incentives to tenants to take premises and pay a higher 'headline' rent. These inducements include rent free periods and capital payments. In the models indicated above, the ERV must be estimated on the assumption that they are free of inducements and headline rents must be adjusted downwards to compensate for the incentives. The rack rented yield will also be difficult to extract from the evidence as very few properties will be sold which are truly rack rented. However, this raises transaction analysis issues which are no different from those raised in analysing reversionary transactions in a rising market and this is addressed in the second half of this chapter.

The major difference between the valuation of a rising reversion and the valuation of an over-rented situation is the added importance attached to tenant strength in the latter circumstances. The ability of the tenant to survive the payment of a rent which is, in our example, double the actual rental value is crucial to the maintenance of the income stream.

The income stream from an over-rented property is basically a bond investment and the quality of the investment has ceased to be based upon traditional property risks and is based upon the ability of the tenant to continue to pay the rent and the unexpired term of the lease. The valuation assumes the rent payment is maintained, therefore if the tenant is at all vulnerable, and there is a chance of bankruptcy, the valuation should be reduced. This is achieved by increasing the yield on the term valuation to represent added default risk and the inability to recapture the over-rented portion of the income upon a re-letting (if one can be secured). It is therefore quite reasonable for the analysis to be based upon 13 per cent while the term income is capitalized at, say, 15 per cent to incorporate the extra risk premium.

However, for a property heavily over-let to a very secure covenant under a lease with more than 15 years unexpired (on upwards only reviews), the term yield could be determined in comparison with a fixed income gilt plus a small risk margin for property illiquidity but without the traditional risks of property such as uncertainty of future income flow. In these circumstances, the term yield could be as little as 1 per cent over gilts, certainly less than the 13 per cent in our example.

THREE-STAGE COMPLEX REVERSIONARY FREEHOLDS

As the valuation gets more complex, the conventional valuation approach gets more subjective. The contemporary models have less difficulty in adapting to these complex situations as they give more help to the valuer in interpreting transaction evidence. In order to illustrate how the contemporary models adapt, three situations will be considered:

1 a property with an abnormal review period before a reversion to a normal 5-year review pattern,
2 a Landlord and Tenant Act improvements situation where there is a reversion to an estimated rental value excluding improvements, before a final reversion to the full estimated rental value including improvements, and
3 a stepped rent situation.

In all these examples, it will be assumed that the target rate of return is 13 per cent and the fully let rack rented capitalization rate is 6 per cent as in Examples 6.1–6.4.

■　EXAMPLE 6.6: ABNORMAL REVIEW PATTERN

A shop property is let on a 63-year lease with 21-year rent reviews. There are now 30 years unexpired and the current net rent passing is £100,000 per annum. The estimated rental value on 5-year rent reviews is £200,000 per annum.

The next review is in 9 years' time. The rent will have to be fixed at the open market rental value for a 21-year review period.

In the UK, a practice of uplifting the rent for the abnormal review term has developed. The level of uplift depends upon the locational and physical characteristics of the property. In a study carried out recently (Crosby and Murdoch 1991–2), it was concluded that a rule of thumb approach is adopted in practice (based upon the number of years between the abnormal and normal review pattern) which would lead to approximately a 15 per cent increase in the rental value. For the purposes of this example, a current rental value of £230,000 per annum on a 21-year review pattern is assumed.

As before, the implied rental growth rate calculation would be carried out for both the growth explicit DCF approach and the real value approach. The results of the analysis are, as before, $e = 13$ per cent, $g = 7.76807$ per cent per annum, $i = 4.85481$ per cent and $k = 6$ per cent (based upon 5-year reviews).

Growth explicit DCF

Rent passing	£100,000	
YP 9 years at 13%	5.1317	
		£513,166
Reversion to ERV (21 years)	£230,000	
A £1 9 years at 7.76807%	1.9607	
	£450,961	
YP 21 years at 13%	7.1016	
PV 9 years at 13%	0.3329	
		£1,066,071
Reversion to ERV (5 years)	£200,000	
A £1 30 years at 7.76807%	9.4342	
	£1,886,833	
YP perp. at 6%	16.6667	
PV 30 years at 13%	0.0256	
		£803,950
Valuation		£2,383,187

Real value

Rent passing	£100,000	
YP 9 years at 13%	5.1317	
		£513,166
Reversion to ERV (21 years)	£230,000	
YP 21 years at 13%	7.1016	
PV 9 years at 4.85481%	0.6527	
		£1,066,071
Reversion to ERV (5 years)	£200,000	
YP perp. at 6%	16.6667	
PV 30 years at 4.85481%	0.2412	
		£803,950
Valuation		£2,383,187

As in previous examples, the only difference between the two solutions is that the growth explicit DCF approach grows the rent at each reversion to its anticipated amount, and discounts the reversion at a fixed income yield, while the real value approach reverts to current rental values and implies that the current rental value will grow in the interim period in the PV yield.

Both valuations capitalize the middle term at 13 per cent (a fixed income yield). The reason for this is that there are no rent reviews in the 21-year period and therefore the income cannot be capitalized at yields that imply growth within that 21-year period (6 per cent or 4.85481 per cent). The real value approach discounts the middle term at the IRFY to imply that the rental value on 21-year reviews will grow over the waiting period of 9 years.

■ EXAMPLE 6.7: LANDLORD AND TENANT ACT 1954 IMPROVEMENTS

A similar shop property to Example 6.6 above is let on a lease with 5-year reviews which has 7 years unexpired. The current rent passing is £100,000 per annum and the next review is in 2 years. The tenant has just carried out improvements with the landlord's consent. The current rental value is estimated at £200,000 per annum ignoring the improvements and £225,000 per annum including them. The rent review clause in the existing lease excludes the value of the improvements from the rent at review.

This example shows how both growth explicit DCF and real value deal with the situation of a middle term which has rent reviews within it. In the previous example the middle term was a fixed income.

In England and Wales the rent upon renewal of the lease excludes tenants' improvements for a period of 21 years from the date they were carried out (see Baum and Sams 1991). As the current review pattern is 5 years, it would be reasonable to assume that the lease on renewal in 7 years time also included 5-year reviews and that the improvements would be excluded from the rent to the landlord for a further 15 years.

These assumptions create a cash flow of £100,000 per annum for the next 2 years, a reversion to a rent of (currently) £200,000 per annum for the next 20 years with reviews every 5 years, and a final reversion to £225,000 per annum into perpetuity, also with 5-year reviews, after 22 years.

Growth explicit DCF

The term and final reversion create no special problems and can be treated in the same way as in a two-stage valuation. The middle term can be approached by way of the DCF formula or by explicitly growing the rent every 5 years until the final reversion is reached. Both methods are illustrated. The first being explicit DCF.

Rent passing	£100,000	
YP 2 years at 13%	1.6681	
		£166,810
Reversion to ERV (excluding improvements)	£200,000	
A £1 2 years at 7.76807%	1.1614	
	£232,279	
YP 5 years at 13%	3.5172	
PV 2 years at 13%	0.7831	
		£639,815
Reversion to ERV (excluding improvements)	£200,000	
A £1 7 years at 7.76807%	1.6882	
	£337,645	
YP 5 years at 13%	3.5172	
PV 7 years at 13%	0.4251	
		£504,792
Reversion to ERV (excluding improvements)	£200,000	
A £1 12 years at 7.76807%	2.4540	
	£490,808	
YP 5 years at 13%	3.5172	
PV 12 years at 13%	0.2307	
		£398,264
Reversion to ERV (excluding improvements)	£200,000	
A £1 17 years at 7.76807%	3.5672	
	£713,447	
YP 5 years at 13%	3.5172	
PV 17 years at 13%	0.1252	
		£314,217
Reversion to ERV (including improvements)	£225,000	
A £1 22 years at 7.76807%	5.1854	
	£1,167,716	
YP Perp at 6%	16.6667	
PV 22 years at 13%	0.0680	
		£1,321,564
Valuation		£3,345,462

A tabular format would be appropriate for such a long valuation. Alternatively, the middle term could be assessed by DCF formula (for derivation, see Chapter 5, page 120).

Rent passing	£100,000	
YP 2 years at 13%	1.6681	
		£166,810
Reversion to ERV (excluding improvements)	£200,000	
Amt £1 2 years at 7.76807%	1.1614	
	£232,279	
YP of a rising income for 20 years (DCF YP)	10.2089	
PV 2 years at 13%	0.7831	
		£1,857,088
Reversion to ERV (including improvements)	£225,000	
Amt £1 22 years at 7.76807%	5.1854	
	£1,167,716	
YP perp. at 6%	16.6667	
PV 22 years at 13%	0.0680	
		£1,321,564
Valuation		£3,345,462

$$\text{DCF YP} = \text{YP 5 years at } 13\% \times \frac{1 - (1.0776807)^{20}/(1.13)^{20}}{1 - (1.0776807)^{5}/(1.13)^{5}}$$

$$= 3.5172 \times \frac{0.6125}{0.2110}$$

$$= 3.5172 \times 2.9025$$

$$= 10.2089$$

Real value

The term and final reversion are dealt with as in a two-stage reversionary valuation. The middle term can be solved by adopting the 3 YP formula to represent the capital value of a rising income for a periodic term.

The 3 YP formula is

$$YP = YP \text{ term of review at } e\% \times \frac{YP \text{ whole term at } i\%}{YP \text{ term of review at } i\%}$$

$$= YP \text{ 5 years at } 13\% \times \frac{YP \text{ 20 years at } 4.85481\%}{YP \text{ 5 years at } 4.85481\%}$$

$$= 3.5172 \times \frac{12.61707}{4.346909}$$

$$= 10.2089$$

Rent passing	£100,000	
YP 2 years at 13%	1.6681	
		£166,810
Reversion to ERV (excluding improvements)	£200,000	
3 YP formula	10.2089	
PV 2 years at 4.85481%	0.9095	
		£1,857,088
Reversion to ERV (including improvements)	£225,000	
YP perp. at 6%	16.6667	
PV 22 years at 4.85481%	0.3524	
		£1,321,564
Valuation		£3,345,462

■ EXAMPLE 6.8: STEPPED RENTS

A similar shop property to the previous two examples has just been let on a 15-year lease with 5-yearly upward only rent reviews. The rent in the first year is to be £150,000 and this will rise to £175,000 in the second year, £200,000 in year 3, £225,000 in year 4 and £250,000 in year 5. The estimated rental value is £200,000 per annum.

During the current recession, it has become more common practice to let property on stepped rents, often starting below current rental value and then rising above it. As in previous examples, the short-cut growth explicit DCF and real value techniques have no problem with this situation, which can introduce over-renting when the steps are to above rental value.

Growth explicit DCF

Year 1	£150,000	
PV 1 year at 13%	0.8850	
		£132,743
Year 2	£175,000	
PV 2 years at 13%	0.7831	
		£137,051
Year 3	£200,000	
PV 3 years at 13%	0.6930	
		£138,610
Year 4	£225,000	
PV 4 years at 13%	0.6133	
		£137,997
Year 5	£250,000	
PV 5 years at 13%	0.5428	
		£135,690
Reversion to ERV	£200,000	
A £1 5 years at 7.76807%	1.4536	
	£290,724	
YP perp. at 6%	16.6667	
PV 5 years at 13%	0.5428	
		£2,629,885
Valuation		£3,311,977

Real value

Year 1	£150,000	
PV 1 year at 13%	0.8850	
		£132,743
Year 2	£175,000	
PV 2 years at 13%	0.7831	
		£137,051
Year 3	£200,000	
PV 3 years at 13%	0.6930	
		£138,610
Year 4	£225,000	
PV 4 years at 13%	0.6133	
		£137,997
Year 5	£250,000	
PV 5 years at 13%	0.5428	
		£135,690
Reversion to ERV	£200,000	
YP perp. at 6%	16.6667	
PV 5 years at 4.85481%	0.7890	
		£2,629,885
Valuation		£3,311,977

The PV for one year is the same as the YP for one year (as the YP is der-ived from PV) and the YP one year deferred one year is equal to the PV for two years. The real value approach treats the fixed income identically to the growth explicit DCF but exhibits the usual difference on the rever-sion; adopting current rental values instead of inflating the rent.

The problem which might arise in this case is that the rental value might not rise enough to overtake the last rent passing, and the upward only review clause would take effect fixing the rent at (in our case) £225,000 per annum for the next 5 years. The growth explicit technique is better at iden-tifying this problem and a separate calculation would have to be introduced into the real value approach to test the rent level at first rent review.

The examples of complex reversionary situations illustrated above indi-cate the flexibility and robustness of the growth explicit contemporary approaches. The solutions obtained are all totally consistent with the nature of the lease structures and the market transaction evidence; and therefore produce logical and defensible valuations. The fact that at present they may well not produce the same solutions as the market is a reason for suggesting that the market may well be interpreting market evidence in an inconsistent manner.

The second half of this chapter examines the new models in comparison with the old to attempt to take this debate further. As the equivalent yield is the most defensible conventional approach (see Chapter 4) and real value is the most similar to the conventional approach (in that it has an identical layout, uses current rental values and only differs on yield choice on the term and on the deferment of reversions), these two models will be used to undertake the comparison.

CONVENTIONAL VERSUS CONTEMPORARY TECHNIQUES

The defense of conventional techniques

The change in the perceptions of investors outlined in Chapter 3 should naturally and logically lead to a change in the valuation model. Our examination of the typical income profile incorporating a growth expectation illustrated that the new model should be based upon an explicit DCF format employing the target rate or equated yield. Why then, 30 years after the appearance of the reverse yield gap, has the technique of valuers remained largely unchanged?

The change in perception led to a model which incorporated three extra variables: the equated yield, the growth rate and the timing of rent increases in the future. Although the timing of future rent increases is based on current or actual review patterns, the equated yield and growth rate are not so simple to estimate.

It has been illustrated in Chapter 5 that, if the equated yield is assumed, the growth rate can be calculated using market analysis. This leaves the problem of subjective equated yield choice.

DCF models which rely on the calculation of implied growth accept, by implication, reliance on the major basis of market valuation: comparable evidence. Logic has been suggested as a major criterion for a valuation model (see Chapter 1): objectivity in the use of comparable evidence becomes another major criterion. The defence of conventional techniques relies on objectivity to a greater extent than it does upon logic. The defence of traditional models in practice relies on the following arguments:

1 the contemporary models have an inherent flaw in assuming an equated yield subjectively; and

2 the crux of a valuation is comparable evidence, and if the comparables are good then the valuer does not have to be subjective in his use of them.

The argument, put simply, is that objectivity is not present in the contemporary models' choice of equated yield, while objectivity is present in the conventional models' use of comparisons. This argument can now be examined.

Equated yield choice

The first part of the argument relates to the subjective choice of equated yield in DCF based models. Most published comment suggests that:

1 conventional gilt-edged stock gross redemption yields should be the major comparison for the property target rate; and
2 a margin of 2 per cent above gilts allows for the additional risks of property (see Chapter 2).

The reasons for using conventional gilts are a natural consequence of a supposition that gilts are a substitute for a risk free investment (ignoring interest rate and inflation risks). The risk margin has little other basis than the historical relationship between prime property yields and gilt yields prior to the reverse yield gap (see Table 3.1). A detailed investigation of the historical relationship (Crosby 1985) confirmed that a margin of 2 per cent was the investor's perception of the risk differential between shop property and gilts prior to the reverse yield gap (Table 6.4). However, this historical analysis of yield choice would suggest a different margin for different sectors (industrials, offices) and classes (prime, secondary) of property.

If a historical basis is valid for equated yield choice then equated yields will vary for each type of property. But equated yield choice in modern times should not be based on historical analysis: a more rational basis must be found.

This basis could be founded upon the qualitative differences between the comparable (gilts) and property. The risks of property have been examined

Table 6.4 Gilt and property yield differentials, 1929–55

	Prime shops	Secondary shops	Prime offices	Ground rents
Yield gap	2.25%	3.03%	3.03%	0.73%

Source: Crosby 1985

in Chapter 2; the possibility of diversifying these risks has also been considered. In the valuation context the difficulties of assessing each risk factor for an individual property has led to a choice of all risks yields which imply these risks. Equated yields in practice are no exception, the only difference being that the rental growth rate and timing of reviews have been explicitly dealt with. The incidence of other risk factors will vary from property to property.

To include a detailed isolation of factors within a market valuation is not, we suggest, a realistic proposition given that each comparable property must be subjected to the same scrutiny. The problems of identifying and quantifying these differences in the market valuation context leaves the valuer to choose a suitable equated yield for each property type and confirms the charge of subjectivity. Although an attempt to quantify the 'risk' of property investments is a relevant area of study in the context of the analysis role (see Chapter 8) we feel that little advantage is to be gained in the market valuation context.

Equated yield choice is therefore a subjective element in the DCF-based valuation process and to that extent the defence of conventional techniques is sound. However, is the valuation sensitive to equated yield choice?

To investigate this, an analysis of fully let freehold and reversionary freehold valuations follows.

Fully let freeholds

Although the contemporary models appear to mirror the change in investors' perceptions since the 1960s, the extra variables necessary in DCF models introduce an element of subjectivity. The previous discussion indicates that subjective equated yield choice impacts upon implied growth rates and hence the valuation. But is this important? We examined the effect of varying the equated yield by undertaking an analysis of valuation ranges produced by a wide variation in equated yields. In the following analysis a range of equated yields between 10 per cent and 20 per cent is utilized and the resulting valuations are compared.

■ EXAMPLE 6.9

Value the freehold interest in a property just let at its rental value of £200,000 per annum on a 5-year review pattern. A similar property has also just been let on a 5-year review pattern and recently sold for a price based on a capitalization rate of 6 per cent.

Conventional analysis and valuation

Analysis

$k = 6\%$ (based upon 5-year reviews)

Valuation

ERV	£200,000 pa	
YP perp. at 6%	16.6667	
Valuation		£3,333,333

Contemporary analysis and valuation

Assume

(i) $e = 10\%$; (ii) $e = 20\%$

Analysis

$$(1 + g)^t = \frac{\text{YP perp. at } k - \text{YP } t \text{ years at } e}{\text{YP perp. at } k \times \text{PV } t \text{ years at } e}$$

(i) at $e = 10\%$, $g = 4.4668\%$ pa, $i = 5.2966\%$
(ii) at $e = 20\%$, $g = 15.3463\%$ pa, $i = 4.0346\%$

Valuation (i): $e = 10\%$

ERV	£200,000 pa	

$$\frac{\text{YP 5 years at } 10\% \times \text{YP perp. at } 5.2966\%}{\text{YP 5 years at } 5.2966\%} \quad 16.6667$$

Valuation		£3,333,333

Valuation (ii): $e = 20\%$

ERV	£200,000 pa	

$$\frac{\text{YP 5 years at } 20\% \times \text{YP perp. at } 4.0345\%}{\text{YP 5 years at } 4.0345\%} \quad 16.6667$$

Valuation		£3,333,333

These two valuations by the real value method are of course short cuts to a full DFC valuation at the equated yield. As a reminder of the point, an explicit DCF approach is set out in Tables 6.5 and 6.6.

The use of a real value hybrid shows a number of interesting points. Although the valuations all reconcile, the variables are extremely diverse. The increase in the equated yield from 10 per cent to 20 per cent obviously shows that a much higher growth rate is required to justify the initial return of 6 per cent. The real return (*i*) shows the opposite effect in this case. As the equated yield choice rises, the real return decreases. At an *e* of 10 per cent, *i* equals 5.3 per cent. At an *e* of 20 per cent, *i* equals 4.03 per cent.

Table 6.5 Explicit DCF approach, equated yield 10%, growth at 4.4668% pa

Years	Income (£)	YP	PV	Present value
1–5	200,000	3.7908	1.0000	758,157
6–10	248,840	3.7908	0.6209	585,716
11–15	309,610	3.7908	0.3855	452,497
16–20	385,220	3.7908	0.2394	349,577
21–25	479,290	3.7908	0.1486	270,067
26–30	596,330	3.7908	0.0923	208,641
31–35	741,960	3.7908	0.0573	161,186
36–40	923,150	3.7908	0.0356	124,525
41–45	1,148,580	3.7908	0.0221	96,202
46–50	1,429,070	3.7908	0.0137	74,321
				£3,080,890

Plus:	Rental value year 50	£1,778,053	
	YP perp. at 6.00%	16.6667	
	PV 50 years at 10%	0.0085	
			£252,440
Valuation			£3,333,330

Note: Error due to rounding of growth rate.

Table 6.6 Explicit DCF approach, equated yield 20%, growth at 15.3463% pa

Years	Income (£)	YP	PV	Present value
1–5	200,000	2.9906	1.0000	598,122
6–10	408,365	2.9906	0.4019	490,797
11–15	833,809	2.9906	0.1615	402,730
16–20	1,702,492	2.9906	0.0649	330,466
21–25	3,476,189	2.9906	0.0261	271,168
26–30	7,097,766	2.9906	0.0105	222,511
31–35	14,492,391	2.9906	0.0042	182,584
36–40	29,590,914	2.9906	0.0017	149,822
41–45	60,419,443	2.9906	0.0007	122,938
46–50	123,365,879	2.9906	0.0003	100,879
				£2,872,017

Plus:	Rental value year 50	£251,891,434	
	YP perp. at 6.00%	16.6667	
	PV 50 years at 20%	0.0001	
			£461,318
Valuation			£3,333,335

Note: Error due to rounding of growth rate.

This is due to the impact of the review pattern because the growth must increase by slightly more than the required rate of return (equated yield) as the growth can only be participated in every 5 years.

The influence of these variations is nil when perfect comparables are present. In Example 6.9 the comparable is perfect (the equated yield result could therefore have been quickly achieved by conventional techniques: see Example 6.1 on page 137).

In the following example, the comparable is let on a different review pattern to the property to be valued.

EXAMPLE 6.10

Assuming the same comparison, value the following properties:

(a) ERV £200,000 per annum on an inflation proof basis (indexed rents, for example).
(b) ERV £200,000 per annum on 3-year reviews.
(c) ERV £200,000 per annum on 7-year reviews.

Example 6.10(a)

The inflation proofed rent assumes a review at each rent payment date. The capitalization can be undertaken at the real return i.

(i) $e = 10\%$, $i = 5.2966\%$

ERV	£200,000	
YP perp. at 5.2966%	18.8679	
Valuation		£3,773,580

(ii) $e = 20\%$, $i = 4.0345\%$

ERV	£200,000	
YP perp. at 4.0345%	24.8139	
Valuation		£4,962,780

The range in answers is very wide. At an e of 10 per cent the valuation is 76 per cent of the valuation at an e of 20 per cent.

Example 6.10(b)

(i) $e = 10$ per cent, reviews every 3 years

ERV	£200,000

$$\frac{\text{YP perp. at } 5.2966\% \times \text{YP 3 years at } 10\%}{\text{YP 3 years at } 5.2966\%} \quad 17.3270$$

Valuation	£3,465,400

(ii) $e = 20\%$, reviews every 3 years

ERV	£200,000

$$\frac{\text{YP perp. at } 4.0345\% \times \text{YP 3 years at } 20\%}{\text{YP 3 years at } 4.0345\%} \quad 18.8461$$

Valuation	£3,769,230

The e at 20 per cent valuation is still higher but the e at 10 per cent valuation is now 92 per cent of the higher equated yield solution.

Example 6.10(c)

(i) $e = 10\%$, reviews every 7 years

ERV	£200,000

$$\frac{\text{YP perp. at } 5.2966\% \times \text{YP 7 years at } 10\%}{\text{YP 7 years at } 5.2966\%} \quad 16.0477$$

Valuation	£3,209,550

(ii) $e = 20\%$, reviews every 7 years

ERV	£200,000 pa

$$\frac{\text{YP perp. at } 4.0345\% \times \text{YP 7 years at } 20\%}{\text{YP 7 years at } 4.0345\%} \quad 14.9187$$

Valuation	£2,983,750

In this case the 20 per cent equated yield choice produces the lower valuation, the e at 10 per cent valuation being 7.6 per cent higher.

When the comparable is on the same review pattern as the property to be valued, there is no discrepancy in the contemporary valuations. Where the comparables are not perfect, discrepancies occur. The greater the divergence of review patterns between comparable and subject properties, the greater the range of valuations produced. It may be thought that a higher discount rate would always produce a lower valuation but this is not the case. A high equated yield choice produces a higher valuation if the property to be valued has a shorter review pattern than the comparable, while the effect is reversed when the review pattern of the comparable is shorter than the property to be valued.

All the solutions are controlled by the consistent relationship between the equated yield, the growth rate and the real return. Table 6.7 sets out implied growth rates and real returns derived from equated yields of between 10 per cent and 20 per cent and capitalization rates of 4 per cent, 6 per cent and 8 per cent, all based on comparables with 5-year review patterns.

Table 6.7 illustrates the slightly higher growth rate required each year to offset the fact that increases in rent are only obtainable every 5 years. This produces a reducing real return as the equated yield increases.

The ranges in valuations shown above are perhaps enough to cast doubts on a method which relies on a subjective choice of equated yield. The wider the review patterns, the more significant the effect of equated yield choice: this is of importance, for example, in the evaluation of constant or equated rents if using growth explicit methods.

Table 6.7 Implied rental growth rates and real returns

Equated yield (%)	Capitalization rates on 5-year returns (%)					
	4.0		6.0		8.0	
	g	i	g	i	g	i
10	6.44	3.34	4.47	5.30	2.33	7.49
11	7.50	3.25	5.57	5.14	3.49	7.26
12	8.57	3.16	6.67	4.92	4.63	7.04
13	9.62	3.08	7.77	4.85	5.77	6.83
14	10.68	3.00	8.86	4.72	6.91	6.63
15	11.74	2.92	9.95	4.59	8.04	6.44
16	12.79	2.85	11.03	4.47	9.16	6.26
17	13.84	2.78	12.12	4.36	10.28	6.09
18	14.89	2.71	13.20	4.24	11.40	5.93
19	15.94	2.64	14.27	4.14	12.51	5.77
20	16.98	2.58	15.35	4.03	13.61	5.62
Average	11.73	2.94	9.93	4.61	8.01	6.49
Range	10.54	0.76	10.88	1.27	11.28	1.33

We are left, then, with the problem that subjective equated yield choice can affect the valuation of unusual fully let freeholds (those for which no perfect comparables exist) and no easy rule can be adopted in that choice.

However, we have demonstrated this problem over a very large range: note that a more realistic range of equated yields would result in very little difference. It should also be emphasized that the DCF-based model is much less sensitive to a change in yield than the conventional model.

Doubling the capitalization rate will halve the conventional valuation of a fully let freehold; doubling the equated yield in a contemporary approach to the same problem has already been shown to have a much reduced effect. The choice is therefore between conventional models, which are intuitive concerning choice of capitalization rate within which all investment qualities are implicit, and contemporary DCF-based models which are intuitive concerning choice of equated yield/target rate, albeit with a partial self-correction (the implied growth rate), within which some investment qualities are implicit (for example, risk) and others may be made explicit (for example, growth). We accept that neither contemporary nor conventional models are wholly objective. But which are the most logical?

Reversionary freeholds

The valuation of reversionary freeholds is more complex than the valuation of fully let freeholds. The perfect comparison is harder to find because of the effect of the existing lease. The fully let freehold is a perfect comparable when let on the same review term as the property to be valued. For reversionary freehold investments, the property is let on an existing lease at a rent which is often at less than the estimated rental value. The perfect comparable is a property which has not only the right physical and locational characteristics but also the same unexpired term and rent received to rental value ratio. Differences in these factors will cause properties to have different growth prospects for any given level of future growth in rental values. It would be useful at this stage to reiterate the defence of conventional techniques.

1 The need for subjective equated yield choice is an inherent flaw in contemporary models. (This has been examined and illustrated to cause variation in the valuation of fully let freeholds when the review patterns are different).

2 The objectivity of conventional models is ensured by their use of comparables. (This has been seen to be nonsense, as it relies upon having the perfect comparable.)

A third factor should also be considered. A single capitalization rate used in the conventional model has to reflect the growth potential of the property as a whole rather than the parts of the valuation. This is the basis of the equivalent yield model (the least dangerous conventional approach, which we use for illustration purposes in the remainder of this chapter in preference to term and reversion or layer methods (see Chapter 4)).

The availability and use of comparables and the effect of equated yield choice in the valuation of reversionary freeholds can now be examined to determine whether any of the models pass the tests of rationality and objectivity. The availability and analysis of comparables is examined first.

The availability and analysis of transactions

The availability of transactions depends on the level of activity in the market place and the level of knowledge of that activity. Up to the early 1980s both of these factors contrived to make comparables hard to find. However, the quantity of transactions has increased during the 1980s in the UK property investment market. IPD (1991) suggest that in the peak years of property trading in 1987 and 1988, the institutions were selling nearly 10 per cent of their portfolios and turning over capital sums equivalent to 25 per cent of portfolio value. At the beginning of the 1980s the sales were less than 1 per cent.

However, secrecy and the nature of the market place still make property transaction information difficult to acquire and interpret.

For a debate on technique these factors, although crucial to the valuation process, are immaterial. Both conventional and contemporary models require transaction evidence as market valuation is a comparison based activity; the differences are a product of how they interpret that evidence.

We argue that the contemporary techniques make better use of the available evidence and that where the evidence is thin, they are better able to produce rational valuations on account of their superior logical basis.

Example 6.11 illustrates how both methods approach the analysis of a reversionary property transaction.

   EXAMPLE 6.11

A property is let at a current rent of £150,000 per annum with 3 years unexpired. The estimated rental value is £200,000 per annum and the property has just been sold for £3,750,000.

Conventional analysis

Income flow (at current values)

Years 1–3	£150,000 pa
Reversion	£200,000 pa

Find equivalent yield (IRR on current income estimates):

Trial rate 5%
Current rent	£150,000 pa	
YP 3 years at 5%	2.7232	
		£408,490
ERV	£200,000 pa	
YP perp. at 5%	20.000	
PV 3 years at 5%	0.86384	
		£3,455,350

Valuation   £3,863,840

Trial rate 5.5%
Current rent	£150,000 pa	
YP 3 years at 5.5%	2.6979	
		£404,690
ERV	£200,000 pa	
YP perp. at 5.5%	18.1818	
PV 3 years at 5.5%	0.85161	
		£3,096,780

Valuation   £3,501,470

Net present value at 5% = £3,863,840 − £3,750,000 = + £113,840
Net present value at 5.5% = £3,501,470 − £3,750,000 = − £248,530
IRR = 5% + [0.5 × (113,840/362,370)] = 5% + 0.157077% = 5.16%

Equivalent yield = 5.16 per cent (although the actual result is 5.147 per cent, the error being due to the assumption of linear interpolation within the formula used above).

Contemporary analysis

This requires a subjective assumption to be made regarding equated yield choice.

(i) Assuming an equated yield of 10 per cent

Current rent		£150,000 pa
	YP 3 years at 10%	
ERV		£200,000 pa
	YP perp. at k%	
	PV 3 years at i%	

The valuation of the term can be determined but the valuation of the reversion requires two unknowns to be assessed. These unknowns are the growth rate (implied in the IRFY in the real value approach) and the capitalization rate. Trial and error is necessary in order to find these two inputs.

Current rent	£150,000 pa
YP 3 years at 10%	2.4869
	£373,035

The reversion has a value of £3,750,000 − £373,035 = £3,376,965. As the capitalization rate and the growth rate are a function of one another at an equated yield of 10 per cent, the trial and error (via a computer) is necessary to determine the solution. In this case it solves to $k = 5.20$ per cent; given that $e = 10$ per cent, $g = 5.28$ per cent and $i = 4.48$ per cent.

(ii) At an assumed equated yield of 20 per cent the term value is: £150,000 × YP 3 years at 20 per cent = £315,970.
   The reversion has a value of £3,750,000 − £315,970 = £3,434,030. The combination of yields and growth rates which fit here are $k = 5.25$%; given that $e = 20$%, $g = 15.97$%, $i = 3.48$%.

It would appear from these analyses that the conventional technique requires no subjective assumptions in the analysis of comparables, whereas the contemporary analysis requires an assumption of equated yield before the implied growth rate can be calculated. This may produce some valuation discrepancies which will only be reduced by narrowing the range of possible equated yields.
   However, it can be seen that there is no problem or error in either contemporary or conventional analysis/valuation where the perfect comparable exists. To be perfect, the comparable must be similar in location and

physical characteristics. It must also have the same ERV to rent received under the existing lease ratio and the same unexpired term.

The comparable in Example 6.12 and the valuation of Example 6.13 illustrates the lack of a need for technique where perfect comparables exist.

■ EXAMPLE 6.12

Rent passing £100,000 per annum with 3 years unexpired. ERV £200,000 per annum; sold for £3,725,000.

Conventional analysis produces an equivalent yield of 5.0034%.

Contemporary analysis:

(i) at 10 per cent equated yield:

$g = 5.4105\%$ pa $k = 5.0627\%$ $i = 4.3539\%$

(ii) at 20 per cent equated yield:

$g = 16.0540\%$ pa $k = 5.1478\%$ $i = 3.4001\%$

The equivalent yield model produces one answer only whereas the equated yield model produces a multiplicity of possible solutions. But we have argued before that if the comparison is perfect then these differences do affect the valuation solution. Example 6.13 illustrates.

■ EXAMPLE 6.13

Value an identical property let with 3 years unexpired at £150,000 per annum; ERV £300,000 per annum (this is the same unexpired term and ERV/rent received ratio as in Example 6.12).

Conventional valuation

Term	£150,000 pa		
YP 3 years at 5.0034%	2.7231		
		£408,460	
ERV	£300,000 pa		
YP perp. at 5.0034%	19.9865		
PV 3 years at 5.0034%	0.8638		
		£5,179,040	
Valuation			£5,587,500

Contemporary valuation

(i) at 10 per cent equated yield

Term	£150,000 pa		
YP 3 years at 10%	2.4869		
		£373,030	
ERV	£300,000 pa		
YP perp. at 5.0627%	19.7522		
PV 3 years at 4.3539%	0.8800		
		£5,214,470	
Valuation			£5,587,500

(ii) at 20% equated yield

Term	£150,000 pa		
YP 3 years at 20%	2.1065		
		£315,970	
ERV	£300,000 pa		
YP perp. at 5.1478%	19.4258		
PV 3 years at 3.4001%	0.9046		
		£5,271,530	
Valuation			£5,587,500

The valuations are identical. The rent passing and the ERV are both one and a half times as much as the comparable, so the solution should be £3,725,000 multiplied by $1\frac{1}{2} = £5,587,500$. Where the perfect comparison exists, no investment valuation is necessary: the direct comparison method is more straightforward.

The debate regarding investment valuation technique is therefore focused upon the use of imperfect comparables.

Examples 6.11, 6.12 and 6.13 illustrate the factors which are important when analysing comparables.

The conventional technique assumes a no growth environment which enables the current rents and rental values to be related to the sale price without any subjective inputs by the valuer. For any given rent, unexpired term, rental value and sale price, there is an equivalent yield which can be found. However, the assumption of no growth is unrealistic producing an apparently objective but obviously irrational analysis. Conventional valuers defend this with the well worn valuation disclaimer 'As you devalue so must you value'. Unfortunately, this only works when perfect comparables exist. However, as it has just been illustrated that no technique is necessary in these circumstances, this defence for conventional techniques is invalid.

The contemporary approach is explicit about future growth but in being so requires the assessment of three variables. These are the rental value growth rate, the required rate of return (equated yield) and future review pattern. Once two of these inputs have been decided, the third can be calculated. The review pattern is usually known, so that only one of the other factors must be assumed. This is usually the equated yield. Having set this, a growth rate can be objectively calculated. We therefore have a more rational model but some subjectivity remains.

So far, after considering the two different types of model's performance in interpreting transactions, no obvious preference emerges. The next examination looks at how the two approaches apply comparable information to the valuation of other properties which are not identical in lease structure to the comparable.

Applying the comparable evidence

In order to look at the relative performance of the equivalent yield and equated yield (real value) models, two reversionary properties will be valued based on the evidence from a third reversionary property.

EXAMPLE 6.14: THE COMPARABLE

A shop property has just been sold for £2,000,000. The current rental value is estimated to be £150,000 and the rent passing is £100,000. The lease has 3 years unexpired. (Differences from £2,000,000 in the following valuations are the result of rounding errors.)

Equivalent yield

Rent passing	£100,000	
YP 3 years at 7.0385%	2.6225	
		£262,247
Reversion to ERV	£150,000	
YP perp. at 7.0385%	14.2075	
PV 3 years at 7.0385%	0.8154	
		£1,737,754
Valuation		£2,000,001

This valuation shows that the equivalent yield of the transaction is 7.0385 per cent. No subjectivity has been required.

Equated yield: assume 10 per cent, 15 per cent and 20 per cent

(i) At 10 per cent equated yield

The analysis is undertaken by trial and error, inserting different capitalization rates into the valuation until the one is found which reconciles with the growth rate, equated yield and the IRFY. This analysis cannot be undertaken by assessing the equivalent yield and then inserting it into the implied rental growth rate formula as the capitalization rate k.

A capitalization rate of 7.0969 per cent implies a growth rate of 3.31723 per cent per annum at a 10 per cent equated yield, and produces an IRFY of 6.4682 per cent. These inputs generate a valuation of approximately £2 million. The following illustrates that it is correct.

Term	£100,000		
YP 3 years at 10%	2.4869		
		£248,685	
Reversion to ERV	£150,000		
YP perp. at 7.0969%	14.0907		
PV 3 years at 6.4682%	0.8286		
		£1,751,309	
Valuation			£1,999,995

(ii) At a 15 per cent equated yield the solution at a valuation of £2,000,004 is

Equated yield	15%
Implied growth	8.8406% pa
Capitalization rate	7.1777%
IRFY	5.6591%

(iii) At a 20 per cent equated yield the solution at a valuation of £1,999,986 is

Equated yield	20%
Implied growth	14.2833% pa
Capitalization rate	7.2411%
IRFY	5.0021%

■   EXAMPLE 6.15: A CLOSE COMPARISON

A similar shop property is let on a lease at a rent of £75,000 per annum. The lease has 4 years unexpired and the ERV is £150,000 per annum.

In this case the unexpired term is 1 year longer and the rent passing is at a lower percentage of ERV than in the comparable property. The comparison is not perfect but it is very close.

Equivalent yield

Rent passing	£75,000		
YP 4 years at 7.0385%	3.3843		
		£253,820	
Reversion to ERV	£150,000		
YP perp. at 7.0385%	14.2075		
PV 4 years at 7.0385%	0.7618		
		£1,623,495	
Valuation			£1,877,315

No subjective adjustments have been made to the valuation, so the solution has been totally objective throughout the analysis and valuation stages. However, the slightly longer unexpired term and the lower rent passing may have induced some valuers to consider changing the equivalent yield subjectively. If those differences had been more marked, most valuers would start to consider amendments to the yield, based entirely upon their intuition.

Equated yield

(i)   At 10 per cent equated yield

Term	£75,000		
YP 4 years at 10%	3.1699		
		£237,740	
Reversion to ERV	£150,000		
YP perp. at 7.0969%	14.0907		
PV 4 years at 6.4682%	0.7783		
		£1,644,918	
Valuation			£1,882,658

The difference in valuation is just over £5,000 (or one-quarter of

1 per cent). The adoption of different equated yields does not produce any major divergence.

(ii) At 15 per cent equated yield

Term at 15% (e)	£214,123
Reversion at 7.1777% deferred at 5.6591%	£1,676,789
Valuation	£1,890,912

(iii) At 20 per cent equated yield

Term at 20% (e)	£194,155
Reversion at 7.2411% deferred at 5.0021%	£1,704,099
Valuation	£1,898,254

The difference between the modern valuations is small. The 20 per cent valuation is approximately £15,000 (or just over three-quarters of 1 per cent) above the 10 per cent valuation. The equated yield choice is not a significant factor in this valuation.

■ EXAMPLE 6.16: A POOR QUALITY COMPARISON

A similar shop property to the comparable is let on a historic lease which has no further rent reviews. The rent passing is £75,000 per annum and the lease has 20 years unexpired. The ERV is £150,000.

The only difference between this property and the previous one is that the unexpired term is 20 years, not 4 years. The equivalent yield could be assumed to be the same as the comparable considering it is a perfect comparison in terms of physical and locational characteristics.

Equivalent yield

Rent passing	£75,000		
YP 20 years at 7.0385%	10.5624		
		£792,179	
Reversion to ERV	£150,000		
YP perp. at 7.0385%	14.2075		
PV 20 years at 7.0385%	0.2566		
		£546,778	
Valuation			£1,338,957

This valuation takes no account of the differences between the comparable and the subject property. It assumes that the only difference is that one property will generate an income of £75,000 per annum more than the other one between years 4 and 20. The yield adopted suggests that the income flows have the same growth potential even though one reverts to a 5-year review pattern in 4 years while the other has no income growth for 20 years.

The growth potential cannot be reflected automatically in the valuation so the valuer is now forced to amend the yield intuitively (subjectively) to make up for the limitations of the technique.

Equated yield

(i)   At 10 per cent equated yield

Term	£75,000		
YP 20 years at 10%	8.5136		
		£638,517	
Reversion to ERV	£150,000		
YP perp. at 7.0969%	14.0907		
PV 20 years at 6.4682%	0.2855		
		£603,426	
Valuation			£1,241,943

(ii) At 15 per cent equated yield

Term at 15% (e)	£469,450	
Reversion at 7.1777% (k),		
deferred at 5.6591% (i)	£694,973	
Valuation		£1,164,423

(iii) At 20 per cent equated yield

Term at 20% (e)	£365,218	
Reversion at 7.2411% (k),		
deferred at 5.0021% (i)	£780,418	
Valuation		£1,145,636

The subjective choice of equated yield at the beginning of the analysis stage has started to be significant. The 10 per cent equated yield valuation is now higher than the 20 per cent valuation and by a significant amount (nearly £100,000 or 7.75 per cent). However, the equivalent yield valuation is obviously too high and all three equated yield valuations are below the conventional approach.

The equivalent yield valuer would therefore have to adjust the yield upwards, but there is no systematic constraint on the amount of the adjustment. The equated yield valuations appear to be relatively consistent despite a 100 per cent variation in the equated yield choice and therefore the subjectivity is subject to constraint.

As the equated yield is raised, the value of the term reduces. In the above valuations, the 10 per cent equated yield generates a term value of £638,517 while at 15 per cent it reduces to £469,450. However, the inflation risk free yield used to defer the reversion falls as the equated yield rises (this is because the implied growth rate increases by more than the equated yield to compensate for the delaying effect of the rent review pattern) and this causes the reversion to be valued higher at the higher equated yield (£603,426 at an e of 10 per cent against £694,973 at an e of 15 per cent). There is a cancelling out effect.

As the equated yield is raised in a reversionary situation, the term value is reduced but the reversion value is increased. The resulting difference in the valuation is smaller than expected and, in situations where the reversion value dominates the capital value, a higher equated yield choice can often produce a higher total valuation.

The extent of the cancelling out process is dependent on the relative ratios of values in the term and reversion, which in turn are dependent on the ratio of the term rent to ERV and the unexpired term of the lease. In order to study this effect, an examination of a number of different capitalization rates and ratios of ERV to current rent received was undertaken with the following ranges:

Capitalization rates	3.5% to 8% (step 0.5%) assuming comparables were rack rented
ERV/rent ratios	25%, 50%, 75%, 100%
Review pattern	5 years
Unexpired term	1–10, 15, 20, 25, 50
Equated yields	10% to 20% (step 1%)

We tested 560 permutations and eleven valuations were carried out for each permutation making a total of 6,160 valuations. The results were then analysed to show the excess of the highest valuation in each case over the lowest valuation in each case. These results are illustrated in Tables 6.8–6.11.

A further analysis was undertaken to assess at what unexpired term the higher equated yield choice did not exhibit the highest valuation for each

Table 6.8 Range of valuations – EY 10% to 20%, rent received/ERV ratio 25%

Unexpired term (years)	Capitalization rate (%)										Average	Standard deviation
	3.5	4.0	4.5	5.0	5.5	6.0	6.5	7.0	7.5	8.0		
1	0.54	0.66	0.79	0.88	0.96	1.06	1.15	1.32	1.42	1.52	1.030	0.309
2	1.09	1.26	1.47	1.65	1.82	2.00	2.26	2.53	2.73	3.02	1.983	0.611
3	1.53	1.80	2.05	2.30	2.62	2.89	3.24	3.52	3.90	4.21	2.806	0.859
4	1.94	2.25	2.56	2.94	3.28	3.69	4.06	4.43	4.82	5.32	3.529	1.073
5	2.34	2.71	3.10	3.50	3.91	4.34	4.78	5.24	5.72	6.21	4.184	1.236
6	2.70	3.15	3.61	4.03	4.52	4.95	5.24	5.93	6.49	6.96	4.782	1.360
7	3.05	3.51	3.98	4.47	5.02	5.53	6.05	6.58	7.11	7.77	5.307	1.497
8	3.36	3.89	4.38	4.93	5.50	6.07	6.56	7.06	7.66	8.14	5.755	1.537
9	3.69	4.24	4.79	5.35	5.83	6.47	6.92	7.57	8.12	8.67	6.165	1.589
10	3.99	4.61	5.17	5.73	6.26	6.88	7.40	7.89	8.36	8.94	6.523	1.568
15	5.50	6.17	6.79	7.33	7.78	8.24	8.48	8.72	8.84	8.81	7.666	1.123
20	6.99	7.69	8.23	8.55	8.86	8.67	8.60	8.11	7.28	6.51	7.949	0.758
25	8.47	9.05	9.37	9.50	9.09	8.45	7.49	6.60	5.51	4.49	7.802	1.649
50	14.42	12.72	10.75	8.32	5.71	9.04	14.53	20.38	28.26	36.89	16.102	9.285
Average (first 10 years)	2.422	2.808	3.190	3.578	3.972	4.379	4.790	5.207	5.633	6.076		
Standard deviation	1.085	1.242	1.383	1.537	1.686	1.861	1.987	2.106	2.247	2.387		
Average (total)	4.257	4.551	4.788	4.963	5.083	5.585	6.214	6.849	7.587	8.384		
Standard deviation	3.540	3.221	2.891	2.579	2.372	2.477	3.174	4.306	6.106	8.179		

Table 6.9 Range of valuations – EY 10% to 20%, rent received/ERV ratio 50%

Unexpired term (years)	Capitalization rate (%)										Average	Standard deviation
	3.5	4.0	4.5	5.0	5.5	6.0	6.5	7.0	7.5	8.0		
1	0.50	0.57	0.69	0.76	0.84	0.98	1.06	1.15	1.24	1.41	0.920	0.283
2	0.86	0.99	1.16	1.30	1.43	1.64	1.78	2.00	2.24	2.40	1.58	0.497
3	1.13	1.34	1.52	1.75	1.94	2.19	2.39	2.59	2.88	3.09	2.082	0.626
4	1.37	1.57	1.79	2.00	2.28	2.51	2.82	2.98	3.31	3.56	2.419	0.706
5	1.50	1.73	1.97	2.21	2.46	2.71	2.97	3.23	3.50	3.77	2.605	0.725
6	1.60	1.85	2.11	2.31	2.58	2.78	3.05	3.32	3.51	3.79	2.690	0.693
7	1.70	1.93	2.10	2.31	2.57	2.78	2.97	3.16	3.43	3.61	2.656	0.613
8	1.73	1.97	2.14	2.30	2.57	2.63	2.89	2.99	3.15	3.20	2.557	0.483
9	1.76	1.96	2.13	2.29	2.36	2.55	2.56	2.71	2.75	2.77	2.384	0.330
10	1.75	1.90	2.07	2.16	2.28	2.30	2.29	2.32	2.22	2.08	2.137	0.180
15	1.78	1.73	1.64	1.53	1.33	1.23	1.07	1.50	2.12	2.82	1.675	0.475
20	1.96	1.81	1.57	1.34	1.88	2.82	3.95	5.38	6.90	8.76	3.638	2.439
25	2.32	2.08	1.69	2.76	4.09	5.92	7.95	10.47	13.18	16.43	6.689	4.909
50	3.90	5.72	9.69	14.91	21.78	29.31	37.47	45.34	52.96	59.82	28.090	19.105
Average (first 10 years)	1.390	1.581	1.768	1.939	2.131	2.307	2.478	2.645	2.823	2.968		
Standard deviation	0.409	0.452	0.471	0.499	0.546	0.551	0.604	0.637	0.697	0.757		
Average (total)	1.704	1.939	2.305	2.852	3.599	4.454	5.373	6.367	7.385	8.394		
Standard deviation	0.753	1.124	2.087	3.383	5.095	6.980	9.043	11.029	12.960	14.737		

Table 6.10 Range of valuations – .EY 10% to 20%, rent received/ERV ratio 75%

Unexpired term (years)	Capitalization rate (%)										Average	Standard deviation
	3.5	4.0	4.5	5.0	5.5	6.0	6.5	7.0	7.5	8.0		
1	0.42	0.52	0.54	0.65	0.72	0.85	0.92	1.06	1.14	1.22	0.804	0.264
2	0.67	0.77	0.91	1.02	1.18	1.29	1.46	1.58	1.70	1.90	1.248	0.389
3	0.78	0.90	1.06	1.18	1.30	1.49	1.62	1.82	2.04	2.18	1.437	0.452
4	0.79	0.91	1.07	1.19	1.32	1.44	1.57	1.77	1.91	2.13	1.410	0.416
5	0.72	0.83	0.94	1.05	1.16	1.27	1.39	1.50	1.61	1.73	1.220	0.322
6	0.62	0.67	0.76	0.80	0.88	0.97	0.98	1.07	1.07	1.14	0.896	0.169
7	0.44	0.47	0.48	0.54	0.48	0.52	0.50	0.46	0.42	0.36	0.467	0.049
8	0.26	0.26	0.20	0.16	0.18	0.20	0.22	0.32	0.51	0.55	0.286	0.129
9	0.15	0.17	0.30	0.39	0.56	0.68	0.82	1.13	1.40	1.69	0.729	0.502
10	0.31	0.44	0.61	0.80	1.07	1.32	1.68	2.07	2.42	2.89	1.461	0.836
15	1.46	1.99	2.62	3.42	4.32	5.27	6.41	7.57	8.84	10.21	5.211	2.834
20	2.55	3.64	4.84	6.30	7.99	9.90	12.04	14.18	16.51	19.01	9.696	5.334
25	3.63	5.14	7.10	9.44	12.15	14.93	18.14	21.43	24.80	28.41	14.517	8.079
50	9.15	14.26	20.80	28.15	35.95	43.56	51.09	58.32	64.79	70.39	36.23	18.552
Average (first 10 years)	0.516	0.594	0.687	0.778	0.885	1.003	1.116	1.278	1.422	1.579		
Standard deviation	0.218	0.249	0.293	0.327	0.367	0.411	0.479	0.548	0.614	0.734		
Average (total)	1.568	2.212	3.016	3.935	4.947	5.978	7.060	8.163	9.226	10.272		
Standard deviation	2.303	3.612	5.288	7.187	9.216	11.205	13.208	15.131	16.894	18.479		

Table 6.11 Range of valuations – EY 10% to 20%, rent received/ERV ratio 100%

Unexpired term (years)	Capitalization rate (%)										Average	Standard deviation
	3.5	4.0	4.5	5.0	5.5	6.0	6.5	7.0	7.5	8.0		
1	0.35	0.40	0.45	0.55	0.60	0.66	0.78	0.84	0.97	1.04	0.664	0.225
2	0.45	0.60	0.63	0.76	0.87	0.95	1.10	1.18	1.27	1.43	0.924	0.303
3	0.42	0.52	0.58	0.65	0.77	0.89	0.97	1.04	1.12	1.27	0.823	0.266
4	0.24	0.32	0.36	0.45	0.49	0.54	0.58	0.70	0.75	0.80	0.523	0.178
5	0	0	0	0	0	0	0	0	0	0	0	0
6	0.32	0.40	0.45	0.56	0.61	0.67	0.79	0.85	0.91	1.05	0.661	0.225
7	0.71	0.86	0.97	1.13	1.30	1.48	1.67	1.80	2.08	2.31	1.431	0.505
8	1.12	1.32	1.58	1.82	2.06	2.38	2.72	3.00	3.30	3.69	2.299	0.822
9	1.53	1.84	2.22	2.58	2.91	3.31	3.37	4.26	4.73	5.23	3.234	1.180
10	1.99	2.24	2.83	3.32	3.85	4.41	4.94	5.56	6.22	6.82	4.236	1.555
15	4.25	5.25	6.29	7.48	8.70	10.16	11.56	13.03	14.59	16.21	9.752	3.848
20	6.24	7.89	9.81	11.81	13.98	16.25	18.68	21.24	23.81	26.49	15.62	6.521
25	8.04	10.40	13.16	16.03	19.19	22.51	26.06	29.59	33.26	36.90	21.51	9.337
50	16.18	22.94	30.27	37.95	45.69	52.94	59.82	66.19	71.57	76.42	48.00	19.80
Average (first 10 years) •	0.713	0.868	1.007	1.182	1.346	1.529	1.728	1.923	2.135	2.364		
Standard deviation	0.603	0.724	0.866	1.006	1.159	1.332	1.495	1.694	1.894	2.083		
Average (total)	2.989	3.940	4.971	6.078	7.216	8.368	9.529	10.66	11.76	12.83		
Standard deviation	4.368	6.092	8.004	9.998	12.04	13.98	15.86	17.63	19.19	20.63		

Table 6.12 Unexpired term (in years) at which highest equated yield does not give highest value

Capitalization rate (%)	Rent received/ERV ratio			
	25%	50%	75%	100%
3.5	50+	50+	10	5
4.0	50+	25/50	9	5
4.5	50+	25	9	5
5.0	50+	20	9	5
5.5	50+	15/20	9	5
6.0	25/50	15/20	8	5
6.5	25/50	10/15	8	5
7.0	25/50	10/15	8	5
7.5	25/50	10/15	8	5
8.0	25/50	10/15	8	5

situation. This represented the point at which the increase in value in the reversion caused by a higher equated yield choice was compensated by the reduction in the term value. At this changeover point the range in values is at a minimum and the choice of equated yield is practically irrelevant (see Table 6.12).

The analyses provided a generalized picture. For unexpired terms of 10 years and less, the range in valuation solutions is very low at 2.2187 per cent. The range increases as the unexpired term increases, and the range also increases as the capitalization rate increases. Therefore the valuation of prime property would appear to be more objective by contemporary techniques than valuations of higher yielding secondary property. The smallest ranges in value are when the rent passing to ERV ratio is high. As the unexpired term increases beyond 10 years, the ranges increase, except where the changeover points illustrated in Table 6.9 are reached. The value for the 160 permutations analysed for over 10 years unexpired show an average range of 15 per cent. (For a more detailed explanation and analysis of Table 6.9, see Crosby (1985).)

TAXATION AND MARKET VALUATION

The effects of taxation on the future flows of income and/or capital are mainly ignored in the market valuation of freehold interests.

The structure of leases within the property investment market can produce a wide variety of taxation implications. The market is made up of a variety of groups or individuals, all having unique exposures to taxation. No two groups of purchasers will be exactly alike; it is thus beyond dispute that taxation is a crucial part of an investment appraisal for an individual purchaser (see Chapter 8). But what of market valuation?

At the time of writing, the two main taxes are those on income (income and corporation tax) and capital gain (capital gains tax) and frequent changes in legislation will alter an individual's incidence of taxation. Conventional appraisal techniques assume that investors make a gross of tax comparison with other investment opportunities and returns on capital are therefore assessed on that basis. Using the conventional model for a rack rented freehold investment, and the pre-1960 assumptions of no growth, a gross of tax or net of tax comparison becomes immaterial, as Example 6.17 shows.

■ EXAMPLE 6.17

Capitalization rate = 6 per cent, tax rate = 40 per cent, ERV = £6,000 per annum.
Valuation (i): Gross of tax

ERV	£6,000 pa	
YP perp. at 6%	16.6667	
Valuation		£100,000

On a net of tax basis, the required return (based on opportunity cost) falls by 40 per cent to 3.6 per cent. The income after tax also falls by 40 per cent to £3,600 per annum.
Valuation (ii): Net of tax

Net ERV	£3,600 pa	
YP perp. at 3.6%	27.7778	
Valuation		£100,000

In times of growth, this conventional approach can become misleading. It suggests that the investor's return is reduced by the tax rate, but this is not the case. A contemporary technique can be used to illustrate that the equated yield is not reduced by 40 per cent.

A 6 per cent capitalization rate implies a growth rate of 5.57142 per cent per annum to achieve a return of 11 per cent, assuming 5-year reviews. If a net of tax return of 6.6 per cent (11 per cent × 0.6) is required and the growth rate of 5.57142 per cent per annum is achieved, the IRFY (or real return if inflation and rental growth achieve the same level) is calculated as

$$i = \frac{1+e}{1+g} - 1 = \frac{1.066}{1.0557142} - 1 = 0.97\%$$

The 3 YP formula generates a capitalization rate of 1.14 per cent which in turn generates a YP in perpetuity of 87.574. This YP applied to the net of tax cash flow of £3,600 per annum produces a valuation of

ERV (net)	£3,600 pa	
YP perp.	87.574	
Valuation		£315,274

This seemingly ridiculous solution (compare £100,000) is produced by a calculation which increases the rents at the same growth rate as for the gross of tax valuation, but discounts the future flows at a net of tax discount rate.

The 40 per cent reduction in the equated yield has produced a relatively much greater reduction in the real return, and therefore the real values of the future flow are discounted at over 5 per cent gross ($i = (1 + e)/(1 + g) - 1 = 1.11/1.0557142 - 1 = 5.14\%$) but at less than 1 per cent net.

The valuation is logical. Assume that the gross rent of £6,000 does increase by 5.57 per cent per annum up to the first review in 5 years' time. The rent on review will be

$$£6,000 \times (1.0557)^5 = £7,868 \text{ pa}$$

After deducting 40 per cent for tax the net ERV at year 5 is

ERV	£7,868 pa
less 40%	£3,147 pa
net ERV	£4,721 pa

The current net of tax income is £3,600 per annum. The increase in rent also represents 5.57 per cent per annum.

$$£3,600 \times (1.0557)^5 = £4,721 \text{ pa}$$

The net of tax ERV grows at the same rate as the gross of tax ERV, so it is not the assumption of rental growth which creates the problem.

The problem lies in the choice of the net of tax equated yield. The equated yield does not fall by the tax rate; it can, however, be correctly assessed by using a real value approach. Tax should be deducted from the real return rather than the fixed income return, that is, the IRFY rather than the equated yield.

net IRFY $= 5.14\% \times 0.6 = 3.085\%$

The equated yield net of tax can be found by a rearrangement of the formula $i = (1 + e)(1 + g) - 1$ to $e = (1 + i)(1 + g) - 1$. As the growth rate is held at its original level of 5.57 per cent per annum the equation becomes

$e = (1.03085)(1.0557) - 1 = 8.829\%$

The 3 YP formula can now be used to calculate a net of tax capitalization rate.

$$YP = YP \text{ 5 years at } 8.829\% \times \frac{YP \text{ perp. at } 3.085\%}{YP \text{ 5 years at } 3.085\%}$$

$$= 3.90760 \times \frac{32.4121}{4.5686} = 27.7186$$

ERV (net)	£3,600 pa	
YP perp.	27.7186	
Valuation		£99,787

$$k = \frac{£3,600}{£99,787} = 3.61\%$$

Only the rounding of yields in the preliminary analysis stage caused the valuation to miss £100,000. This approach can therefore be used to appraise the net of tax equated yield for an individual by:

1 analysing the implied growth rate from the gross of tax capitalization rate;
2 calculating the gross of tax real return (i);
3 reducing the real return by the investor's rate of tax; and
4 calculating the net of tax equated yield using $e = (1 + g)(1 + i) - 1$.

This valuation assumes a perpetual holding period but if the investor sells the property after, say, 10 years, it can be shown that the investor does achieve a net of tax return of 8.829 per cent, a marginal tax rate of only 20 per cent on the gross of tax return of 11 per cent.

This assumes that any growth in capital value should be exempt from tax on account of the capital gains tax indexing provisions (this assumes a static real value; inflation and growth being equal). Only if rental growth does not match inflation will the holding period materially affect the net of tax returns.

Table 6.13 Explicit DCF net of tax valuation

Years	Outflow (£)	Inflow (£)	PV at 8.829%	PV (£)
0	(100,000)		1.0000	(100,000)
1		3,600	0.9189	3,308
2		3,600	0.8444	3,040
3		3,600	0.7759	2,794
4		3,600	0.7130	2,567
5		3,600	0.6552	2,359
6		4,721	0.6020	2,843
7		4,721	0.5532	2,612
8		4,721	0.5084	2,401
9		4,721	0.4671	2,206
10		4,721 + 17,1951	0.4293	75,854

Note: Net present value = 0.

An explicit DCF valuation is used above to show how the return will be achieved and to illustrate that the real value approach has correctly appraised the situation. The two valuations – one perpetual, one for 10 years – equate.

On the basis of a 10-year holding period the purchase price of £100,000 will produce a fixed rent of £3,600 net for the next 5 years, a reversion to £4,721 net in years 5–10 and a sale price of £171,951 in year 10 (assuming the growth rate of 5.57 per cent per annum is achieved and capitalization rates remain static) (see Table 6.13).

Reversionary freehold investments, however, are more difficult to value on a net-of-tax basis. Reversionary properties enjoy an inherent real growth produced by the lease structure. As the reversion to a higher rent gets closer, the capital value increases even if the ERV does not increase. In a rising market a capital gains tax liability will arise even if growth in rents only matches inflation.

■ EXAMPLE 6.18

Current rent £10,000 per annum, unexpired term 10 years, ERV £100,000 per annum, tax 40 per cent. The conventional valuation of the reversionary freehold at a 6 per cent equivalent yield is as follows:

Current rent	£10,000 pa	
YP 10 years at 6%	7.3601	
		£73,601
Reversion to ERV	£100,000 pa	
YP perp. at 6%	16.6667	
PV 10 years at 6%	0.5584	
		£930,660
Valuation		£1,004,261

In one year's time the capital value will have risen to £1,054,520 on account of the approach of the reversion. In 10 year's time the capital value will have risen to £1,666,667 (ERV × YP perp. at 6 per cent) on the reversion to the ERV of £100,000 per annum. This assumes no rental growth. The increase in value would be subject to the capital gains tax, as it is a real rather than an inflationary gain.

Net of tax flows		
Income years		
1–10	£10,000 pa	
Less tax at 40%	£4,000 pa	
Net of tax income	£6,000 pa	
Sale price on lease		
renewal in year 10	£1,666,667	
Less purchase		
price	£1,000,000	
Gain	£666,667	
Tax at 40%	£266,667	
Sale price		£1,666,667
Less tax		£266,667
Net proceeds of		
disposal		£1,400,000
Inflows		
Years 1–10	£6,000 pa	
Year 10	£1,400,000	

The net of tax internal rate of return is 3.38 per cent.

A 40 per cent reduction from the gross of tax yield of 6 per cent would give a net of tax yield of 3.6 per cent. However, a conventional valuation carried out on the net of tax basis would give a different result.

Current rent	£6,000 pa	
YP 10 years at 3.6%	8.2748	
		£49,649
ERV	£60,000 pa	
YP perp. at 3.6%	27.7778	
PV 10 years at 3.6%	0.7021	
		£117,176
Valuation		£1,219,825

Introducing the growth element implicit in current market conditions complicates the valuation process still further. The same example of a reversionary freehold was assessed at a 6 per cent gross capitalization rate because of the implied future growth. A real value or equated yield valuation to show an equated yield of 11 per cent and a rack rented capitalization rate of 6 per cent would have produced a slightly different gross of tax solution.

$$k = 6\%, \ e = 11\%, \ g = 5.57\% \text{ pa}, \ i = 5.14\%$$

Current rent	£10,000 pa	
YP 10 years at 11%	5.8892	
		£58,890
ERV	£100,000 pa	
YP perp. at 6%	16.6667	
PV 10 years at 5.14%	0.6068	
		£1,009,440
Valuation		£1,068,330

Adopting a real value net of tax approach, the IRFY is reduced to 3.0853 per cent, assuming a 40 per cent tax rate. The equated yield can be assessed by $e = (1 + i)(1 + g) - 1$, that is, $(1.03085 \times 1.0557) - 1 = 0.08829$ or 8.8292. The valuation becomes (at a net of tax equated yield of 8.829 per cent and a net of tax IRFY of 3.0853 per cent):

Current rent (net of tax)	£6,000 pa	
YP 10 years at 8.829	6.4664	
		£38,798
ERV (net)	£60,000 pa	

$$\frac{\text{YP perp. at } 3.0853\% \times \text{YP 5 years at } 8.829\%}{\text{YP 5 years at } 3.0853\%}$$

	27.7187	
PV 10 years at 3.0853%	0.73796	
		£1,227.318
Valuation		£1,266,116

The solution is no clearer. The different capital gains tax treatment of real and inflationary gain makes the use of 'short-cut' valuation models extremely dangerous when the complexities of taxation are involved. Even the growth explicit models as applied above ignore the capital gains tax liability inherent in reversionary investments. Practices such as assessing a gross of tax redemption yield (equated yield) and then reducing this to a net of tax redemption yield by deducting the income tax rate are fraught with danger. The danger becomes extreme in certain cases. For example, growth explicit models which discount at net of tax equated yields based on a simplistic reduction from gross equated yields will produce valuations which suggest investments have infinite values when the net of tax equated yield is lower than the growth rate.

Given the difficulties of carrying out market valuations on a net of tax basis it is not surprising that gross of tax comparisons are commonplace. If all income flows were taxed similarly then the problem would be a minor one. In essence initial incomes are taxed at the investor's own marginal income tax rate, inflationary capital gains are exempt from tax, but real capital gains are not. A gross equated yield is made up of real return and growth, and growth can be made up of real growth/loss and inflationary growth. The initial return can be made up of all ranges of these elements; so generalizing on the taxation incidence of a particular investment property for the typical purchaser is dangerous. This is not to say that an individual purchaser should not consider the taxation implications of a purchase: this is the role of analysis and is a crucial element in an appraisal for investment worth, fully covered in Chapter 8. At this point, let it suffice to say that contemporary models are of infinitely greater value than conventional models in assessing tax implications.

It has already been established that, when using the conventional basis, comparisons should have similar lease structures, locational and physical similarities, similar unexpired terms and ERV/rent received ratios. Added to this list is similar taxation profiles (although the last factor flows from the preceding). A consideration of the effect of tax reinforces the need for quality comparisons.

Contemporary models, on the other hand, require a subjective equated yield choice based on other investments (probably conventional gilts). Part of the yield differential should be the product of different taxation implications. Freehold property has advantages over gilts. Although the capital gain from gilts is exempt from tax, prime properties invariably produce lower initial returns than gilts. This implies greater capital gains for prime property, and given that such gains may be largely or wholly exempt from capital gains tax as a result of index-linking, net of tax prime property returns may be relatively higher for the same gross of tax return. This problem is mitigated by the influence of non-taxpaying institutions on both gilt and property prices.

Our suggested approach to tax in freehold valuations is to ignore taxation and to make comparisons on a gross of tax basis, undertaking the valuation using a DCF approach. Taxation is nonetheless a crucial factor in the analysis of investments (see Chapter 8).

CONCLUSIONS

The material in this chapter isolates the limitations and flaws in any methodology used to assess the market value of income flows from freehold investment property. The basis of market value is comparable properties but property investments are individualistic and therefore valuers require a logical approach which helps them in their use of non-perfect comparisons.

Given the nature of the task, there are a number of alternative approaches to valuation. We believe that the advantages of the growth explicit methods are irrefutable and it is gratifying to note that at the time of writing many leading UK practitioners are coming around to this way of thinking. The catalyst for this change has been the current recession and the problems associated with over-rented properties.

It is ironic that the real advantage of the growth explicit models has been recognized during the worst fall in property values in living memory. The conventional methodology has failed practitioners and some have now looked to alternatives for help. We believe that the contemporary models give that help. The main issues are summarized below.

The charge of subjectivity in the use of comparables is at the heart of the debate and the charge is not unfounded when applied to contemporary models. But the effect of the subjectivity is minimal for reversionary property with under 10 years unexpired. Given the range of equated yields used in the analysis, which should be reduced by future research (10 per cent is an excessive range given today's knowledge of comparative investment appraisal), the reliability of valuation can be improved.

The charge of subjectivity should also be addressed to equivalent yield models, which have an unbridled degree of manipulation in the valuation stage. The claim for objectivity is a mirage, unless the number of transactions in the market is enough to give almost perfect comparisons every time.

A logical market valuation model which helps the valuer to manipulate the non-perfect comparison while retaining as much objectivity as possible is needed. The equivalent yield model does not pass the test, while the equated yield model can pass the test especially if a more rigorous basis for equated yield choice is found. Even if a more rigorous basis is not available, the compensating effects inherent within freehold reversionary valuation by contemporary techniques would lead to more consistent valuations in practice.

However, the over-riding issue is that the conventional models are not based in the logic of the market in which they operate. They can therefore not adapt to changes in that market. The 1990–3 period in the UK has exposed them to problems which they could not adequately handle. The growth explicit models are based in logic and therefore can adapt to changing circumstances. It is no accident that the growth explicit models have been able to adapt to over-renting with minimal adjustment while the conventional models have collapsed.

7

Contemporary leasehold market valuations

INTRODUCTION

In this, the final chapter which deals with pricing or market valuations, we look at the valuation of leasehold interests. As in the previous chapter, we set out the application of the contemporary market valuation model to a number of examples before comparing and contrasting the conventional and contemporary approaches in the market valuation role.

Again, we must first make the point that any model being used for pricing or market valuation purposes should be based on comparisons with prices in the market place. So why is the fundamental concept underlying the conventional model the sinking fund?

This concept assumed that the re-investment provided enough capital upon expiry of the leasehold interest to buy another leasehold interest of equal length. A repetition of this purchase at the subsequent expiry dates into infinity turned the terminable leasehold into a perpetual interest. The reason for this approach, which made a leasehold like a freehold, was to enable comparisons to be made with the freehold market simply because fewer leasehold interests are sold.

The quantity of information on leasehold transactions is likely to be less than the information concerning freeholds, therefore it is useful if the recommended contemporary techniques can adapt to cope with this problem. So we shall also look at the freehold market for comparables, and then apply the results to contemporary valuations of the leasehold interest.

The range of leasehold examples that can be concocted is almost limitless due to the inter-relationship of at least two leases. In this chapter we use a few examples to illustrate how the principles of the contemporary models can be applied in practice.

Contemporary transaction analysis goes further than determining the capitalization rate of the interest. It relies on the estimation of a rack rented perpetual capitalization rate, an implied rental growth rate and an equated yield for the freehold interest. For all the examples in this chapter, we shall assume that a freehold rack rented property, in the same location as the leasehold interest to be valued, will sell for a capitalization rate/all risks yield of 6 per cent if let on 5-year reviews.

In order to analyse this transaction, the same approach as before is utilized.

$$(1 + g)^t = \frac{\text{YP perp. at } k\% - \text{YP } t \text{ years at } e\%}{\text{YP perp. at } k\% \times \text{PV } t \text{ years at } e\%}$$

$$(1 + g)^5 = \frac{\text{YP perp. at } 6\% - \text{YP } 5 \text{ years at } 13\%}{\text{YP perp. at } 6\% \times \text{PV } 5 \text{ years at } 13\%}$$

$$= \frac{16.6667 - 3.5172}{16.6667 \times 0.5428}$$

$$= \frac{13.1494}{9.0460} = 1.4536$$

$$g = (1.4536)^{1/5} - 1 = 0.0776807 = 7.76807\%$$

Before setting out some examples of how the valuations work, a few comments on the nature of the growth rate are necessary. The growth rate, subject to the limitation of being a constant average, represents the freeholder's need for growth to obtain the required rate of return. It therefore represents the implied rate of growth in the rental value of all similar property in the particular location and can therefore be used in the valuation of other interests in that location, including leaseholds.

The required return or equated yield for a leasehold will be discussed in detail in the second part of this chapter. For the time being, and in order to illustrate the application of the model, we could adopt a small margin above the freehold rate to quantify the supposed additional risk of the leasehold interest (say 1 or 2 per cent).

However, the discussion in the second part will illustrate the fact that different leasehold structures demand different yields dependant upon how much of the cash flow is generated by future growth. The risk attached to certain leasehold cash flows would suggest extremely high discount rates while other cash flows have more in common with a fixed income gilt than any other property investment. For the purposes of setting out the application of the contemporary model, we shall undertake all the following valuations at an equated yield of 18 per cent.

FIXED LEASEHOLD PROFIT RENTS

 EXAMPLE 7.1

A property has 6 years unexpired at a ground rent of £20,000 per annum. The headlessee has sublet the property for the remainder of the term at £300,000 per annum with no further reviews. Assuming an equated yield of 13 per cent (as before) for a freehold, assume 18 per cent for the leasehold to reflect increased risk.

The risk of this particular investment is almost solely dependent upon the covenant strength of the sublessee. If the sublessee is very strong or the market for this type of property is very active, then the cash flow is similar to a fixed income gilt and the yield adopted would be much lower than 13 per cent. If the tenant is weak and the market poor the income could turn into a liability very easily and is a high risk investment.

Explicit DCF

The calculated values are given in Table 7.1. Given that fixed rents are received and paid, there is no advantage in a tabular layout. Capitalization of the profit rent is possible by a YP multiplier, in this case for 6 years at 18 per cent. A conventional layout is preferred.

Profit rent	£280,000 pa	
YP 6 years at 18%	3.4976	
Valuation		£979,330

Table 7.1

Year	Rent received (£)	Rent paid (£)	Profit rent (£)
1	300,000	20,000	280,000
2	300,000	20,000	280,000
3	300,000	20,000	280,000
4	300,000	20,000	280,000
5	300,000	20,000	280,000
6	300,000	20,000	280,000

Real value

The real value technique would give the same solution to this fixed profit rent case, but the similarity hides a fundamental difference between the explicit DCF and real value approaches in application.

The real value approach does not require the determination of profit rent but is based upon a separate capitalization of the two income flows in order that growth profiles, which may differ between the two, can be separately reflected (see following pages).

Rent received	£300,000 pa	
YP 6 years at 18%	3.4976	
Value of rent received		£1,049,280
Less rent paid	£20,000 pa	
YP 6 years at 18%	3.4976	
Value of rent paid		£69,950
Valuation		£979,330

GEARED LEASEHOLD PROFIT RENTS

Reviewable rent received, fixed rent paid

 EXAMPLE 7.2

A shop property is let on ground lease with 50 years unexpired at a fixed rent of £50,000 per annum. The property has just been sublet at its estimated rental value of £300,000 per annum on 5-year reviews. Similar freehold properties sell for 6 per cent capitalization rates when let on 5-year review patterns.

A fixed rent paid coupled with the perceptions and expectations of future rental growth creates a situation that pre-1950s valuers did not envisage. The expectation for a pre-reverse yield gap investment was no growth. The ability of the rent to grow was no advantage over the fixed ground rent; indeed, the lack of ability to change was seen as the advantage of security (the yield on ground rents being below the yield on rack rents). The valuation technique of assessing profit rent and capitalizing from the unexpired term fitted these perceptions, and the expected income flow was as shown in Figure 7.1.

The obvious solution was to assess the difference in rents and capitalize at the appropriate rate, assessed as more risky than a freehold. The expected

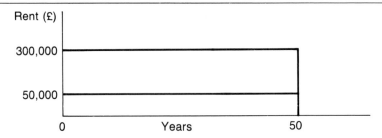

Figure 7.1 Fixed profit rent income profile

income profile takes on a different shape given a perception of growth (see Figure 7.2).

Two factors are apparent. The net income is expected to grow and the growth rate is not the same as the equivalent freehold (see below). In addition the growth will be different depending on the ratio of rent received to the rent paid. The problem can be illustrated by two identical profit rents based on different rents.

(1) Rent received	£10,000	(2) Rent received	£100,000
Rent paid	£1,000	Rent paid	£91,000
Profit rent	£9,000	Profit rent	£9,000

Assuming 10 per cent per annum growth, in case (1) a rent review in year 5 will increase the rent received to

£10,000 × A £1 5 years at 10% (1.61051)   £16,105 pa
less rent paid   £1,000 pa
Profit rent   £15,105 pa

In case (1), the increase from £9,000 to £15,105 represents an increase of 67.8 per cent over 5 years or 10.9 per cent per annum.

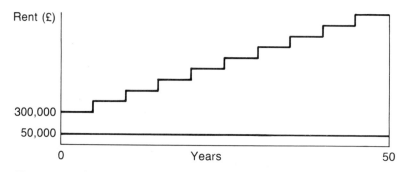

Figure 7.2 Geared profit rent growth income profile

In case (2) the same assumptions produce a review rent of:

£100,000 × A £1 5 years at 10% (1.6105)	£161,051 pa
less rent paid	£91,000 pa
Profit rent	£70,051 pa

The increase from £9,000 to £70,051 represents an increase of 678 per cent or 50.7 per cent per annum.

In the following 5 years the increases are as follows:

	Freehold	Leasehold (1)	Leasehold (2)
Growth in ERV	61.05%	61.05%	61.05%
Growth in net income	61.05%	65.09%	140.36%
Increase pa	10.00%	10.55%	19.17%

The gearing effects are as follows.

1 Except where the rent paid is a peppercorn, the rental growth is at a greater rate for a leasehold than for an equivalent freehold.
2 The rate of growth is dependent on the ratio of the rent received to the rent paid.
3 The rate of growth diminishes at each subsequent review and tends towards the rate of growth in the ERV in perpetuity.

Explicit DCF

In an explicit DCF approach all future rent changes are incorporated into the income flow so that the gearing effects are taken into account. Assuming the same freehold analysis as before ($e = 13$ per cent, $k = 6$ per

Table 7.2

Years	Rental value	Growth at 7.76807%	Rent received	Rent paid	Profit rent
1–5	300,000	1.0000	300 000	50,000	250,000
6–10	300,000	1.4536	436,086	50,000	386,086
11–15	300,000	2.1130	633,902	50,000	583,902
16–20	300,000	3.0715	921,452	50,000	871,452
21–25	300,000	4.4648	1,339,440	50,000	1,289,440
26–30	300,000	6.4901	1,947,040	50,000	1,947,040
31–35	300,000	9.4342	2,830,250	50,000	2,780,250
36–40	300,000	13.7137	4,114,100	50,000	4,064,100
41–45	300,000	19.9344	5,980,340	50,000	5,930,340
46–50	300,000	28.9771	8,693,140	50,000	8,643,140

Table 7.3

Years	Profit rent	YP at 18%	PV at 18%	Present value
1–5	250,000	3.1272	1.0000	781,790
6–10	386,086	3.1272	0.4371	527,750
11–15	583,902	3.1272	0.1911	348,880
16–20	871,452	3.1272	0.0835	227,600
21–25	1,289,440	3.1272	0.0365	147,200
26–30	1,947,040	3.1272	0.0160	94,660
31–35	2,780,250	3.1272	0.0070	60,640
36–40	4,064,100	3.1272	0.0031	38,750
41–45	5,930,340	3.1272	0.0013	24,710
46–50	8,643,140	3.1272	0.0006	15,740
Valuation				£2,267,730

cent), this leads to a growth rate of 7.766807 per cent per annum. Assuming the same risk adjustment (+ 5 per cent), the equated yield model is based on the following inputs: $e = 18$ per cent, $g = 7.76807$ per cent per annum. Tables 7.2 and 7.3 give the results.

Real value

The income flow is capitalized in two parts. The capital value of the right to receive the rent from the sublessee is found and the capital value of the liability to pay the ground rent is then deducted. The remainder is the capital value of the net income to the headlessee. The risk rate used in both parts of the calculation is the risk rate for the headlessee's net income. In this case the whole of the rental value is capitalized at 18 per cent and the liability to pay the ground rent is also capitalized at 18 per cent, to leave a residue of the headlessee's interest, by implication valued at an 18 per cent yield.

$$i = \frac{1.18}{1.0776807} - 1 = 9.4944\%$$

Rent received	£300,000 pa	

YP 5 years at 18% ×
$$\frac{\text{YP 50 years at } 9.4944\%}{\text{YP 5 years at } 9.4944\%}$$
$$\frac{3.1272 \times 10.4196}{3.8403} \qquad 8.4848$$

Value of rent received		£2,545,440	
Rent paid	£50,000 pa		
YP 50 years at 18%	5.5541		
Value of rent paid		£277,710	
Valuation			£2,267,730

Synchronized reviews in head- and sub-leases

■ EXAMPLE 7.3

A similar shop property to the previous examples is held from the free-holder on a lease with 20 years unexpired. The rent is geared to the subletting which is for the remainder of the term with 5-year reviews. The rent has just been agreed at the estimated rental value of £300,000 per annum and the headlease specifies that the rent payable to the freeholder is to be 50 per cent of ERV. Assume the same equated yield and growth rate as before.

In this case, the profit rent will behave in exactly the same way as the rent received from the subletting. If the rental value grows by the implied growth rate, so will the profit rent.

Table 7.4

Years	Rental value	Growth at 7.76807%	Rent received	Rent paid	Growth at 7.76807%	Rent paid
0–5	300,000	1.0000	300,000	150,000	1.0000	150,000
6–10	300,000	1.4536	436,086	150,000	1.4536	218,043
11–15	300,000	2.1130	633,902	150,000	2.1130	316,951
16–20	300,000	3.0715	921,452	150,000	3.0715	460,726

Table 7.5

Years	Profit rent	YP at 18%	PV at 18%	Present value
0–5	150,000	3.1272	1.0000	469,076
6–10	218,043	3.1272	0.4371	298,046
11–15	316,951	3.1272	0.1911	189,376
16–20	460,726	3.1272	0.0835	120,327
Valuation				£1,076,825

Explicit DCF

See Tables 7.4 and 7.5.

Real value

In this case there is no need to separate the rent received capitalization from the rent paid. However, this is the only occasion when the profit rent can be directly capitalized, unless the rent paid is a peppercorn. The valuation is therefore set out below in a form which will suit all situations.

Rent received   £300,000

YP 5 years at 18% ×

$$\frac{\text{YP 20 years at 9.4944\%}}{\text{YP 5 years at 9.4944\%}}$$

$3.1272 \times \dfrac{8.8158}{3.8403}$ $\underline{7.1788}$

Value of rent received   £2,153,649

Less rent paid   £150,000

YP 5 years at 18% ×

$$\frac{\text{YP 20 years at 9.4944\%}}{\text{YP 5 years at 9.4944\%}}$$

$3.1272 \times \dfrac{8.8158}{3.8403}$ $\underline{7.1788}$

Value of rent paid   £1,076,824

Valuation   £1,076,825

REVERSIONARY LEASEHOLDS

Reviewable rent received, fixed rent paid

 EXAMPLE 7.4

A similar shop property to the previous examples is held from the free-holder on a lease with 23 years unexpired. The rent was fixed at the beginning of the lease 40 years ago at £4,000 per annum and the property is now sublet on a modern lease with 5-year rent reviews at £200,000 per annum. The estimated rental value is £225,000 per annum and the next review is in 3 years' time.

Explicit DCF

See Tables 7.6 and 7.7.

Real value

The real value approach to reversionary leaseholds is consistent with its approach to reversionary freeholds. The valuation of the rent received

Table 7.6

Years	Rental value	Growth at 7.76807%	Rent received	Rent paid	Profit rent
1–3	200,000	1.0000	200,000	4,000	196,000
4–8	225,000	1.2516	281,613	4,000	277,613
9–13	225,000	1.8194	409,358	4,000	405,358
14–18	225,000	2.6447	595,051	4,000	591,051
19–23	225,000	3.8443	864,977	4,000	860,977

Table 7.7

Years	Profit rent	YP at 18%	PV at 18%	Present value
1–3	196,000	2.1743	1.0000	426,157
4–8	277,613	3.1272	0.6086	528,379
9–13	405,358	3.1272	0.2660	337,236
14–18	591,051	3.1272	0.1163	214,937
19–23	860,977	3.1272	0.0508	136,857
Valuation				£1,643,566

consists of a term income which is fixed for the next 3 years. This income is therefore valued at the equated yield. Upon review, the income reverts to rental value and is then reviewed every 5 years over the next 20 years.

As the income has a 20-year term and 5-year reviews, it is valued using the 3 YP formula which incorporates the total term, the review pattern and the rental growth rate which is implied by the use of the IRFY. The fact that the rental value is also expected to grow over the interim period while the valuation only reverts to ERV, is taken into account by deferring the reversion at the IRFY to imply the growth.

Term rent	£200,000		
YP 3 years at 18%	2.1743		
		£434,855	
Reversion to ERV	£225,000		
YP 5 years at 18% ×			
$\dfrac{\text{YP 20 years at 9.4944\%}}{\text{YP 5 years at 9.4944\%}}$	7.1788		
PV 3 years at 9.4944%	0.7618		
		£1,230,440	
Value of rent received		£1,665,294	
Less rent paid	£4,000		
YP 23 years at 18%	5.4321		
Value of rent paid		£21,728	
Valuation			£1,643,566

Reviewable rent received, unsynchronized reviewable rent paid

 EXAMPLE 7.5

Assume a similar property and location to all the previous examples. The shop property is held from the freeholder on a 63-year lease with rent reviews every 21 years. There are now 30 years unexpired and the current net rent passing is £100,000 per annum. The estimated rental value based upon 5-year reviews is £200,000 per annum. The property is sublet on a 15-year lease with 5-year reviews which now has 13 years unexpired and the rent passing is £175,000 per annum.

It is unreasonable to expect that all rent reviews in the leases which make up a leasehold investment will be synchronized or even on the same review pattern. In this example the subletting is subject to a normal modern lease but the property is held from the freeholder on an old lease subject to what is now an abnormal review pattern. The result is that the unexpired term does not fit easily into the review pattern of the sublease. If the headlessee continues to sublet the property on leases with 5-year reviews after the current sublease expires, eventually there will be a fagend of 2 years.

This example is derived from Example 6.6 in the previous chapter with a subleasehold interest introduced. The problems raised by the abnormal review pattern were considered then and it was decided that the letting on a 21-year review would be at a rent 15 per cent above that obtainable under a normal 5-year review (see page 150). In current rental value terms this assumes a rent of £230,000 instead of £200,000.

Figure 7.3 illustrates the complexity of the cash flow to the headlessee.

Explicit DCF

The profit rent has periods of being both positive (years 1–9 and 14–30) and negative (years 10–13). See Tables 7.8 and 7.9.

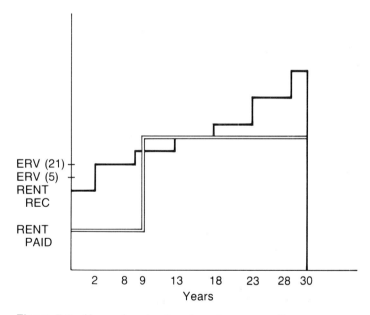

Figure 7.3 Unsynchronized reviews income profile

Table 7.8

Years	Rent/rental value	Growth at 7.76807%	Rent received	Rent paid	Growth at 7.76807%	Rent paid
1–3	175,000	1.0000	175,000	100,000	1.0000	100,000
4–8	200,000	1.2516	250,323	100,000	1.0000	100,000
9	200,000	1.8194	363,874	100,000	1.0000	100,000
10–13	200,000	1.8194	363,874	230,000	1.9607	450,961
14–18	200,000	2.6447	528,934	230,000	1.9607	450,961
19–23	200,000	3.8443	768,868	230,000	1.9607	450,961
24–28	200,000	5.5882	1,117,641	230,000	1.9607	450,961
29–30	200,000	8.1231	1,624,624	230,000	1.9607	450,961

Table 7.9

Years	Profit rent	YP at 18%	PV at 18%	Present value
1–3	75,000	2.1743	1.0000	163,070
4–8	150,323	3.1272	0.6086	286,108
9	263,874	0.8475	0.2660	59,492
10–13	– 87,087	2.6901	0.2255	– 52,817
14–18	77,973	3.1272	0.1163	28,355
19–23	317,907	3.1272	0.0508	50,533
24–28	666,680	3.1272	0.0222	46,322
29–30	1,173,663	1.5656	0.0097	17,846
Valuation				£598,909

Real value

Rent received
Term rent	£175,000		
YP 3 years at 18%	2.1743		
		£380,498	
Reversion to ERV	£200,000		

YP 5 years at 18% ×

$$\frac{\text{YP 27 years at } 9.4944\%}{\text{YP 5 years at } 9.4944\%}$$

$3.1272 \times \dfrac{9.6227}{3.8403}$	7.8358		
PV 3 years at 9.4944%	0.7618		
Value of rent received		£1,193,819	
			£1,574,316
Less rent paid			
Rent passing	£100,000		
YP 9 years at 18%	4.3030		
		£430,302	
Reversion to ERV (21 year reviews)	£230,000		
YP 21 years at 18%	5.3837		
PV 9 years at 9.4944%	0.4421		
Value of rent paid		£547,371	
			£977,673
Valuation			£596,644

For the first time there is a significant difference in the two approaches even though it is only £2,265. This difference relates to the treatment of the 2-year unexpired term after the last rent review in year 28. The explicit DCF approach has used the rent based upon 5-year rent reviews to value the last 2 years. Theoretically, this rent should be reduced for the shorter period between rent revision in the last 2 years (in the same way as it would be increased if the review pattern was longer than 5 years). The real value approach builds the reduced rental value of the last 2 years into its calculation and is therefore more theoretically accurate.

Using the implied rental growth rate and the leasehold equated yield, the reduced rental value can be calculated by comparing the capital value of a 5-year review pattern with the capital value of the 2-year review pattern. Using real value principles, the value of a 5-year review pattern is

Rental value on a 5-year review £200,000

YP 5 years at 18% $\times \dfrac{\text{YP perp. at } 9.4944\%}{\text{YP 5 years at } 9.4944\%}$ 8.5768

£1,715,352

The capital value of a 2-year review pattern let at an unknown rent is

Rental value on a 2-year review £x

YP 2 years at 18% $\times \dfrac{\text{YP perp. at } 9.4944\%}{\text{YP 2 years at } 9.4944\%}$ 9.4371

£9,4371x

Assuming the capital value should remain the same for a property let under 2-year reviews at a lower rent as it is for the property let on 5-year reviews:

$9.4371x = £1,715,352$
$x \qquad = £181,767$ pa

If this new rental value is now plugged into the DCF approach for years 29–30, the value of those last 2 years falls by £2,251 to £596,658 as compared with £596,644 by the real value approach. Apart from a rounding error, real value and explicit DCF approaches now equate.

Over-rented leaseholds

In Chapter 6 we looked at a valuation of a heavily over-rented office block in the centre of London. We complete our examination of the application of contemporary growth explicit models to leasehold valuation by valuing a headleasehold interest in a similar property.

■ EXAMPLE 7.6

An office block in Central London is held on lease with 22 years unexpired at a rent passing of £800,000 fixed 3 years ago. The lease provides for upward only rent reviews as and when the sublease is reviewed to 50 per cent of rental value. The property is sublet to a good covenant tenant for the remainder of the term with a review in 2 years' time and every 5 years thereafter. The rent passing is £1,600,000 per annum. The rental value is now estimated to be only £750,000 per annum and similar freehold properties sell for capitalization rates of 8 per cent. Value the headleasehold interest.

As the lease rents are geared to each other, this is a relatively straightforward case. The first step in either approach is to calculate the implied rental growth rate from the freehold transaction evidence. At an 8 per cent all risks yield and a 13 per cent equated yield, the implied rental growth rate is 5.7739 per cent per annum (see Chapter 6, Example 6.5, pages 146–50).

The next step is to assess when the ERV will overtake the rent passing.

At first review	$£750,000 \times (1.057739)^2 = £839,109$
At second review	$£750,000 \times (1.057739)^7 = £1,110,991$
At third review	$£750,000 \times (1.057739)^{12} = £1,470,969$
At fourth review	$£750,000 \times (1.057739)^{17} = £1,947,583$

As the rent passing is £1.6 million, this suggests the overage (or froth, as it is sometimes called) will be eliminated by the fourth review in 17 years time.

Explicit DCF

As there are only two parts to the valuation, it has been set out in conventional format.

Rent received	£1,600,000	
Less rent paid	£800,000	
Profit rent	£800,000	
YP 17 years at 18%	5.2223	
		£4,177,867
Reversion to inflated ERV		
(see above)	£1,947,583	
Less rent paid to free-		
holder at 50%	£973,790	
Profit rent	£973,791	
YP 5 years at 18%	3.1272	
PV 17 years at 18%	0.0600	
		£182,652
Valuation		£4,360,519

Real value

Calculate IRFY: $i = (1.18/1.057739) - 1 = 11.5587\%$

Rent received	£1,600,000		
YP 17 years at 18%	5.2223		
		£8,355,734	
Reversion to ERV	£750,000		
YP 5 years at 18%	3.1272		
PV 17 years at			
11.5587%	0.1558		
		£365,303	
Value of rents receivable			£8,721,037
less Rents paid	£800,000		
YP 17 years at 18%	5.2223		
		£4,177,867	
Reversion to ERV (50%)	£375,000		
YP 5 years at 18%	3.1272		
PV 17 years at			
11.5587%	0.1558		
		£182,652	
			£4,360,519
Valuation			£4,360,518

In Chapter 6, we finished our look at freehold market valuations by comparing the conventional and contemporary models with each other. We complete our examination of market valuations by carrying out a similar exercise for leaseholds.

CONVENTIONAL VERSUS CONTEMPORARY TECHNIQUES

Our critique of leasehold valuation by conventional techniques in Chapter 4 illustrated that changes in investors' perceptions in the 1950s and 1960s introduced a variety of problems which led to the conclusion that a rational and logical basis for appraisal had been lost.

Any defence of the continued use of years' purchase dual rate, tax adjusted, capitalization factors applied to current profit rents must, as in a defence of freehold appraisals, be based on objectivity, such objectivity to be based on the analysis of similar transactions.

While a debate exists regarding whether a sufficient quantity and quality of comparables exists for the typical freehold valuation, there is no doubt that good leasehold investment comparisons are usually very hard to find. To be a perfect comparison a leasehold investment must be similar in terms of a wide variety of criteria.

These criteria change depending on the nature of the subject leasehold investment. The fixed income leasehold, where the headlease and the sublease have no more reviews and expire at the same time, creates a property investment where the property characteristics (location and so on) are of very little importance compared with the quality of tenant (see Baum and Butler 1986). The investment comprises a fixed income stream and can be valued by direct comparison or by reference to other fixed income investments.

When rising or falling rents are introduced in either lease, the criteria for a good comparison change. The usual characteristics of a similar tenant, a similar position, a similar physical condition, and so on, are necessary, but similarity in this situation also requires the same unexpired term, the same relationship between rent passing and ERV in the sublease, and the same relationship between rents received and rents paid to the superior landlord.

The use of initial yields in order to effect a comparison of unidentical leasehold investments is, in the authors' opinion, highly dangerous.

In our investigation of freeholds, we were able to examine in some detail the criteria of rationality and objectivity and, while coming down on the side of contemporary models on both counts, conventional and contemporary models often reach very similar conclusions. Those who still use and defend leasehold conventional techniques have no such comfort. The valuation method is totally illogical and produces random answers.

The reason for this is not the usual debate regarding the use of dual rate or single rate and tax or no tax. Using single rate net or gross of tax will not solve any major problems. Debates about this constitute red herrings, as are such irrelevancies as double sinking fund, Pannell's and other tricks to 'solve' the mathematical problems of reversionary dual rate valuations.

The real problem is that since the appearance of the reverse yield gap around 1960, the conventional approach ceased to be an investment method and became a comparison model. The core of the valuation is the all risks yield. As the cash flow only considers the current levels of rent and rental value, the yield has to imply all the risks and the future behaviour of the cash flow. There are two major fundamental constraints to this comparison within leasehold valuation.

The first is the inadequacy of the all risks yield in dealing with the complex structure of the cash flow created by the relationship between the two leases. This complexity was illustrated in Example 7.2 (pages 195–9) where it was shown that identical current profit rents could be derived from very different rental levels within leases and produce different future cash flows. Gearing distorts the shape of future cash flows to create complex interests which are incapable of simplistic comparison.

The second major constraint is the nature of the all risks yield. The all risks yield is only meaningful when used to compare perpetual cash flows. It is often a surrogate for a higher target return (equated yield) coupled with an implied rental value growth rate and, in these circumstances, the same all risks yield can imply different growth rates or equated yields if used within YPs for a number of specific terms.

Consider the following example.

■ EXAMPLE 7.7

Value the leasehold interest in property held at a peppercorn rent for the next 15 years. The property is sublet for the remainder of the term at the estimated rental value of £100,000 per annum with reviews in years 5 and 10. A similar freehold fully let on a 5-year review pattern had just sold on the basis of a 6 per cent capitalization rate.

It might be assumed, as the profit rent would grow at the same rate as the ERV, that a direct comparison could be made between freehold and leasehold. Assuming no risk adjustment is required to distinguish between the freehold and leasehold in this case, and that a 13 per cent equated yield is required, the growth rate needed to increase an initial 6 per cent to an equated yield of 13 per cent, assuming 5-year reviews, is 7.768 per cent per annum in perpetuity.

The conventional application of the comparable to the leasehold using a capitalization rate of 6 per cent would produce a gross single rate valuation as follows:

Profit rent	£100,000 pa	
YP 15 years at 6%	9.7122	
Valuation		£971,220

If, as suggested, the 6 per cent capitalization rate is a short cut to assuming 7.768 per cent per annum rental growth, receivable every 5 years, then the internal rate of return over the 15 years should be 13 per cent, as it would be for the freehold. Unfortunately, this is not the case. A DCF approach does not produce the same answer. Using the real value 3 YP formula to illustrate:

$$i = \frac{1.13}{11.07768} - 1 = 0.04855 = 4.855\%$$

| Profit rent | £100,000 pa |

YP 15 years at 4.855% × $\dfrac{\text{YP 5 years at } 13\%}{\text{YP 5 years at } 4.855\%}$

$$= 10.48196 \times \frac{3.5172}{4.3469} \qquad\qquad \underline{8.4813}$$

| Valuation | £848,130 |

As the direct use of the capitalization rate gives a solution nearly 15 per cent higher than the equated yield approach (which is explicit regarding the growth rate), the capitalization rate of 6 per cent must imply a much higher growth rate than 7.768 per cent to produce an internal rate of return of 13 per cent. The growth rate implied by a 6 per cent capitalization rate for 15 years to produce an (IRR) of 13 per cent is in fact 11.1 per cent per annum. To add to the confusion, the capitalization rate of 6 per cent implies completely different growth rates for every different unexpired term. Table 7.10 and Figure 7.4 illustrate the implications of a perpetual capitalization rate of 6 per cent for terminable incomes on 5-year reviews. From Table 7.10, it is possible to conclude that the required all risks yield on a 15-year term to imply 7.76807 per cent per annum growth and obtain an equated yield

Table 7.10 Capitalization rates of terminable incomes

Years	YP at 6%	3 YPs	Required yield to be used with YP single rate to equate with 3 YPs
5	4.2124	3.5172	13.00%
10	7.3601	6.2922	9.50%
15	9.7122	8.4816	8.15%
20	11.4699	10.2088	7.50%
25	12.7834	11.5716	7.10%
50	15.7619	15.1091	6.30%
75	16.4558	16.1904	6.10%
100	16.6175	16.5217	6.04%
Perp.	16.6667	16.6667	6.00%

Note: YPs at $k = 6$ per cent, $e = 13$ per cent, $g = 7.76807$ per cent per annum, $t = 5$ years.

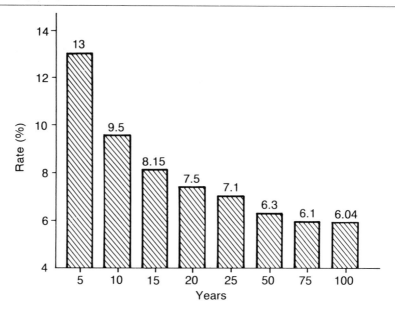

Figure 7.4 Terminable capitalization rates

of 13 per cent is 8.15 per cent. The valuation of the 15-year income flow required for Example 7.7 should have been as follows.

Profit rent	£100,000 pa
YP 15 years at 8.15%	8.4816
Valuation	£848,160

(Error due to rounding.)

Had the valuation been of a 25-year leasehold the all risks yield should have been 7.1 per cent. A 50-year term would not need much adjustment from the perpetual all risks yield of 6 per cent (to 6.3 per cent).

The valuer must either dispose of the all risks yield approach or guess the adjustment. The use of comparisons which do not have the same unexpired term invalidates growth implicit capitalization rate comparisons.

There remains very little to be said regarding the conventional technique. It is a comparison technique which relies on evidence of transactions. The yield choice should be based upon the evidence of sales of similar properties but, on the assumption that it is unlikely that many of these will be leaseholds, these will be freehold. The 'risks' hidden within the all risks yield are different for freeholds and leaseholds, and so different that the investments have almost nothing in common except the fact that they are secured on real property. The time has come to lay the conventional techniques to rest once and for all, provided the alternatives stand up to scrutiny. In our opinion the contemporary alternatives are clearly better as they are more closely related to the rationale of the property investment market. However, they also suffer from a number of limitations and the remaining part of this chapter isolates these limitations.

THE LIMITATIONS OF THE CONTEMPORARY MODELS

Real value or explicit DCF techniques reconcile (or can be reconciled) and the limitations are therefore common to both.

When used as market pricing/valuation models, they utilize evidence of market transactions. Leasehold transaction may be rare but, if they can be found, they must constitute the best evidence of market value. Although it is possible to analyse leasehold transactions by growth explicit methods, the next section highlights the difficulties inherent in interpreting these transactions if they can be found.

Analysis and valuation using leasehold comparables

In order to illustrate the possible use of comparisons, it is assumed that a similar property in terms of physical and locational characteristics is available.

■ EXAMPLE 7.8

A leasehold interest has sold for £736,000. The rent paid to the freeholder is £100,000 per annum on a lease with 10 years unexpired and with no further reviews. The lessee had just sublet for the remainder of the term, with a review in 5 years, at the estimated rental value of £200,000 per annum.

A conventional analysis (on a single rate gross of tax basis) would simply find the capitalization rate on the basis of a 10-year term at the current profit rent.

Profit rent	£100,000 pa
YP 10 years at ?%	x
Sale price	£736,000

£736,000 = £100,000x $x = 7.3600$
YP 10 years at 6% = 7.3600
Capitalization rate = 6%

In practice, this information would then be applied directly to any property of similar locational and physical characteristics; at worst disregarding any lease structure differences, at best amending the capitalization rate intuitively to reflect perceived differences.

The contemporary analysis is more complex. In order to find the equated yield of the investment the valuer must either assume a growth rate or assess an implied growth rate by using freehold comparisons. Adopting the first alternative, an assumed growth rate of 5 per cent per annum would produce an equated yield of 10.25 per cent by trial and error (see below).

Current profit rent	£100,000 pa		
YP 5 years at 10.25%	3.7667		
		£376,670	
ERV	£200,000 pa		
Amt £1 in 5 years at 5%	1.2763		
Inflated rent	£255,260 pa		
Less rent paid	£100,000 pa		
Profit rent	£155,260 pa		
YP 5 years at 10.25%	3.7667		
PV 5 years at 10.25%	0.6139		
		£359,030	
Valuation			£735,700
Sale price			£736,000

This analysis is based on pure speculation of the anticipated growth rate. It could alternatively have been based on an assumption of a freehold equated yield from which a growth rate could have been assessed.

Freeholds provide much more market evidence. For example, assume that the freehold interest in a property similar to the subject of Example 7.8, recently let on a lease with 5-year reviews at its estimated rental value, has been sold on the basis of a capitalization rate of 4 per cent.

The analysis for implied growth rate gives the following growth rates, depending upon the equated yield selected.

1 Equated yield 10 per cent: rental growth 6.44 per cent per annum.
2 Equated yield 20 per cent: rental growth 16.98 per cent per annum.

The application of the information to the valuation of a leasehold investment can now be considered.

■ EXAMPLE 7.9

The leasehold interest in a property similar to the subject of Example 7.8 (in terms of locational and physical factors) is let on a lease with 20 years unexpired at a fixed rent of £200,000 per annum. The property has just been let at its estimated rental value of £300,000 per annum on a 20-year lease with 5-year reviews.

Two transactions are now available for analysis. The leasehold interest which indicated the 6 per cent capitalization rate over 15 years and a free-hold interest sold to show a yield of 4 per cent.

The conventional valuation is likely to be undertaken with no intuitive adjustment of yield using the 6 per cent capitalization rate backed up by a lower yield on the freehold interest which would be perceived to be less risky.

Profit rent	£100,000 pa	
YP 20 years at 6%	11.4699	
Valuation		£1,146,990

Contemporary analysis produces two alternative implied growth rates at the freehold equated yields of 10 per cent and 20 per cent. These are 6.44 per cent and 16.98 per cent respectively. These are appropriate indicators, given that what is needed is the market perception of the rate at which the property's ERV is expected to increase, a factor quite independent of tenure. The analysis for leasehold equated yield can therefore be repeated at these two growth rates.

The analysis of the comparison by trial and error produces the following solutions. At a growth rate of 6.44 per cent per annum the equated yield is 11.4 per cent, and at a growth rate of 16.98 per cent per annum the equated yield is 19.1 per cent.

The valuation of Example 7.9 can now be attempted using each of these sets of results.

(i) $e = 11.4\%$, $g = 6.44\%$, $i = 4.66\%$

Rent received   £300,000 pa

YP 20 years at 4.66% ×

$\dfrac{\text{YP 5 years at } 11.4\%}{\text{YP 5 years at } 4.66\%}$

= 12.8295 × 3.6590	10.7409	
Value of rent received		£3,223,230
Less rent paid	£200,000 pa	
YP 20 years at 11.4%	7.7594	
Value of rent paid		£1,551,890
Valuation		£1,671,340

(ii) $e = 19.10\%$, $g = 16.89\%$, $i = 1.81\%$

Valuation   £2,203,630

The valuation results show a considerable variation between the two contemporary approaches; but note that both the contemporary solutions are in excess of the conventional approach. To compare the results, the internal rates of return of the comparable and the property to be valued are assessed for each solution at different prospective growth rates (Table 7.11).

The results indicate that the valuations are true to their assumptions. The conventional valuation reconciles with the comparison with a no growth assumption (that is, the subject property purchased for the conventional

Table 7.11   Comparison of the performance of the comparable property and the subject property at different rental growth rates (expressed as a total return (IRR) over the life of the investment)

Valuations	Rental	Growth	Rates
	0% pa	6.44% pa	16.98% pa
Comparison			
£736,000	6%	11.4%	19.1%
Conventional			
£1,146,990	6%	15.5%	28.0%
Equated yield at 10%			
£1,671,340	1.8%	11.4%	23.6%
Equated yield at 20%			
£2,203,630	negative	8.7%	19.1%

valuation and the comparable would both give a total return of 6 per cent per annum if there was no rental growth over the life of the investment). The two contemporary valuations reconcile with the comparison at the growth rates implied from the relevant equated yield assumption for the freehold.

All the valuations are fraught with problems but they indicate that the assumptions are vital to producing a reasonable valuation. Valuers are more likely to be accurate if they make an attempt to rationalize the equated yield choice (and therefore make an assumption on the future behaviour of the cash flow) rather than rely on the all risks yield. It is only when nil growth assumptions are valid that the simplistic all risks yield analysis has any meaning.

Analysis and valuation using freehold comparables

All the examples in the first part of this chapter were based on valuations of leasehold interests derived from analyses of freehold transactions. This, the more usual approach to the valuation of leaseholds, highlights the two main problems involved in using the contemporary model.

The first is the subjective choice of equated yield necessary when assessing the growth rate implied in the price paid for the freehold. In freehold valuation, this has been shown to be an insignificant problem, but this does not hold for leaseholds.

The second problem is the adjustment of the yield upwards for the additional risk of the leasehold interest. This adjustment was arbitrarily chosen at 5 per cent (13 per cent to 18 per cent) in the examples.

These two yield adjustments combine to create a situation where the subjective inputs made by the valuer are very significant. An example will illustrate.

■ EXAMPLE 7.10

A headleasehold interest is to be valued. The property comprises a shop which is held from the freeholder on a lease with 20 years unexpired at a fixed rent of £100,000 per annum. The property has just been sublet for the remainder of the term on a lease with 5-year reviews at the estimated rental value of £200,000. There are no leasehold comparables available but similar freehold properties let on 5-year review patterns sell for rack rented capitalization rates of 7 per cent.

The first step in the valuation is the analysis for implied rental growth which is derived from the choice of the equated yield for the freehold. In the analysis of freehold interests in the previous chapter the yield choice was varied from 10 per cent to 20 per cent, a wide variation to prove the insignificance of the equated yield choice. A more reasonable variation is taken at 5 per cent, from a risk free return of, say, 10 per cent up to a required return of 15 per cent incorporating a risk premium of 5 per cent.

The implied rental growth rate is calculated as follows:

$$(1+g)^t = \frac{\text{YP perp. at } k\% - \text{YP } t \text{ years at } e\%}{\text{YP perp. at } k\% \times \text{PV } t \text{ years at } e\%}$$

$$(1+g)^5 = \frac{\text{YP perp. at } 7\% - \text{YP } 5 \text{ years at } 10\%}{\text{YP perp. at } 7\% \times \text{PV } 5 \text{ years at } 10\%}$$

$$= \frac{14.2857 - 3.7908}{14.2857 \times 0.6209}$$

$$= \frac{10.4949}{8.8700} = 1.1832$$

$$g = (1.1832)^{1/5} - 1 = 0.034209\% = 3.4209\%$$

If the equated yield is raised to 15 per cent the implied rental growth rate becomes 9.0109 per cent per annum.

The next stage of the valuation is to determine the equated yield for the leasehold interest. This choice is also subjective in the hands of the valuer. Due to the individual nature of leasehold interests, the possible range is limitless; for the purposes of the example we shall assume from no risk adjustment over the freehold interest (10 per cent) to a 10 per cent risk premium over the freehold.

Table 7.12 gives the contemporary solutions to Example 7.10 given this range of assumptions of freehold and leasehold equated yield.

The most dominant factor in the level of the valuation is the risk premium

Table 7.12 Leasehold valuations based upon ranges of freehold and leasehold equated yields

Leasehold equated yield	Freehold equated yield	
	10%	15%
10%	1,173,558	
15%	807,314	1,250,883
20%	595,084	851,724
25%		619,666

adjustment from freehold to leasehold. If the same risk premium is adopted, the valuations remain fairly constant regardless of the equated yield choice in the original freehold analysis. This focuses attention on the choice of risk premium from freehold to leasehold. Are leaseholds more risky than freeholds and by how much?

Risk will be examined in detail in the next chapter but a few observations are warranted in the context of pricing/market valuation. It has already been suggested that the problem with leaseholds is their individuality; caused by the presence of two leases and their unique relationship to each other. A risky valuation is one where the possible variation of inputs into the model causes significant differences in the solution. Our two analyses of the variation caused by the valuer's subjective inputs indicate that the leasehold valuation is more sensitive to these inputs, and therefore it is a more risky valuation than that of the freehold.

The individuality of leasehold interests means that there is more variation in the possible returns from these investments. For example, a short lease-hold interest, held on a fixed rent until expiry, and sublet on a fixed rent until expiry, is a fixed income investment based upon the covenant of the subtenant and may attract very little risk premium above the gilt market. A highly geared interest would attract a substantial risk premium, especially if most of the value was based upon future rental growth and the current profit rent is very small. The need for focusing attention on the equated yield choice in a leasehold valuation is the single most important factor and, at present, this is a subjective, qualitative choice in the hands of the valuer. Once achieved, a rational valuation based on market transactions can be produced.

There is no doubt that, over the past 20 years or so, the rapid change in lease structures led to investment opportunities for alert investors in the leasehold market. Geared cash flows, secured on good covenant tenants and purchased from vendors still advised on the basis of traditional valuation methods, have produced enormous annual returns. Stories of 30 per cent and 40 per cent per annum total returns over long periods are common-place. This suggests a serious undervaluation of worth over a long period of this asset class.

The adoption of more rational pricing models would lead to more rational price levels in the leasehold investment market.

TAXATION AND MARKET VALUATION

Leasehold initial yields are high to make up for disadvantages in comparison with freeholds, such as:

1 no capital gain to redemption through asset appreciation as a result of inflation;
2 loss of the historic cost as a result of the wasting nature of the asset.

Given higher initial yields, more income is produced for a given outlay. This extra income is taxed. Freehold property investments, largely free of capital taxes and providing low income yields, are generally subject to a low tax incidence. In the leasehold market, on the other hand, high taxpayers have to obtain a much higher return gross of tax to compensate for its significant reduction by taxation (see Example 8.1 on pages 233–41). It is not surprising therefore that high taxpayers do not participate to a great extent in the leasehold investment market (especially short leaseholds): this reinforces the view that taxation should not be a consideration in leasehold market valuation but, as for freeholds, is a crucial element in an analysis for individual worth.

However, where it is possible to identify a group of potential purchasers subject to a common tax incidence, so that tax implications become relevant in market valuation, the following approach may be utilized.

■ EXAMPLE 7.11

Value the headleasehold interest in a property held on a lease with 20 years unexpired at a fixed rent of £50,000 per annum. The property has just been sublet for the remaining 20 years, with 5-year reviews, at the ERV of £200,000 per annum. Assume an equated yield of 15 per cent, growth of 6 per cent per annum and income tax at 40 per cent.

The real net yield should not be the net of tax equated yield (see page 185), but should instead be the net of tax real return.

The gross of tax real return is $(1 + e)/(1 + g) - 1$, so $(1.15)/(1.06) - 1 = 8.4906$ per cent, which at 40 per cent tax gives a net real return of 5.0943 per cent. The net of tax equated yield is therefore the product of the net of tax i and the growth rate $(1 + g)(1 + i) - 1$.

Net of tax equated yield $= (1.06 \times 1.050943) - 1 = 11.40$ per cent.

Net of tax IRFY approach

Rent received (net of tax)   £120,000 pa

$$\frac{\text{YP 20 years at } 5.0934\% \times \text{YP 5 years at } 11.4\%}{\text{YP 5 years at } 5.0934\%}$$

10.4758

Value of rent received		£1,257,100
Less rent paid	£30,000 pa	
YP 20 years at 11.4%	7.7594	
Value of rent paid		£232,780
Valuation		£1,024,320

Many valuers might argue that the identification of the tax position of a dominant group of purchasers in a submarket is unlikely and difficult unless the group concerned is the gross fund (the tax-exempt pension funds and charities). The effect of tax upon market valuation techniques is therefore debatable, whether conventional or contemporary methods are employed.

The same is not true in analysis, which is dealt with in the following chapter.

CONCLUSIONS

The valuer must accept that the valuation of leasehold investments is a much more difficult problem than for freeholds. Market pricing is a comparative exercise and the quality of the valuation ultimately rests on the quality of the information.

It is widely accepted that many leasehold valuations are based upon freehold transaction evidence and our analysis of the conventional model shows that it fails to accurately interpret this evidence. This leads to valuations which have no basis and no logic. They should be abandoned.

The alternative contemporary approach is preferable. It enables the valuer to make reasoned qualitative decisions and to translate those decisions into a rational mathematical model.

Although the valuation is subject to wide variation by the possible different interpretations of market information, it lends itself to the next obvious progression in practical valuation. This progression is the increasing acceptance of the fact that the valuation is a best estimate around a range of possible estimates, and should begin to be reported as such. If the valuer is unsure about certain inputs into the model, information technology makes the production of a number of solutions a simple affair, and therefore an analysis of the risk of a valuation is an easily obtained by-product.

In the same way that the owner of a picture would not expect the art valuer to precisely predict the selling price at auction, clients can readily accept that the individuality of property causes valuation to be an imprecise science or a fairly precise art. Valuation reports quoting mean and standard deviations for more sophisticated clients and ranges for other clients should become the norm in the not too distant future. The only forseeable problem would be to stop lending institutions adopting the lowest value in the range for loan purposes.

It is true to say that the market valuation of highly individual property assets like leaseholds is very likely to lead to a possible range of values, dependent on the subjective risk premium choice. It is impossible, then, to deny that this produces a halfway house between the objective pricing process and the subjective assessment of worth. The two processes are likely to become less and less separate as property assets become more unique and as pricing models become more rational.

The final part of this book deals with the assessment of worth. Any similarity in the methods we propose for pricing and the methods set out for the assessment of worth in the next chapter is absolutely intentional because although the market valuation techniques put forward in this text are based on the interpretation of comparable evidence, the use of more explicit models will ultimately lead to a more rational basis of pricing using more deterministic applications of technique.

Part four

VALUATION: THE ASSESSMENT OF WORTH

8

Property investment analysis: The assessment of worth

INTRODUCTION: A MODEL FOR ANALYSIS

Valuation, the assessment of worth or property investment analysis, was explained in Chapter 1 as an exercise differentiated from pricing or market valuation by its subjectivity. It is the estimation of the worth of a property investment to an investor. For our purposes, the investor is likely to be an institutional fund or a property company.

Worth may be expressed in three forms. Where the price of an investment is known, for example, in a retrospective analysis after a sale, or where negotiations for a purchase by private treaty have neared completion, then the worth of the investment must be expressed either as a rate of return or as an excess value over the price (net present value) at a given target rate (see Chapter 2). Where the price is unknown, for example, where an investment is to be sold by auction, the analysis is aimed at an assessment of the capital value of the investment, or the maximum price that can be paid, given a target rate of return.

We utilize a single model for all types of analysis. Such a model may be more explicit than that used in market valuation (see Baum 1984b), because it is no longer necessary to generalize. For example, the tax implications of an investment purchase to a particular investor may be ascertained, while net of tax appraisals in market valuation are usually avoided because a market tax rate cannot be generalized. In fact, the model should be absolutely explicit in order that the assumptions upon which the net present value or internal rate of return are predicated are exposed.

In order to be accurate, the rate of return needs to be an overall rate of return based upon an explicit projection of the cash flow likely to be produced by the investment. This rate of return has appeared throughout this book as the internal rate of return, the required or equated yield or the redemption yield.

We need to be careful to stress, however, that we are aiming at analyses of net returns, i.e. returns remaining after all expenses have been stripped away. This is not always the case when terms of overall return are used: for example, redemption yield as used by the *Financial Times* for the analysis of gilts is gross of tax and gross of transaction costs. Consequently, given that the purpose of property investment analysis is to facilitate investment comparison, and therefore decision-making, the analyst must be careful to adjust such measures to the same, absolutely net, terms in pursuit of accurate comparisons.

We do not, however, base our analysis upon the estimation of real returns, that is returns remaining after the effects of inflation have been stripped away. We recognize that real return analysis (to produce real return estimates or to estimate capital value given a target real return) is increasingly desirable and possible since the introduction of index-linked gilts and given the practices of several investment management companies. However, for reasons we have already stated in Part 1, the concentration of this book is upon monetary returns.

We have no doubt that in the near future this may have to be reconsidered. In pursuit of this, the models presented in this chapter and throughout this book are immediately adaptable to real return analysis and the analyst can amend the outlines presented herein accordingly.

Property investment analysis has been particularly aided by the popularization of personal computers in recent years and the introduction of spreadsheet software. Our own work has developed in this way. Consequently our model has taken shape as an explicit cash flow projection in monetary terms and in spreadsheet (row and column) format. We see the goal as an analysis of risk against return (see page 240): but before considering using our model for this purpose, we need to build it.

THE VARIABLES

The return from a property investment is a function of income, capital return and psychic income (see Chapter 2). We make no attempt to measure the latter, and for shorter leaseholds we may not expect a capital return. Thus our gross cash flow will be made up of income and (perhaps) capital. The income may increase at reviews. Estimation of a capital return depends upon the timing of a sale; therefore, we need to estimate a likely holding period. Holding costs will be incurred during the period of ownership, and these will need to be estimated. Purchase and sale transfer costs will be payable; at each rent review a fee will be payable; letting or reletting costs may have to be faced; and management fees may be incurred. Taxes on income and capital gain will be charged. Leaseholders may be faced with dilapidations claims. The income may be inclusive, so that (unusually) the investor pays rates out of the rent received; and a service charge may not cover the cost of service provision. Properties have to be repaired and refurbished: even then the impact of building depreciation may have to be faced.

The estimation of each of these factors will help us to reach an explicit net cash flow projection. If the price is known, the rate of return becomes the dependent variable in the analysis. If the price is not known, the target rate has to be added to the above list of independent variables, the capital value becoming the dependent variable. The same spreadsheet model can accommodate either variation.

All variables will now be briefly considered.

The holding period

For purely technical reasons – specifically, to avoid an infinitely long cash flow projection in a freehold analysis – a finite holding period must be utilized in the analysis model. For freeholds, this implies the assumption of a resale. For leaseholds, the holding period will usually equate with the remaining term.

The overriding concern in the choice of holding period must be the intentions of the investor. Discussions with the investor might reveal his likely or intended period of ownership. Where no intention to sell is apparent, the holding period becomes arbitrary.

In either case, there are reasons for forcing the coincidence of the resale date with the end of an occupation lease or a rent review period. This reflects likely practice, as a suspicion that fuller and fairer prices are achieved immediately after review or with a tenant under a new lease in harness appears to be common. (It is clear from earlier chapters that conventional valuation techniques may contribute to this policy, although risk aversion is a mighty influence.)

While the holding period is of no effect upon a market valuation in explicit DCF form, the introduction of costs, taxes and so on in investment analysis will destroy this consistency. Consequently, while periods of 10 or 15 years are often settled on for convenience, it should be noted that slight changes in holding period return may be achieved by shortening or lengthening the holding period, and this type of exercise is one of several uses of the model. Our analyses utilize holding periods which coincide with rent reviews or lease ends and usually fall in the 10–20 year range.

Resale price

In the cases of freeholds and long leaseholds the selection of a holding period will trigger the assumption of a resale at that date. The resale price has to be projected as the most likely selling price at that date. If the most common method of market pricing is the years' purchase method, and given that the sale will usually coincide with a review, the freehold resale price is given by

Estimated rental value (ERV) × YP in perpetuity

or

$$\frac{\text{ERV}}{\text{Capitalization rate } k}$$

This requires the projection of two variables: ERV at the resale and k at resale.

Estimated rental value

A projection of rental value to the point of resale in property investment analysis should not be based upon a market-implied growth rate (see Chapter 5). While this may be a guide, it should be remembered that the implied growth rate is an average rate in perpetuity; it is also net of depreciation. Further, it is a function of the price that is being analysed. In an estimate of worth an attempt has to be made to forecast rental growth year by year and depreciation should be explicitly accounted for. This is further discussed and illustrated from page 229 onwards.

Capitalization rate

The prediction of a capitalization rate for the subject property 10 or 15 years hence requires the estimation of two distinct trend lines. First, yields for the type of property under consideration may be expected to change over the period. If so, the extent to which the market yield will change must be estimated. However, it may be hypothesized that the expectations of the property investment market over the past century have been of generally stable prime yields (see Chapters 3 and 4), so that this may not be as large a task as it appears. Second, the movement in yield of the subject property against an index of yields for such properties in a frozen state over the holding period needs to be estimated. In other words, the extent of depreci-ation likely to be suffered by an ageing building (see pages 231–2) needs to be estimated. A cross-section analysis may facilitate this process: if the sub-ject property is 10 years old, and the appropriate capitalization rate is 7 per cent, given an expectation of stable yields over time the best estimate of the resale capitalization rate after a 10-year holding period is the current yield on similar but 20-year old buildings.

Gross income flow

Forecasting rental growth over the holding period is important both in the estimation of the rental flow and in the prediction of the resale price. Again, a two-tier approach is necessary. First, the rental value of the frozen property over time is to be forecast. Forecasting a variable such as this might be based upon any of three methods.

Extrapolation of time series data

A time series is a series of figures, for example rental values, over time. From the time series it may be possible to identify a long-term trend in rental values, but a cyclical pattern will almost certainly obscure this to some extent. In addition there may be non-recurring influences – rent freezes, for example – which need to be smoothed away. Extrapolation involves continuation of the time series line into the future, reflecting both cyclical variations and the long-term trend.

Identifying causal relationships

Analysis of past relationships can often give a clue to the future. Fore-casting future economic variables by statistical analysis of these relation-ships (econometrics) is an integral forecasting tool used, for example, by economic forecasters. The analyst forms a hypothesis relating to causal relationships and tests that hypothesis by using statistical tests of data ana-lyses. For example, the lagged impact of interest rates (the independent vari-able) upon property yields (the dependent variable) might be tested by regressing one factor against the other over time and measuring the strength and significance of the relationship between the two. If correlation is high, a simple prediction may be made.

The ideal situation for the forecaster would be where the independent variables are seen to move in advance of the dependent variable. Analysis of the business cycle is often undertaken to find indicators which lead the economy and those leading indicators form the basis of models which predict changes in the economy.

A combined approach

The most common method of forecasting utilized in the property market is an approach which combines extrapolation with a causal analysis, almost certainly in an informal framework. Gilt yields might be used as an indicator of prime property yields: when they fall, property yields might follow. However, this is not always the case. At the time of writing the first edition of this book, falling gilt yields coincided with rising prime property yields, so that an extrapolated forecast would conflict with a simple causal forecast based only on gilt yields.

In such circumstances the analyst is likely to base projections primarily on extrapolation coloured by causal influences (the forthcoming supply of new property in the sector, for example). If such an approach is used, the cyclical and long-term trends in a time series should be differentiated.

While the science of forecasting in the property market has far to go there have been rapid strides since the first edition of this book was published. Forecasting services, of which several are now available by subscription, form the foundation of the strategies and property investment decisions of many institutional investors. It may be a coincidence that at the time of writing the second edition, gilt yields had begun to drive property yields, albeit in a lagged manner.

Rental values

The estimation of gross income flow requires the estimation of rental values for the subject property as it ages in comparison to the projected value of the 'frozen' property. Again, this allows for building depreciation resulting from the ageing process (see page 231), and is again possible by means of a cross-section analysis (see Baum 1991).

In this type of analysis, the rent of the subject is expressed as a percentage of its frozen equivalent over time. To continue the example begun on page 229 above, the current ERV of the subject 10-year old building is £25 per square foot. A rental growth estimate of 6 per cent per annum over the 10-year holding period is projected. Fifteen-year-old similar buildings let at £22 per square foot: 20-year-old buildings let at £18 per square foot.

The projected rental values are as follows:

Years 1–5 $= £25.00$
Years 6–10 $£22 \times (1.06)^5 = £29.44$
Year 10 (resale) $£18 \times (1.06)^{10} = £32.24$

As the resale capitalization rate is predicted as 8 per cent, the resale price is therefore

$$\frac{\text{rent}}{\text{yield}} = \frac{£32.24}{0.08} \quad \text{per square foot}$$

$$= £402.94 \quad \text{per square foot}$$

At current yields of 7 per cent, the price is $£25/0.07 = £357.14$ per square foot. The gross cash flow is therefore as shown in Table 8.1. The internal rate of return of this investment – gross of all costs – is 8.37 per cent.

The gross income flow is termed gross effective income in North American texts (see, for example, Greer and Farrell 1984) to distinguish between maximum potential income when the property is fully let and the actual income likely to remain after voids. In this projection of income flow, an assumption has been made that 100 per cent occupancy is achieved. If voids in a multi-let building are expected, the gross income flow should be reduced to a gross effective income flow by deducting an allowance for voids.

Depreciation

Allowances for depreciation have been referred to above. Both rental value and resale capitalization rate are adjusted in the example used to effect a loss of value caused by ageing.

Note that the complexity of property depreciation is illustrated by an ageing building producing a rising rental income. This may be explained by the split of investment into site and building (see Chapter 2): while the site may appreciate or depreciate in value in real terms, the building must

Table 8.1

Years	Outlay (£)	Income (£)	Realization (£)
0	(357.14)		
1–5		25.00	
6–10		29.44	
10			402.94

normally depreciate. It is, however, impossible to test this effect accurately without abundant evidence of the rental value of bare sites, which is rare in the UK.

Thus, while the depreciation in real terms of a property investment may be attributable to site or building factors, typically it is the latter which is primarily responsible for the income pattern declining in comparison to a 'frozen' index of values. The cross-section analysis referred to earlier is recommended as an accessible method of estimating a depreciation-prone investment income pattern.

Acceptance of differential building and site value performance over time leads to a necessary check in the analysis of a property investment. Given an ageing and declining building on an inflation-proof or improving site, the time will come when the net value of the site (after demolition and clearance) exceeds the value of the developed property. This may happen within the holding period, and if so the analysis must reflect that fact, subject to legal considerations (the tenant may not be removable until the lease end).

In the example, assume the net site value is initially 50 per cent of the total value and is expected to grow at the same rate as the 'frozen' rent index (6 per cent). At the resale date it is worth £12.50 $(1.06)^{10}$ = £319.79. This is exceeded by the property resale value (£403): but in different circumstances, especially where a longer holding period is used, this may not be the case, and a check needs to be built into the model. Estimates of the current net site value and the rate at which it will increase are therefore needed. The latter should equate with the rate at which newly prime property rental values are expected to increase: the former requires comparable evidence.

Regular expenses

Implicit within the gross cash flow from a property investment is a series of regularly recurring expenses. These include management costs, either fees charged by an agent or the time of staff. In the former case they may be based upon a percentage of gross rents; in the latter, they need more careful estimation, and may have to be increased over time. Repairs and maintenance will normally be covered, like insurance, by the tenant's obligations under a full repairing and insuring (FRI) lease; if not, they must be accounted for, as must the exceptional burden of rates.

While the investor who provides services, for example, to the common parts of a multi-tenanted office building or shopping centre, will usually expect to recover these expenses in a service charge, the amount received may not quite match the cost of provision through a lagging effect or other causes, in which case an allowance needs to be made.

All expenses not tied to rent must be subject to an allowance for anticipated cost inflation.

Periodic expenses

While FRI leases place the burden of normal repairs upon tenants, dilapidations claims are not always met with the required response; in addition to
this, improvements may be necessary to make the property marketable.

Thus at the end of an occupation lease the investor will be faced with the
prospect of redeveloping, refurbishing, repairing or redecorating the
property. If the lease end falls within the building period, the prospect must
be allowed for, again with an inflation factor.

Fees

In order to strip out all costs to leave a net return estimate, acquisition fees
and sale fees at the end of the holding period need to be removed from the
cash flow. These will normally be based upon purchase and sale prices.

Rent review fees, based upon the new rent agreed, need to be allowed for
at each review, and re-leasing fees, again based on the new rent agreed, have
to be provided for at the lease end. Advertising costs may be additional to
both sale and re-leasing fees. VAT should be added to all expenses where
appropriate.

Taxes

Property investment analysis for the individual investor or fund can, and
should, be absolutely specific regarding the tax implications of the purchase. Thus capital and writing down allowances should be taken into
account where appropriate. Income or corporation tax should be removed
from the income flow. Capital gains tax payable upon resale can be precisely projected by the model's insistence upon estimation of purchase
price, sale price, intervening expenditure, holding period and intervening
inflation. The effect of tax upon return is illustrated by Example 8.1.

Examples

 EXAMPLE 8.1

A leasehold investment property has just been sold for £750,000. It is held
from the freeholder on a lease with 10 years unexpired at a fixed rent of

£47,500 per annum. The property has just been sublet on a lease which expires at the same time as the headlease at a rent of £200,000 per annum with one review in 5 years' time.

Forecasts of the market sector a future rental growth rate of 8.71 per cent per annum (3 per cent real, adjusted for inflation).

Analysis for gross of tax IRR

Cost	£750,000	
Income	Years 1–5	£152,500 pa
		[£200,000 − £47,500]
	Years 6–10	£200,000 pa
		$\times (1.0871)^5$
	=	£303,653
	less	£47,500
	=	£256,153

The internal rate of return of this investment gross of tax is 20.48 per cent.

Analysis for net of tax IRR (assuming the investor pays tax on income at 40 per cent)

Cost	£750,000	
Income	Years 1–5	£152,500 × 0.6 = £91,500
	Years 6–10	£256,153 × 0.6 = £153,692

The internal rate of return of this investment net of tax is 8.85 per cent. A 40 per cent tax rate has resulted in a 57 per cent reduction in return.

Of course, a large sector of the property market is dominated by the tax-exempt purchaser, and this can greatly simplify the analysis process, as demonstrated below.

Example 8.2 is presented in annual format, with all income and expenses assumed to be received at the year end. This is unrealistic in the UK market, and the model applied in practice must be amended to reflect the actual timing of expenses.

The client, a potential purchaser, is assumed to be tax-exempt; the property is a single-tenanted building where no voids are expected and no periodic expenses are anticipated.

■ EXAMPLE 8.2

Property investment analysis: 10-year model

Data

Price	£357.14
Capitalization rate (year 0)	7%
Capitalization rate (year 10)	8%
ERV (year 0)	£25.00 per square foot
ERV (year 5)	£22.00 per square foot
ERV (year 10)	£18.00 per square foot
Rental growth	6%
Site value percentage	50
Resale site value	£319.79
Resale property value	£402.94
Expected realization	£402.94
Management percentage	10
Voids percentage	0%
Periodic expenses	See schedule
Inflation	5%
Purchase fees	3%
Review fees	7%
Letting fees	15%
Sales fees	2.75%
Income tax	0%
Capital gains tax	0%
Target rate	13%

Periodic outlays: schedule

See Table 8.2.

Cash flow

See Table 8.3.

Table 8.2

Year	Cost (£)
0	0
1	0
2	0
3	0
4	0
5	0
6	0
7	0
8	0
9	0
10	0

Table 8.3

Year	Rent (£)	Voids (£)	Gross effective income (£)	Outlay/ resale (£)	Expenses (£)	Fees (£)	Periodic outlays (£)	Net cash (£)
0	0	0	0	− 357.14	0	10.71	0	− 367.85
1	25	0	25		2.5		0	22.5
2	25	0	25		2.5		0	22.5
3	25	0	25		2.5		0	22.5
4	25	0	25		2.5		0	22.5
5	25	0	25		2.5	2.06	0	20.44
6	29.44	0	29.44		2.94		0	26.50
7	29.44	0	29.44		2.94		0	26.50
8	29.44	0	29.44		2.94		0	26.50
9	29.44	0	29.44		2.94		0	26.50
10	29.44	0	29.44	402.94	2.94	11.08	0	418.36

Analysis 1		*Analysis 2*	
Price	£357.14	Price	£357.14
Target rate	13%	Target rate	6.5%
NPV	− £123.80	NPV	£13.267
IRR	6.98%	IRR	6.98%

The decision depends on choice of target rate. The internal rate of return (IRR) produced is 6.98 per cent. Compare this with the gross IRR of 8.37 per cent (see page 231). At any target rate less than 6.98 per cent, a positive net present value (NPV) is produced, and the decision is to accept, or purchase. For example, at a target rate of 6.5 per cent, a positive NPV of £13.27 is the result: an outlay of an extra £13.27 would still produce the target rate. However, at a target rate of 13 per cent, a negative NPV of nearly £124 indicates that the outlay is £124 too great, and a reduction in price of this amount would be needed to tempt a purchaser.

■ EXAMPLE 8.3

The same example has been amended to illustrate the effect of voids, periodic outlays, tax and a price reduction on the decision.

The property is now assumed to be priced at £250, but an immediate outlay of £100 is essential (for, let us say, repairs). A further outlay of £50 at the end of the holding period, for improvements prior to a sale, is allowed for and made subject to an inflation allowance. Income tax of 30 per cent of net income is payable. Capital gains tax of 30 per cent on the net real gain produced by the sale price (less fees and the outlay in year 10) over the initial outlay, fees and initial improvement expenditure is provided for. In this case a net capital loss produces a tax benefit, for set-off against other profits, of £28.86.

The after-tax IRR is 7.36 per cent, which should be compared, for example, with the after tax redemption yield net of expenses (transfer costs and so on) on gilts. At a net of tax target rate of 6.5 per cent, the decision is to purchase at this price.

Property investment analysis: 10-year model

Data

Price	£250.00
Capitalization rate (year 0)	7%
Capitalization rate (year 10)	8%
ERV (year 0)	£25.00 per square foot
ERV (year 5)	£22.00 per square foot
ERV (year 10)	£18.00 per square foot
Rental growth	10%
Site value percentage	70
Resale site value	£453.90
Resale property value	£583.59
Expected realization	£583.59
Management percentage	10
Voids percentage	20

Continued overleaf

Continued

Price	£250.00
Periodic expenses	See schedule
Inflation	5%
Purchase fees	3%
Review fees	7%
Letting fees	15%
Sales fees	2.75%
Income tax	30%
Capital gains tax	30%
Target rate	6.5%

Periodic outlays: schedule

See Table 8.4.

Cash flow

See Tables 8.5 and 8.6.

Analysis

Price	£250.00
Target rate	6.5%
NPV	£26.172
IRR	7.36%

Table 8.4

Year	Cost (£)
0	100
1	0
2	0
3	0
4	0
5	0
6	0
7	0
8	0
9	0
10	50

Table 8.5

Year	Rent (£)	Voids (£)	Gross effective income (£)	Outlay resale (£)	Expenses (£)
0	0	0	0	– 250	0
1	25	5	20		2
2	25	5	20		2
3	25	5	20		2
4	25	5	20		2
5	25	5	20		2
6	35.43	7.09	28.34		2.83
7	35.43	7.09	28.34		2.83
8	35.43	7.09	28.34		2.83
9	35.43	7.09	28.34		2.83
10	35.43	7.09	28.34	583.59	2.83

(continued)

Fees (£)	Periodic outlays (£)	Net cash (£)	Income T (£)	Capital gains tax (£)	After-tax cash flow (£)
7.50	100.00	– 357.50			– 357.50
	0	18	5.4		12.6
	0	18	5.4		12.6
	0	18	5.4		12.6
	0	18	5.4		12.6
2.48	0	15.52	4.66		10.86
	0	25.51	7.65		17.86
	0	25.51	7.65		17.86
	0	25.51	7.65		17.86
	0	25.51	7.65		17.86
16.05	81.44	511.61	7.65	– 28.86	540.48

The target rate of return

The principal purpose of property investment analysis in the form discussed in this chapter is the facilitation of decision-making. The basic criterion for decision-making in investment, risk considerations apart, is the expected or required rate of return. This is termed the *target rate* (sometimes the *hurdle rate*) of return.

The target rate has already appeared in Chapter 2 as I. It was seen from Fisher's work (see Chapter 2) that the rate of return I can be built up from three factors: expected inflation d, risk r and time preference i. $I = (1 + d)(1 + r)(1 + i) - 1$; I is a compensation for these three factors, these three deterrents to the setting aside of capital for a period.

The target rate should be based upon the return required by the investor to compensate him for the loss of capital employed in the project which could have been employed elsewhere, that is, the opportunity cost of capital (for example, the redemption yield on similar maturity gilts) plus a risk premium.

It is common to see no distinction between the required return on borrowed and equity funds. This is, however, unrealistic. Financial markets cannot be assumed to be efficient. The opportunity cost of equity to an equity investor such as a pension fund and the actual cost of equity (dividends required by investors) to an equity/debt investor such as a property company will not equate with the actual cost of borrowing capital. Consequently, the analyst should rely upon the concept of opportunity cost (and not the actual cost of capital) in the estimation of target rate.

(In certain circumstances the cost of borrowing may be taken into account by using the weighted average cost of capital. For a fuller discussion of the weighted average cost of capital see Brigham (1985) and Brealey and Myers (1984).)

The target rate will be treated in simple terms for the remainder of this chapter, which is devoted to the fundamental focus of property investment analysis: risk–return analysis.

RISK–RETURN ANALYSIS

Introduction

The focus of this chapter is the analysis of property investment opportunities by means of discounted cash flow (DCF) techniques. While several markets throughout the world exhibit a reluctance to abandon initial yield based analysis, consumer-led and computer-aided improvements in service have produced, and continue to produce, widespread refinements in DCF methods. Investors should now expect no less than a present value or IRR analysis based upon income and expense projections. This is a first and base level of analysis. Analysts are, as a result, increasingly forced to use market analysis to predict the uncertain, or, as stated in the introduction to this chapter, to make an explicit projection of the cash flow likely to be produced by the investment.

This element of uncertainty demands another level of decision-aiding analysis. However, risk analysis, well explored in financial theory, has not yet been the subject of comprehensive examination in the real estate sector, and empirical tests of real estate risk have not yet been developed to a point which enables risk–return analysis to be widely practised in property markets. There is an absence of reported data regarding the riskiness of individual real estate investments, in terms of both quantum and source, although developments are being made: see, for example, the research of Brown (1991).

Despite this vacuum, a third level of analysis is rapidly being developed, both in theoretical and empirical terms. Recognition of portfolio risk, spurred by dominance of the real estate market by institutional investors in the UK and by a similar increasing influence in the USA, has produced applications of the capital asset pricing model (CAPM) (see Chapter 2) to real estate investment in recent years. The intellectual appeal of CAPM coupled with a well-documented burst of real estate buying by UK institutions aiming towards real estate/fixed interest security/equity diversification has established risk—return analysis at the portfolio level as the subject of much research interest in the UK; a similar movement is discernible in the USA.

The intention in this section is to link these levels of decision aid in a logical manner, and to establish the interdependence of the underlying techniques. Each succeeding level of analysis subsumes the previous level; deficiencies at any level are therefore compounded. It is important, therefore, to identify both theoretical and practical problems in the application of each level of analysis before proceeding to the next.

All levels of decision technology for real estate investment discussed herein are based on DCF analysis and utilize a return measure. Estimation of return may be by net present value (NPV) or internal rate of return (IRR). These alternatives, introduced in Chapter 2, are assessed briefly below.

Net present value or internal rate of return?

It appears clear that in the general finance area the debate concerning a theoretical preference for NPV or IRR has been well settled in favour of the former. Brigham (1985) is positive enough:

> the NPV method exhibits all the desired decision rule properties and, as such, it is the best method for evaluating projects. Because the NPV method is better than IRR we were tempted to explain NPV only, state that it should be used as the accepted criterion, and go on to the next topic.

Brigham's only reason for not doing so is continued use of IRR in the market. This preference for NPV is dependent, of course, upon the 'desired decision rule properties', which are in essence aimed towards maximization of shareholder wealth. In real estate terms, this translates simply to maximization of present asset values, the normal aim of a limited-resource investor.

Greer and Farrell (1984) therefore express surprise that in real estate literature IRR continues to find favour.

> While the internal rate of return has little substantive advantage over alternative methods of applying discount rates to projected cash flows, it does have serious weaknesses not found in the alternatives. Persistent support of a favoured technique might be admirable were there no substitutes that possess equal power to discriminate between acceptable and unacceptable opportunities. Such is not the case, however, with the IRR approach. Its continued advocacy is therefore somewhat curious.

It does not seem curious to the authors that IRR continues to find favour, because it is simpler to use. This should not be a factor acting in its favour when the alternative, NPV, is almost as simple, but the intuitive appeal of return expressed in a single point return measure, with no requirement upon the analyst to assess a target or hurdle rate, is obvious. Nonetheless, Jaffe (1977) considers that IRR remains popular in real estate simply because real estate research and debate lag behind general financial literature. It will eventually be clear in real estate practice that IRR is flawed where reinvestment of returns is likely. Given that IRR incorporates a risk premium (see below), the implicit assumption where reinvestment is likely that cash flows of any amount can be reinvested to earn the same rate is unrealistic. Modified IRR and financial management rate of return techniques (see Newell 1986; Robinson 1985) have merit in their intended solution of this IRR defect; but, as the appeal of the accepted technique is simplicity, such modifications may be superfluous. The prospect of multiple IRR solutions with cash flow sign changes such as are typical in a real estate investment (which may require refurbishment or repair or fall vacant at any time) is a further restriction.

Comparison of mutually exclusive projects requiring different initial outlays is more logically dealt with by NPV; in this situation incremental analysis (see Baum and Mackmin 1989) is another example of a superfluous theoretical advance designed to enable IRR to produce the same result as NPV. In conclusion, NPV is clearly preferable as a decision aid, but IRR has attractions for practitioners.

Both NPV and IRR will be utilized in the following discussion of risk–return analysis, which will be based around the following example.

■ EXAMPLE 8.4

The property investment analyst has been appointed advisor to a tax-exempt investment fund which has to make a choice between two alternative property investments which it has been offered. Investment A is a leasehold shop; investment B is a small freehold office building. Each is for sale at £130,000, and the following information is available.

Investment A

The property comprises a single shop unit which is arranged on three floors with a total net floor area of 2,875 square feet. The current leaseholder holds the property on a net lease for a term of 35 years expiring 5 years after the purchase is likely to be completed, at a fixed rent of £2,250 per annum. The entire property is let on a net lease to the current occupier for a term expiring 2 days before the headlease at a rent of £45,000 per annum, subject to a review to open market rent 2 years before the lease expires. The current open market rental value is £52,500 (net) per annum. Acquisition fees are estimated at 3 per cent of purchase price. Rent review fees are estimated at 7.5 per cent of the revised rent. Management costs are 10 per cent of rent collected per annum. Rents have been growing in this part of the UK at 5 per cent per annum and little change is expected in the short term.

Investment B

The property is a small freehold office building with a total area of 3,000 square feet, let with 5 years (at likely completion date) of the current lease to run. Last year's rent was £20,000 and around 30 per cent of this rent was lost in outgoings, including management fees. Acquisition and sale fees are estimated at 5 per cent of price. Rents are annually reviewable in line with the retail price index (RPI). Current capitalization rates are between 10 and 12 per cent.

General

RPI increased by 3.5 per cent last year. British government fixed interest securities, medium dated, currently yield around 11 per cent if held to maturity. Rents from each property can be assumed to be received annually in arrear. All fees can be regarded as reliable cost estimates.

A basic NPV/IRR analysis of each transaction might be presented as follows:

Investment A

Data

Current rent received	£45,000 pa
Head rent paid	£2,250 pa
Remainder of lease	5 years
Term of review	3 years
Acquisition fees	3%
Rent review fees	7.5%
Management costs	10%
Price	£130,000
Target rate	11%

Variables

Rental value	£52,500 pa
Rental growth	5% pa

Appraisal

See Table 8.7.

Table 8.7

End of year	Rent in (£)	Rent out (£)	Review fees (£)	Management fees (£)	Outlay (£)	Acquisition fees (£)	Net cash (£)
0	0	0	0	0	130,000	3,900	(133,900)
1	45,000	2,250	0	4,500	0	0	38,250
2	45,000	2,250	0	4,500	0	0	38,250
3	45,000	2,250	4,558	4,500	0	0	33,692
4	60,775	2,250	0	6,078	0	0	52,448
5	60,775	2,250	0	6,078	0	0	52,448
						NPV	£21,913
						IRR (%)	16.9029

Investment B

Data

Current rent received	£20,000
Term to review	1 year
Sale fees	5%
Acquisition fees	5%
Rent review fees	0.00
Management costs etc.	3%
Price	£130,000
Target rate	11%

Variables

RPI growth	3.5% pa
Resale capitalization rate	11% pa

Appraisal

See Table 8.8

The results, employing the data and variables as listed, show investment B to be preferable to investment A by both NPV and IRR criteria. (It should be noted that NPV and IRR will not always indicate the same decision, referring us back to the conclusion that, when in doubt, NPV should always be followed.)

However, this fails to take account of the risks of these investments. In Chapter 2 risk was defined as 'uncertainty regarding the expected rate of return from an investment'. In this case, each investment suffers from two major uncertainties. For investment A, these are the estimated current rental value and the anticipated rate of rental growth. For investment B,

Table 8.8

End of year	Rent in (£)	Resale (£)	Management fees (£)	Outlay (£)	Acquisition/ sale (£)	Net cash (£)
0	0		0	130,000	6,500	(136,500)
1	20,700		6,210	0	0	14,490
2	21,425		6,427	0	0	14,997
3	22,174		6,652	0	0	15,522
4	22,950		6,885	0	0	16,065
5	23,754	215,943	7,126	0	10,797	221,773
					NPV	£42,270
					IRR (%)	18.2503

they are the resale capitalization rate and the rate of change in the RPI. The remainder of this chapter is devoted to methods of dealing with these uncertainties.

Sensitivity analysis

Sensitivity analysis was developed as a means of identifying the independent variable which causes the greatest change in the dependent variable. Many other simple explorations of risk are made possible by this technique.

The two uncertainties (risky variables) in investments A and B may not turn out to be as expected and shown in the basic analysis above. Given this, it will be useful to know what the effect of likely changes will be upon return. Sensitivity analysis can be used to explore the question: 'what if?'

Let us assume that a reasonable margin of error in each case is determined to be plus or minus 20 per cent. What is the effect of a 20 per cent change in each and then both variables? The results are given in Tables 8.9 and 8.10. With investment A every outcome indicates that the investment

Table 8.9 Investment A

		NPV (£)	IRR (%)
Rental value	+20%	34,945	19.863
Rental value	−20%	8,882	13.563
Rental growth	+20%	23,793	17.351
Rental growth	−20%	20,069	16.456
Both variables	+20%	37,200	20.343
Both variables	−20%	7,406	13.156

Table 8.10 Investment B

		NPV (£)	IRR (%)
Resale capitalization rate	+20%	72,706	22.476
Resale capitalization rate	−20%	21,979	15.019
RPI growth	+20%	47,556	19.050
RPI growth	−20%	37,115	17.451
Resale capitalization rate	+20% }	79,035	23.305
RPI growth	−20% }		
Resale capitalization rate	+20% }	17,501	14.241
RPI growth	−20% }		

is worthwhile at a target rate of 11 per cent. The same is true of investment B. The worst outcome is better than the worst outcome in A and the best is also better than the best outcome in A. It continues to appear to be the better buy.

However, this rudimentary form of sensitivity analysis has failed to consider whether a 20 per cent increase or reduction in each variable is equally likely. Let us assume that market research shows that this is patently not the case here. While rental growth in the south of England may show a 20 per cent variation from the expected, the estimated market rental may only vary from the expected by up to 5 per cent. On the other hand, RPI changes may vary by 30 per cent from the expected, and a thin market means that the resale capitalization rate could lie anywhere between 8 and 14 per cent. Revised figures on these more realistic estimates are as shown in Tables 8.11 and 8.12.

This more realistic form of sensitivity analysis leaves investment B as the better choice, but begins to raise questions. The worst outcome of A is now better than the worst outcome of B, which now complicates the decision somewhat. If the target rate were to increase to 13 per cent, the implications are more vital: with some outcomes, investment B should not be undertaken, while at all outcomes investment A remains viable. Given this

Table 8.11 Investment A

		NPV (£)	IRR (%)
Rental value	+5%	25,171	17.674
Rental value	−5%	18,655	16.108
Rental growth	+20%	23,793	17.351
Rental growth	−20%	20,069	16.456
Best outcome		27,145	18.131
Worst outcome		16,904	15.670

Table 8.12 Investment B

		NPV (£)	IRR (%)
Resale capitalization rate	8%	87,924	24.373
Resale capitalization rate	14%	16,182	14.018
RPI growth	+30%	50,249	19.450
RPI growth	−30%	34,585	17.051
Best outcome		98,266	25.630
Worst outcome		9,794	12.861

information, some investors would choose A, as they would not be prepared to face the slightest prospect of a loss.

Sensitivity analysis therefore allows a more informed decision to be made. It does, however, fail to address a vital point. What are the chances of the possible variations becoming fact? It may be, for example, that there is only the slightest of chances that RPI growth will be more than 20 per cent in excess of the expected, whereas it is almost impossible to estimate a likely resale capitalization rate due to a paucity of market evidence. This will surely qualify the above analysis. What is now implied is an element of qualitative or subjective judgement. The best outcome in A is less profitable than the best outcome in B: but the latter may be much less likely than the former. This element of risk must be taken into account in a full analysis. It is not enough to say what could happen; it is necessary to qualify such hypotheses by probabilities, and to some extent the next set of techniques – and certainly the mean–variance criterion (see page 257) – attempt to do this, leaving sensitivity analysis behind as a somewhat rudimentary (albeit objective) risk analysis technique.

Risk-adjustment techniques

Both the potential variation and the chances of variation in the outcome from the expected must be taken into account in a full risk–return analysis. Yet the decision-maker will demand as clear an indication as possible. Risk-adjustment techniques satisfy these demands. Unfortunately, they leave rather large questions unanswered en route. Nonetheless, they are widely practised, both consciously and unconsciously, in both wider investment markets and in real estate.

Three manifestations of risk-adjusted technique will be considered here. They are risk-adjusted discount rates; the certainty equivalent technique; and a hybrid of these, suitable for UK property investment analysis, termed here the sliced income method.

Risk-adjusted discount rate

Whether by NPV or IRR, the estimation of a single point return estimate has to cope with varying risks (defined here as variance of possible returns) between alternatives. Choosing on the basis of IRRs alone where risks differ presumes indifference to risk, which undermines a whole stream of accepted finance wisdom (see Chapter 2). Given that most investors are risk averse to a degree, a choice on the basis of IRR involves a risk adjustment.

Adjustment may be to discount rate or to income. The use of the risk-adjusted discount rate is in accord with Fisher's work, as presented in Chapter 2. The interest (or discount) rate I can be constructed from the function $(1 + i)(1 + d)(1 + r) - 1$ where i represents a return for time preference, d represents a return for expected inflation and r represents a return for risk. The risk free rate (RFR), 11 per cent in the sensitivity example, is a function of i and d: $(1 + i)(1 + d) - 1$, so $I = (1 - \text{RFR})(1 + r) - 1$. This is the risk-adjusted discount rate. The greater the amount of perceived risk, the higher is r.

Note that this is not the way the risk-adjusted discount rate (RADR) is normally constructed in practice. Instead, the RADR is usually found by $\text{RFR} + r$. The difference is usually small, and can be shown to be unimportant as the choice of r is arbitrary. For example, suppose $\text{RFR} = 0.11$ and $r = 0.05$. $(1 + \text{RFR})(1 + r) - 1 = 16.55$ per cent; $\text{RFR} + r = 16$ per cent. Such fine distinction in the RADR would normally be pointless.

The use of risk-adjusted discount rates implies that more return is required to compensate for greater risk. How much more is impossible to determine objectively: this depends upon the risk–return indifference curve of the investor, a subjective matter. Figure 8.1 below illustrates this concept. Most investors – and the market, in accepted finance theory – show

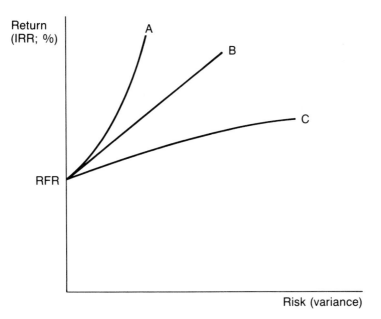

Figure 8.1   Risk–return indifference curves

behaviour which is risk-averse, where an increase in risk would lead to an increase in required return (see Chapter 2). In the case of A, the proportionate increase in measured return would exceed the proportionate increase in risk; A is therefore risk-averse.

So solidly entrenched in financial theory is the acceptance of risk-aversion that investor B, who requires more return in exact proportion to the increase in risk, is called in some texts (see, for example, Gitman and Joehnk (1984)) risk-indifferent! This leaves us in some confusion concerning the position of C, typically termed risk-seeking, yet still requiring more return for some more risk. In fact all three are risk-averse.

The subjectivity of the risk–return trade-off makes it difficult for the analyst to rank investments which are subject to risk by IRR alone (while the capital asset pricing model (see page 40) can be used to avoid this problem, its application to real estate is in question (see page 241)). By practice the analyst may be able to build up helpful experience, but marginal cases will always devalue the reliability of advice. If, on the other hand, NPV techniques, which are to be preferred, are relied upon, what then? The risk adjustment has necessarily to be made to the target or hurdle rate. The problem of quantum adjustment to account for risk is exactly the same as for IRR. Hence the use of risk-adjusted discount rates in this first level of analysis is subject to charges of subjectivity in discount rate choice.

Nonetheless, investment B was shown by sensitivity analysis to be riskier than investment A. Even without the advantage of such an analysis – which does not, it should be remembered, make a decision – the experienced investor or analyst should be capable of discerning such differences and, hence, make reasonable adjustments to the RFR to produce different RADRs.

Assume 12.5 per cent is chosen for A and 17.5 per cent is chosen for B. The results are as follows:

Investment A

	NPV	£15,833
	IRR	16.903%

Investment B

	NPV	£3,710
	IRR	18.250%

Note that on the basis of NPV A becomes preferable. On the basis of IRR too, A produces a greater yield margin over the target rate. Yet if RADRs of 12.5 per cent and 15 per cent respectively are used, the results are as follows:

Investment A

NPV	£15,833
IRR	16.903%

Investment B

NPV	£17,092
IRR	18.250%

Now, on the NPV criterion, B should be bought. This brings to light the major problem with the RADR method. There are no agreed criteria for the determination of the RADR, and relatively slight changes may reverse a decision. The analyst's perception of risk may not equate with the investor's. Who decides?

Additionally, the use of the RADR implies an increasing discount applied to future returns, and therefore that cash flows become riskier the longer the investor has to wait to receive them. The inappropriateness of such a by-product of the technique is demonstrated by the pre-let development project not subject to a fixed price building contract. The riskier cash flows are in the earlier, and not the later, years.

Finally, risk premiums have to be determined individually for each project. No two property investments are alike: risk is a complex function of gross incomes, operating expenses and capital returns.

Consequently, RADR is difficult to use reliably in practice. It continues to be used due to its simplicity and ease of application. In property investment analysis the following method is hardly used at all, but is probably superior.

Certainty equivalent cash flows

At this level, subjective adjustment of the discount rate is not attempted. Adjustment of the income stream is the only remaining means of reflecting risk in value. The second vital input into real estate investment analysis is the projected income flow, a function of a complex relationship of gross rental, operating expenses, financing arrangements, taxation and capital return, all of which are subject to potential variance and hence risk.

The certainty equivalent technique utilizes the concept of risk-aversion by theorizing a single point income level which the investor would trade for the variable cash flows actually in prospect. In relation to the expected (average) income flow utilized in risk-adjusted discounting, the certainty equivalent income flow for a risk-averse investor will be lower. Because risk–return indifference is unique to the investor, the certainty equivalent cash flow is best determined in a process of dialogue between analyst and investor.

The selection of the certainty equivalent cash flow by way of the certainty equivalent inputs (rental growth, initial rental value, resale capitalization rate and others) is, nonetheless, not ideally performed in this manner where the investor may, as might usually be suspected in real estate investment, suggest that the onus of analysis should fall not upon the investor but upon the analyst. An objective, analyst-performed selection of a certainty equivalent income may be produced by use of the capital asset pricing model (see Brealey and Myers 1984: 188); we prefer a simpler route, utilizing standard deviation analysis.

Our use of the standard deviation is designed to replace the best estimate of the cash flows by a certainty equivalent cash flow which there is approximately an 84 per cent chance of bettering and only a 16 per cent chance of failing to achieve. Assuming a normal distribution of possible cash flows, one standard deviation (SD) either side of the expected (best estimate) cash flow includes 68 per cent of all possible outcomes. The remaining 32 per cent includes 16 per cent which lie below the expected cash flow less one SD, and 16 per cent which lie above the expected cash flow plus one SD. Consequently, the use of the expected cash flow less one SD as the certainty equivalent results in the 84:16 chance of bettering it, thus reflecting a generous (but objectively determined in all cases) degree of risk-aversion on behalf of the investor.

In the example, each investment has two variables. Assume that the potential outcomes and associated probabilities for each variable are represented by the following samples from a continuous distribution.

Investment A

Rental value	£49,875	£52,500	£55,125
Probability	0.2	0.6	0.2
Rental growth	0.04	0.05	0.06
Probability	0.3	0.4	0.3

Investment B

RPI growth	0.0245	0.035	0.0455
Probability	0.333	0.334	0.333
Resale capitalization rate	0.08	0.11	0.14
Probability	0.3	0.4	0.3

Calculation of the SD is performed as follows. (This calculation assumes, incorrectly, that the observations are derived from a finite population. See page 265 for a discussion of this problem.)

1 Calculate the expected value:

$$\text{expected value } (\bar{r}) = \Sigma(p \times \hat{r})$$

where p is the probability of each sample outcome and $\hat{r}$ is each sample outcome.

2 Calculate the variance:

$$\text{variance } (\sigma^2) = \Sigma p(\hat{r} - \bar{r})^2$$

3 Calculate the SD:

$$\text{SD (population)} = \sqrt{\sigma^2}$$

The results are given in Table 8.13.

We can now calculate the certainty equivalents for these variables. These are given in Table 8.14.

Table 8.13

	Expected value	Variance	Standard deviation
Investment A			
Rental value	£52,500	£2,756,250	£1,660.195
Rental growth	0.05	0.00006	0.007745
Investment B			
RPI growth	0.035	0.000073	0.008568
Resale capitalization rate	0.11	0.000540	0.023237

Table 8.14

	Expected value	Standard deviation	Certainty equivalent (rounded)
Investment A			
Rental value	£52,500	£1,660.195	£50,840
Rental growth	0.05	0.007745	0.04225
Investment B			
RPI growth	0.035	0.008568	0.02643
Resale capitalization rate	0.110	0.023237	0.13324

These values can now be fed back into the analysis model using the risk free target rate of 11 per cent (remember that the investments are now effectively risk free: the values of the variables chosen represent certainty, or risk free, equivalents of their expected values). The results are given in Table 8.15.

Table 8.15

	NPV	IRR
Investment A	£18,467	16.061%
Investment B	£15,606	13.907%

This produces the same decision as the RADR (NPV) method at RADRs of 12.5 per cent and 17.5 per cent respectively and suggests that the safer investment, A, should be purchased.

This interpretation of the certainty equivalent technique has the apparent advantage over RADR of objectivity. While using SDs to compute certainty equivalents of the variables ignores the investor's risk–return indifference function, and is only therefore of use where it is not possible to establish it, this is a major theoretical deficiency which is of little practical importance. The investor's risk–return indifference is extremely difficult to measure. Moreover, the choice of certainty equivalent need not be expected value minus 1 SD: any proportion or multiple of 1 SD can be used instead to reflect the investor's risk-aversion. Consequently we favour the use of this technique in preference to risk-adjusted discount rates, and suggest it as a practicable means of general risk analysis.

The sliced income approach

While the certainty equivalent technique may represent an improvement over risk-adjusted discount rates, particularly when the standardization allowed by use of SDs is incorporated, the technique lends itself to further rational development in the special case of property investment analysis in the UK and other markets with rents fixed under leases. By combining risk-adjustment and certainty equivalent methods a 'sliced' view of a property investment can be moulded for use where property investment cash flows lend themselves to differential treatment.

Such cases exist wherever a minimum rental is guaranteed (certain) and an extra rental is possible (risky). Examples are (in the USA) contractually pre-determined level or stepped rents in shopping malls with extra percentage rents paid subject to retail turnover performance; or (in the UK) property let, as it typically is, subject to 5-yearly rent reviews which are upward only. In effect, a minimum rent equal to the previous contract rent is (ignoring default risk) guaranteed; any overage is a bonus.

The guaranteed income (assuming a quality tenant) should be discounted at a risk free rate, in accordance with its certain nature. The overage, or possible bonus, is then calculated by comparing the expected – most likely – income stream (calculated exactly as per risk-adjusted discount rate techniques) with the certain (not certainty equivalent, which would typically be higher) income and producing a top-slice income which due to its leveraged nature is extremely sensitive to changes in variables (rental value, rental growth, operating expenses and so on) and is therefore highly risky. Commensurate with this, it is discounted at a highly risk-adjusted rate.

This technique is best illustrated by investment A. Upward only rent reviews in the sublease will guarantee a rent on reversion equal to the current rent paid by the subtenant. This is therefore risk free in terms of the uncertainty of rental growth (but not default).

The certain income is calculated in this example as the cash flow that would be received if the upward only rent review in year 3 resulted in the same rent being paid. The overage is the difference between this and the expected rent based on the expected values of the two variables of ERV and rental growth. The resulting certain income is discounted at the RFR of 11 per cent.

The overage is more risky than the expected income flow. Consequently, where 12.5 per cent was the overall risk-adjusted discount rate previously used to produce an NPV of £15,833, a higher rate (15 per cent in this example) should be used in the valuation of the overage rent. A total NPV of £14,267 is produced: no IRR can be calculated, as there are two separate cash flows and only one outlay. The result is close to those produced for investment A by both RADR and certainty equivalent techniques (see Table 8.16).

The sliced income method is inappropriate for investment B, which is best analysed using certainty equivalent techniques. The conclusion from these analyses is best based on the preferred NPV technique. Using the sliced income technique, investment A produces an NPV of £14,267. Using the certainty equivalent technique, investment B produces an NPV of £15,606. The decision is a marginal one.

Ideally, all three first-level techniques should produce similar results. This cannot be guaranteed, however. It will only happen if the subjectivity of the risk-adjusted rates in risk-adjusted discount rate and sliced analysis

Table 8.16 Appraisal, investment A, sliced income

End of year	Rent in (£)	Rent out (£)	Review fees (£)	Management fees (£)	Outlay (£)	Acquisition (£)	Net cash (£)	Certain (£)	Overage (£)
0	0	0	0	0	130,000	3,900	−133,900		
1	45,000	2,250	0	4,500	0	0	38,250	38,250	0
2	45,000	2,250	0	4,500	0	0	38,250	38,250	0
3	45,000	2,250	4,558	4,500	0	0	33,692	33,692	0
4	60,775	2,250	0	6,078	0	0	52,448	38,250	14,197
5	60,775	2,250	0	6,078	0	0	52,448	38,250	14,197
								PV: £132,990	PV: £15,176
									Total NPV: £14,266

coincide in effect with the arbitrariness of the certainty equivalent income. It is the subjective and arbitrary nature of these techniques which harbours a wealth of criticism.

The major criticism of all techniques which incorporate risk-adjusted discount rates, that is, that future returns are increasingly heavily penalized without consistent justification, remains.

This first level of analysis, however applied, has the merit of producing a single comparative decision aid: purchase if NPV is positive; where investments are mutually exclusive, purchase the investment with the higher NPV. This is a criticism as well as a merit. The decision-maker may not appreciate the analyst's roughshod disregard of his individual risk–return indifference. He may therefore prefer separate measures of risk and return, and to base his decision on these two results, rather than upon the single NPV measure.

The mean–variance criterion

The subjectivity of the risk–return indifference function for the investor may render an objective decision-aiding analytical technique dangerous in the hands of the analyst. Risk-adjustment techniques encourage the analyst to presume to replace the subjective function by objective experience, but

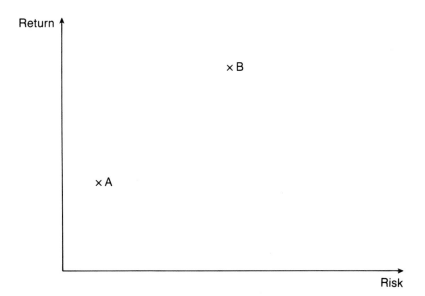

Figure 8.2 The two investment case: 1

the sophisticated investor may not be satisfied with this. (For example, utility (see Byrne and Cadman 1985) may affect his position. This is largely ignored in this analysis but further reference to the point should be made by the serious reader.) He may wish to judge the merits of two alternative investments against each other by comparing their expected return and their risk in combination, represented graphically as follows. Assume investment A is low risk, low return, and investment B is high risk, high return (see Figure 8.2).

Some investors will prefer A while others will prefer B. This will depend on their risk-aversion, as represented by risk−return indifference curves (see Chapter 2). Suppose investor Z is highly risk-averse, while Y is not. (It is assumed that all investors will accept the RFR for a risk free investment.) See Figure 8.3.

Investor Z would buy investment A, because the expected return is more than enough to compensate for the risk involved. He would not, however, buy B. Investor Y, on the other hand, would probably prefer B to A because the margin of return over the minimum required is higher.

If, however, investment B were riskier than A but produced less return, then any risk-averse investor would choose A (see Figure 8.4).

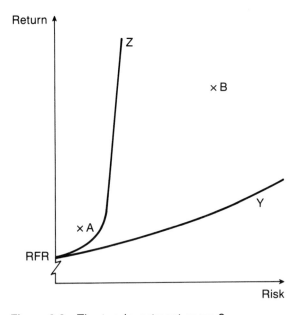

Figure 8.3 The two investment case: 2

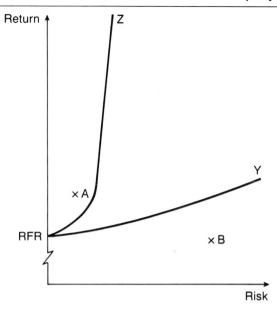

Figure 8.4   The two investment case: 3

This leads directly to the mean–variance criterion. This is a decision rule, which states the following.

Purchase investment A if, and only if,

the return on A > return on B
and the risk of A ⩽ risk of B

This applies to all risk-averse investors (thought to be the vast majority) and is therefore an objective decision rule, regardless of the risk–return indifference of the investor.

We have already concluded that return may be measured in two ways: NPV or IRR. The rule might therefore be

Purchase investment A if, and only if,

IRR A > IRR B   or   NPV A at RFR > NPV B at RFR
and the risk of A ⩽ the risk of B

Given that risk is separately measured, it follows that the NPV must be at the RFR. But how is risk to be measured? It has already been shown that standard deviation (σ, or SD) offers a quantitative risk measurement device.

It has been applied to the input variables; but now it must be applied to the return. What is the potential variability of the return from the expected return?

The following discussion continues the unrealistic presumption made to date that the observed values of the variables are part of a discrete, and not continuous, distribution. (This understates risk, and standard deviation, but may not be misleading in a comparison of similar investments.) Given this, there are nine potential IRRs from investment A. These are given in Table 8.17.

The expected (weighted average) return is given by $\Sigma(p \times r)$, which in this case is 16.898 per cent (note the typical slight difference between this and the result of the most likely rental value in combination with the most likely rental growth). The SD of these returns is 0.605 per cent.

For NPV, the appropriate figures are as given in Table 8.18.

This computation was relatively straightforward. The assumption of a discrete distribution of cash flows in place of the more probable continuous distribution has cut down the number of possible cash flows from infinite to nine. In addition, perfect serial correlation of cash flows in years 3, 4 and 5 simplifies the exercise. The combination of a particular rental growth and a particular rental value (nine in all) predicts the cash flows in each of these years, as it determines the rent review fee to be deducted in year 3 and the level rents received in years 4 and 5. If this were not so the number of possible cash flows would have been 729.

Table 8.17

	Rental growth		
Rental value	4% (0.3)	5% (0.4)	6% (0.3)
49,875 (0.2)	15.670% (0.06)	16.108% (0.08)	16.547% (0.06)
52,500 (0.6)	16.456% (0.18)	16.903% (0.24)	17.351% (0.18)
55,125 (0.2)	17.219% (0.06)	17.674% (0.08)	18.131% (0.06)

Note: Probabilities in parentheses.

Table 8.18

	Rental growth		
Rental value	4% (0.3)	5% (0.4)	6% (0.3)
49,875 (0.2)	16,904 (0.16)	18,655 (0.08)	20,441 (0.06)
52,500 (0.6)	20,069 (0.18)	21,913 (0.24)	23,793 (0.18)
55,125 (0.2)	23,235 (0.06)	25,171 (0.08)	27,145 (0.06)

Notes: $\bar{r} = \Sigma(p \times \bar{r}) = £21,924$; $\sigma = £2,516$. The SD of NPVs is the same as the SD of total present values of the nine possible cash flows.

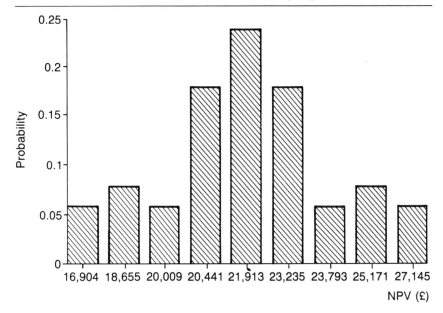

Figure 8.5 Distribution of net present values

The degree of simplification employed is illustrated by investment B. There is no serial correlation between cash flows. Even assuming three discrete RPI growth figures – unrealistic, of course – the number of potential cash flows is $3 \times 3 \times 3 \times 3 \times 3$: combining the effect of three discrete resale capitalization rates produces a total number of possible cash flows of (again, by coincidence) 729. Even a powerful small computer will take some time to produce estimates of SDs and expected IRR and NPV when the assumption of a discrete distribution is relaxed and this number approaches infinity.

So, for illustration purposes only, and to aid the completion of the mean–variance analysis, investment B will be analysed making the following two simplifying assumptions.

1 Cash flows are perfectly serially correlated from year to year. For example, 3 per cent RPI growth in year 1 predetermines 3 per cent RPI growth for each year from 1 to 5. This overstates the risk of the investment.
2 The values of variables form a discrete distribution. This slightly understates the risk of the investment.

The results are given in Table 8.19. A comparison of the results for investments A and B is given in Table 8.20.

Table 8.19 Analysis, investment B

| RPI growth | Resale capitalization rate | | |
	0.08	0.11	0.14
IRRs[a]			
0.0245	23.111% (0.06)	17,051% (0.08)	12.861% (0.06)
0.035	24.373% (0.18)	18.250% (0.24)	14.018% (0.18)
0.0455	25.635% (0.06)	19.450% (0.08)	15.175% (0.06)
NPVs[b]			
0.0245	77,970 (0.06)	34,585 (0.08)	9,794 (0.06)
0.035	87,924 (0.18)	42,270 (0.24)	16,182 (0.18)
0.0455	98,266 (0.06)	50,249 (0.08)	22,810 (0.06)

Notes: [a] $\bar{r} = \Sigma(p \times \hat{r}) = 18.817$ per cent; $\sigma = 4.109$ per cent.
[b] $\bar{r} = \Sigma(p \times \hat{r}) = £48,201$; $\sigma = £28,687$.

Table 8.20 Comparative results

| | IRR | | NPV | |
	Expected value	Standard deviation	Expected value	Standard deviation
Investment A	16.898%	0.605%	£12,924	£2,516
Investment B	18.817%	4.109%	£48,201	£28,687

The expected return of A is less than that of B, but the risks of B are higher than those of A. This means that a decision using the mean–variance criterion is impossible, and we are referred back to the risk–return indifference of the investor. The risk-averse investor would choose A; the risk-indifferent would choose B.

A problem to be tackled in many cases is the difference in size of investments. These are identical. But what if A cost £130,000 while B cost £220,000? While the return measures may be capable of direct comparison (NPV is preferable in such a case (see Brigham 1985), the SD of returns from a large project would inevitably be higher than the SD of returns from a small project of identical risk. Consequently standardization is necessary and is achieved by using the coefficient of variation, a measure of risk relative to the size of the project. This could be

$$\frac{\text{SD of PVs}}{\text{expected PV}} \quad \text{or} \quad \frac{\sigma \text{ PV}}{\overline{\overline{\text{PV}}}}$$

For investment A, in the preceding analysis, this is

$$\frac{£2,516}{£155,824} = 0.01615$$

For investment B, it is

$$\frac{£28,687}{£165,187} = 0.17366$$

The conclusion to be drawn from these figures is that B is over ten times riskier per unit of investment size than A.

The coefficient of IRR/NPV variation

Another interpretation of the coefficient of variation proposed by Reilly (1985) and Brigham (1985) has more immediate appeal and more general an application in decision-making. The mean–variance criterion will not provide a decision where the project of higher risk produces a higher return: yet this is to be expected in a competitive market for investments. An objective measure of risk per unit of return may be useful for the investor, or analyst, without a clear picture of subjective risk–return indifference.

Either NPV or IRR might be used in a coefficient of variation for measuring risk against return. The IRR version is calculated as follows:

$$\frac{\text{SD of IRR}}{\text{expected IRR}} \quad \text{or} \quad \frac{\sigma \text{ IRR}}{\text{IRR}}$$

For investment A, this is

$$\frac{0.605\%}{16.898\%} = 0.03580$$

For investment B, it is

$$\frac{4.109\%}{18.817\%} = 0.21837$$

This shows that investment B is much riskier (around six times) than investment A per unit of return and would prompt all but the least risk-averse investor to choose investment A.

In NPV terms, the measure is

$$\frac{\text{SD of NPV}}{\text{expected NPV}} \quad \text{or} \quad \frac{\sigma \text{ NPV}}{\text{NPV}}$$

For investment A, this is

$$\frac{£2,516}{£21,924} = 11.476\%$$

For investment B, this is

$$\frac{£28,687}{£48,201} = 59.515\%$$

This comparison almost exactly repeats the result of the coefficient of IRR variation.

There are again reasons for preferring the NPV measure. The coefficient of IRR variation should only be used where two acceptable investments are being compared: otherwise, an apparently superior (lower risk per unit of return) investment may be preferred when it is expected to fail to produce a return equal to or exceeding the target rate (and would therefore be unacceptable). The coefficient of NPV variation does not suffer from this problem (an unacceptable project would produce a negative coefficient).

Standard deviations in risk analysis: some problems

Reaching this stage has only been possible with the aid of some simplifying assumptions regarding the nature of the probability distributions of the variables employed and, hence, a rather robust use of SDs. In this section we consider further the possible problems we have to date circumnavigated by the use of these assumptions.

Measures of investment risk are more difficult to achieve where the possible values of variables are drawn from a continuous, rather than a discrete, distribution, where the values are drawn from a skewed distribution, and where the values of variables from year to year are not perfectly serially correlated. In our property investment analysis model the first of these problems is exemplified by the fact that rental growth has to be represented as a minimum, expected and maximum value (say 4 per cent, 5 per cent and 6 per cent) when average rental growth per annum could theoretically take any value between minus infinity and plus infinity to any number of decimal places. Second, the problem of lack of serial correlation is exemplified by the fact that rental growth achieved over a second rent review period may have no relationship with the equivalent value of the first review period, and so on, radically complicating the analysis.

Sample standard deviation

The former problem is easily avoided by use of sample statistics. Use of the sample SD puts into effect the truism that the discrete SD (or SD of a population, σ_p) understates the risk of a variable drawn from a continuous distribution. Given that the population SD = variance^2, the sample SD (σ_s) can be found as follows:

$$\text{variance} = \sigma_p{}^2$$

$$\sigma_s \quad = \sqrt{\left[(\sigma \text{ variance})\frac{n}{n-1}\right]}$$

where n is the number of samples taken from the population.

For example, assuming maximum, expected and minimum values of rental growth of 4 per cent, 5 per cent and 6 per cent with probabilities of 0.2, 0.6 and 0.2 respectively, variance $= \Sigma(\hat{r} - \bar{r})^2 p$, where $\hat{r}$ is the observed value of the variable, $\bar{r}$ is the expected value of the variable and p is the probability of occurrence of observed value.

$$\begin{aligned}\text{variance} &= \Sigma(0.04 - 0.05)^2\, 0.2 + (0.05 - 0.05)^2 (0.6) \\ &\quad + (0.06 - 0.05)^2\, 0.2\end{aligned}$$

$$= (0.00002 + 0.00002)$$

$$= 0.00004$$

$$\sigma \quad = \sqrt{\left[(\text{variance})\frac{n}{n-1}\right]}$$

The use of n, the number of observations, is problematic. Estimates of rental growth are unlikely to be made by sampling a population. Forecasting is more likely to be undertaken by a combination of time series extrapolation and causal analysis (see pages 229–30). However, it is possible to hypothesize that rental growth for each of the last 10 years may be taken as the population from which samples of 4 per cent, 5 per cent and 6 per cent may be drawn. In that case, n is 10.

$$\sigma = \sqrt{[(0.00004)(10/9)]}$$

$$= \sqrt{[(0.00004)(1.1111)]}$$

$$= \sqrt{(0.00004444)}$$

$$= 0.006667$$

Note that if the sample were drawn from 100 observations, $\sigma_s = 0.006356$. As the number of samples taken increases, σ_s reduces and approaches σ_p ($\sigma_p = \sqrt{r}$, so that $\sqrt{(0.00004)} = 0.006325$).

Of the variables listed in Example 8.2 on page 235 only the scale-based fees can be regarded as suitable for this type of sample analysis, and they are unlikely to be of major importance. The major variables are ERV at years 0, 5 and 10, rental growth and the resale capitalization rate. All samples are drawn from continuous infinite populations. The choice, therefore, between the more correct sample SD, hypothesizing a number of samples, and the population SD is a marginal one, given the likely small difference in result.

Skewness

Skewness describes the tendency of a distribution of values of a variable to differ from the normal curve. This occurs where the median value does not equate with the mean or the mode, and the area of the curve to one side of the expected (mean) value does not equate with the area of the curve to the other side; in other words, the value of the subject variable is more likely to be higher than lower, or vice versa, than the mean value. In a normal distribution it is equally likely that a higher or a lower value will be the outcome.

The SD used as the risk measure for much of this chapter may be used as a measure of dispersion in all symmetrical and even moderately skewed distributions. However, it becomes misleading as a measure of risk where the distribution is highly skewed.

This is not likely to be a large problem in property investment analysis. The variables discussed in this chapter are likely to be drawn from relatively normal distributions. However, problems may be encountered at rent reviews, which are typically 'upward-only' in the UK. In a non-inflationary context, upward-only rent reviews may significantly skew the distribution of potential rents at review, and this is a factor which must be considered within a risk–return analysis which relies upon the SD measure. It is an argument in favour of the sliced income method, described on page 254.

Serial correlation between cash flows

Where a multi-period analytical model is used, many variables have to be estimated at more than one point in time. For example, rent review fees may be 7 per cent in the current market, and it would usually be presumed that they would continue at that level. Perfect serial correlation between succeeding levels of rent review fee percentages is thereby assumed. However, average rental growth per annum between years 0 and 5 is unlikely to predict, except in an extremely complex manner, average rental growth per annum between years 6 and 10. In other words, there is unlikely to be strong serial correlation between succeeding values of expected rental growth (for empirical evidence of this, see Brown 1985: 257).

Even allowing for the effect of the UK 5-yearly rent review stabilizer, this is a considerable problem. Given a simple model with three major variables (ERV, resale capitalization rate and rental growth) the extension of the time period for analysis beyond 5 years to a typical 15 increases the number of cash flow possibilities (even taking only three values of what are continuously distributed variables from infinite ranges) from 27 to 6,561. A mean–variance analysis of the type presented for purposes of comprehension in this chapter is thereby made unworkable.

There are four possible solutions to this problem.

Assuming serial correlation

The first is the method adopted to date in this chapter, that is, to assume perfect serial correlation between cash flows. This confines the number of possible cash flows in this case to 27, but overstates the riskiness of the project. Given that the purpose of the analysis may be a relative judgement rather than an absolute measure of risk, this need not be a problem. However, it will be misleading where the shapes of the distributions of the variables in the two projects are considerably different as the riskier project may be excessively penalized. Wider comparisons (for example, with alternative investments) may also become invalid as a result of this simplification.

Interpolation

Robinson (1987) suggests a simple robust solution: interpolation of the SD or coefficient of variation, measured between the extremes of perfect serial correlation and independence between cash flows (see Example 8.5). The advantages and disadvantages of such an approach are relatively self-evident: accuracy is not guaranteed, but a simple solution is attainable within a reasonable time.

Hillier and Sykes

A third solution is the type of algebraic approach adapted from the work of Hillier (1963) to real estate by Sykes (1983b).

As Robinson (1987) shows, a maximum value for a project's risk is given by the SD measure where the values of variables over time are independent of their preceding values, and a minimum value of the same project's risk is given by the SD measure where each variable is perfectly serially correlated.

■ EXAMPLE 8.5

Cost of project	£1,000
Return in year 1	£50 (0.5p) or £75 (0.5p)
Return in year 2	£1,500 (0.5p) or £1,750 (0.5p)

Possible net cash flows: perfectly independent

Year 0	(£1,000)	(£1,000)	(£1,000)	(£1,000)
1	£50	£50	£75	£75
2	£1,500	£1,750	£1,500	£1,750
NPV at 10%	£285.12	£491.74	£307.85	£514.46
SD of NPVs	£103.93			

Possible cash flows: perfectly serially correlated (so that an income of £75 in year 1 predicts the larger return in year 2)

Year 0	(£1,000)	(£1,000)
1	£50	£75
2	£1,500	£1,750
NPV at 10%	£285.12	£514.46
SD of NPVs	£114.67	

Within these two extremes lies the possibility that cash flows are partially correlated. The above cash flow might represent the result of the interplay of many variables, some of which are independent of their preceding values (for example, repair expenses) and some of which are perfectly serially correlated (for example, gross rent between reviews). If there is partial correlation between the cash flows above, the SD of the NPVs lies between £103.93 and £114.67; beyond this it is only possible to say that a precise measure would be extremely difficult, necessitating the estimation of partial correlation coefficients between all the cash flows. (Robinson's approach, however, is simple interpolation: use (say) £109.30 as a midpoint SD measure.)

Sykes suggests that the fortunate aspect of property investment analysis in this respect is the fact that cash flows are either perfectly correlated or independent, and not partially correlated. (This ignores the complex effects of expenses, fees and so on.) Thus, while rents between reviews are perfectly correlated, Sykes posits that rents immediately before and after review are, in an inflationary environment and given normal depreciation, independent.

Hillier's equation for the SD of independent cash flows and perfectly correlated cash flows respectively are as follows:

$$\sigma^2 \text{ NPV} = \sum_{j=1}^{\hat{}} \frac{\sigma^2 j}{(1+i)^2 j}$$

$$\sigma^2 \text{ NPV} = \left[\sum_{j=1}^{\hat{}} \frac{\sigma j}{(1+i)^j} \right]^2$$

Sykes then derives a formula for establishing the SD of a property investment (ignoring outgoings) as follows. Assuming a 10-year holding period, the cash flow is made up of five variables. These are as follows.

1 *The outlay* The outlay is known and risk free. The SD of the NPV is identical to that of the total present value of a cash flow. Thus, in estimating the risk of an investment where the outlay is risk free, the outlay may be ignored.

2 *Rent, years 0–5* This will usually already have been negotiated at the time analysis is carried out and is thus risk free, in the absence of default risk. The SD is nil, and this variable may be ignored in a combined expression of the risk of the investment.

3 *Rent, years 6–10 and 11–15* These are perfectly correlated, although the two expressions are independent of each other and of the starting rent. Thus the expression for the SD of the present value of the rent between years 6 and 10 is

$$\sigma^2 = \sigma \left[\sum_{j=6}^{10} \frac{1}{(1+i)^j} \right]^2$$

where j is the number of years and i is the target rate. The equivalent for years 11–15 is

$$\sigma^2 = \sigma \left[\sum_{j=11}^{15} \frac{1}{(1+i)^j} \right]^2$$

4 *Resale price*   This is an independent risky variable (c). The total expression is therefore

$$\sigma^2 \, \text{NPV} = \sigma \left[\sum_{j=6}^{10} \frac{1}{(1+i)^j} \right]^2 + \left\{ \sum_{j=11}^{15} \left[\frac{1}{(1+i)^j} \right] \right\}^2 + \left[\frac{\sigma^c}{(1+i)^{15}} \right]^2$$

This is the expression for total risk of an investment with perfect correlation within reviews and assuming no correlation between different period review rents and resale price.

As Sykes points out, the resale price presents a problem, as it represents the result of resale capitalization rate (independent) and ERV at the resale date. This complicates the estimation of SD by formula, but Sykes suggests formulae employing partial derivatives (see Sykes 1983b).

Sykes' adaptation of Hillier's work to UK property is a useful advance. It is questioned by Brown (1985) who is critical of its assumption of complete independence of rents between review, ignoring as it does the many complications created by outgoings and upward only reviews. It is of necessity, therefore, a short cut. The same is only true to a much reduced extent in the case of the following, fourth, solution to the problem of independence cash flows.

Simulation

We referred earlier in this chapter to 6,561 potential cash flows from a simple property investment.

It would be quite possible to program a modern computer to estimate the NPV of all 6,561 cash flows and to calculate the SD of the results. It would, however, be difficult to program a small computer to do this in a reasonable amount of time; and, in any event, 6,561 is a small number of potential cash flows.

A solution to this is (Monte Carlo) simulation. Given estimates of the worst, expected and best outcomes of all variables and the associated probabilities, many programs are available to select, at random, combinations of variables, calculating and storing the NPV produced by the resultant cash flow, and repeating the exercise strictly in accordance with the probabilities given. If the analyst specified a 60 per cent chance of repairs being necessary at a cost of £5,000 at the lease end, then six times out of ten the cash flow thrown out by the simulation will include this expense. Simulation programs can run this exercise repeatedly, calculate NPVs and produce the SD of the results. It is to be expected that the shape of the curve of a distribution of a high number of simulations will be identical to the shape of the curve of the population, so that the SD measure will be accurate.

The advantage of the numeric simulation technique is its ability to accurately take into account all variables, unlike the adaptation of the algebraic Hillier technique described above. It can also deal with the problems of serial correlation (or lack of it) within a variable and a divergence between sample and population SD measures. Care must be taken where there is a suspicion of interdependence (correlation) between variables, for example, where a high rate of RPI growth might imply rises in capitalization rates, in which case a simple simulation exercise would understate risk to some extent. On balance, however, simulation is of considerable aid in the decision.

Simulation is therefore now used to compare investments A and B.

Simulation in practice Using the mean–variance criterion for investment decision-making necessitates the estimation of possible values for each of two variables in each case.

For investment A, the variables are rental value and average rental growth. Pessimistic, expected and optimistic values for these variables are given in Table 8.21, with associated probabilities.

For investment B, the variables are the average increase in RPI and the

Table 8.21

Rental value	p	Rental growth	p
49,875	0.2	4%	0.3
52,500	0.6	5%	0.4
55,125	0.2	6%	0.3

Table 8.22

RPI growth	p	Resale capitalization rate	p
2.45%	0.2	0.14	0.3
3.5%	0.6	0.11	0.4
4.55%	0.2	0.08	0.3

resale capitalization rate. Pessimistic, expected and optimistic values for these variables, with probabilities, are given in Table 8.22.

In a simulation program, the analyst need not be restricted to pessimistic, expected and optimistic values, depending upon the parameters established in the program used. Any number of value bands for each variable may be employed.

In the simulation program we constructed, we chose five value bands for each variable. The value bands used for investment A (which are broadly consistent with previous pessimistic, expected and optimistic values for the two variables in investment A) are given in Table 8.23. (New subjective probability estimates for these value ranges have been assigned (strictly, the possibilities of rents below £49,219 and above £55,781 should be included in the outlying ranges).)

Simulation programs work by generating random numbers within the chosen value bands in a frequency determined by the probability assumptions made. Hence, given sufficient cycles, 40 per cent of all simulated cash flows will be on the basis that the rental value will be between £51,845 and £53,156; 20 per cent of all simulated cash flows will be on the basis of growth of between 4.26 per cent and 4.75 per cent. Random number generation selects any value within these ranges and not a finite central point.

The first ten results in our simulation exercise are given in Table 8.24.

Already, the probability distribution of variables is being reflected in the random generation of values. The average ERV is £52,347, close to the expected £52,500; the average growth is 5.27 per cent, close to the expected 5 per cent, but likely to become much closer to it over 200 cycles (see page 275, it becomes 5.06 per cent).

For investment B, the appropriate value bands with new probabilities are as shown in Table 8.25. The first ten results are as given in Table 8.26.

Table 8.23

	Rental value (p)	Rental growth (p)
Pessimistic	49,875 (0.2)	0.04 (0.3)
Expected	52,500 (0.6)	0.05 (0.4)
Optimistic	55,125 (0.2)	0.06 (0.3)
Band 1	49,219–50,531 (0.1)	0.0375–0.0425 (0.15)
Band 2	50,532–51,844 (0.2)	0.0426–0.0475 (0.2)
Band 3	51,845–53,156 (0.4)	0.0476–0.0525 (0.3)
Band 4	53,157–54,469 (0.2)	0.0526–0.0575 (0.2)
Band 5	54,470–55,781 (0.1)	0.0576–0.0625 (0.15)

Table 8.24

Cycle	ERV (£)	Growth (%)	NPV (£)	IRR (%)
1	51,770	5.96	22,788	17.11
2	50,736	5.90	21,365	16.77
3	55,381	4.44	24,388	17.49
4	52,355	6.23	24,045	17.41
5	53,962	4.14	22,099	16.95
6	49,828	5.70	19,837	16.40
7	51,854	4.63	20,437	16.55
8	51,977	4.84	20,966	16.67
9	52,958	5.64	23,689	17.33
10	52,650	5.18	22,428	17.03

Table 8.25

	RPI growth (%) (p)	Resale capitalization rate (p)
Pessimistic	2.45 (0.2)	0.14 (0.3)
Expected	3.5 (0.6)	0.11 (0.4)
Optimistic	4.55 (0.2)	0.08 (0.3)
Band 1	2.1875–2.7125 (0.1)	13.26–14.75 (0.15)
Band 2	2.7126–3.2375 (0.2)	11.76–13.25 (0.2)
Band 3	3.2376–3.7625 (0.4)	10.26–11.75 (0.3)
Band 4	3.7626–4.2875 (0.2)	8.76–10.25 (0.2)
Band 5	4.2876–4.8125 (0.1)	7.26–8.75 (0.15)

Table 8.26

Cycle	Capitalization rate (%)	RPI growth (%)	NPV (£)	IRR (%)
1	12.43	4.19	33,014	16.84
2	11.99	2.50	25,410	15.58
3	9.88	3.53	56,350	20.29
4	11.27	3.52	39,474	17.83
5	11.12	3.18	38,538	17.68
6	12.55	3.39	26,514	15.77
7	10.09	3.22	51,015	19.52
8	10.17	4.51	60,340	20.87
9	8.99	4.45	77,943	23.18
10	14.29	2.91	10,641	13.02

Two hundred cycles of each cash flow were recorded. Arguably, this is insufficient a number to ensure that the simulation is absolutely representative of the totality of possible cash flows, but for purposes of illustration 200 will suffice.

Again the mean–variance criterion can be employed in decision-making. This time, however, the problem of choice of sample or population SD is effectively avoided, as a large number of cycles will cause the two to equate. Serial correlation between cash flows can also be easily avoided in the simulation exercise (although our simple simulation exercise was not designed to overcome this problem). The problem of skewness is effectively avoided by the use of realistically normal probability distributions for each variable in each case, resulting in a normal distribution of IRRs and NPVs. Hence the results shown in Table 8.27 are satisfactory for our purpose.

The interpretation of the results is as follows.

For investment A, the average NPV is £21,879. There is a 68.26 per cent probability that the NPV will lie between £21,879 ± £2,195, that is, £19,684 and £24,074; a 95.46 per cent probability that the NPV will lie between £21,879 ± (2 × £2,195), that is, £17,489 and £26,269; and a 99.74 per cent probability that the NPV will lie between £21,879 ± (3 × £2,195), that is, £15,294 and £28,464.

For investment B, the average NPV is £47,861. There is a 68.26 per cent probability that the NPV will lie between £47,861 ± £23,587, that is, £24,274 and £71,448; a 94.46 per cent probability that the NPV will lie between £47,861 ± (2 × £23,587), that is, £687 and £95,035; and a 99.74 per cent probability that the NPV will lie between £47,861 ± (3 × £23,587), that is, £22,900 and £118,622.

A comparison of the results is given in Table 8.28.

Table 8.27

	Investment A	Investment B
Number of cycles	200	200
Average IRR	16.89%	18.87%
σ of IRR	0.53%	3.39%
Minimum IRR	15.64%	12.51%
Maximum IRR	18.19%	27.12%
Average NPV	£21,879	£47,861
σ of NPV	£2,195	£23,587
Minimum NPV	£16,779	£7,856
Maximum NPV	£27,400	£111,446
Average rental growth/RPI growth	5.06%	3.56%
Average rental value/resale capitalization rate	£52,376	10.89%

Table 8.28 Comparison of discrete and simulated results

	Investment A		Investment B	
	Discrete mean–variance	*Simulation*	*Discrete mean–variance*	*Simulation*
Average expected IRR (%)	16.90	16.89	18.817	18.869
σ IRR (%)	0.61	0.53	4.11	3.39
Coefficient of IRR variation (%)	3.58	3.12	21.837	17.971
Average expected NPV (£)	21,924	21,879	48,201	47,861
σ NPV (£)	2,516	2,195	28,687	23,587
Coefficient of NPV variation (%)	11.48	10.03	59.52	49.28

Note how the original discrete test overstates risk by a small amount, as a result of the discrete variable values, the effect of the new probabilities and/or the effect of using the overstated measure of population SD (σ_p) in the original analysis. The nine cash flows analysed earlier will thus inevitably produce a higher population SD than the 200 used in simulation, all other things being equal; hence the simulation results are to be preferred as being more accurate.

In practice, the discrete mean–variance test, using optimistic, expected and pessimistic values, can hardly be said to be inadequate. The above results show a clear decision on the basis of coefficient of variation measures: the differences between the results of the two approaches are hardly significant. Nonetheless, given that the effort involved in carrying out a simulation need not be greater than alternative less rigorous methods, it is to be recommended.

In conclusion, while the mean–variance criterion allows no clear decision, the coefficient of IRR variation indicates that investment A is to be preferred by all but the risk-indifferent and risk-seeking investor: while B will probably be more profitable than A, the investor takes on considerably more risk per unit of return.

Figures 8.8 and 8.9 illustrate graphically the relative risks and returns of the two investments.

Portfolio risk

In Chapter 2 we discussed the work of Markowitz and Sharpe in developing modern portfolio theory (MPT). They showed how the combination of two or more investments whose returns fluctuate in different conditions but in opposite directions can reduce risk without at the same time reducing

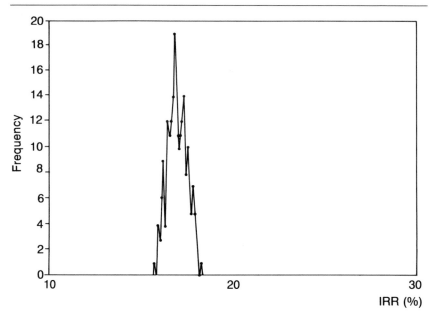

Figure 8.6   Investment A, distribution of possible returns

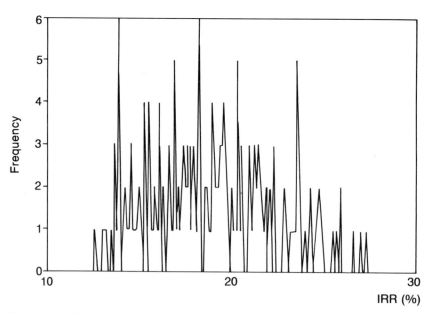

Figure 8.7   Investment B, distribution of possible returns

return. Further, the conclusion of MPT must be that a riskier investment may be preferred to a safe investment, as the effect of including that investment may, if it shows inverse correlation with the existing portfolio, be to reduce portfolio risk without paying for that benefit in loss of return.

This may be the case if in our example investment B were a US investment (let us say, Texas). Investment A may be less risky than B.

However, if the fund holds only UK real estate, and if US real estate has a tendency to perform well when UK real estate performs badly, then B may be preferable.

The difficulties of applying this logic are in quantifying the relative attraction of the two investments to the holder of a portfolio and in the assumptions which must be made in order to progress the measurement process.

The capital asset pricing model (CAPM, see Chapter 2) requires at least one major assumption to be made. The difficulties of measuring the covariance of a real portfolio and the relative variance of potential new investments are enormous, and the CAPM proceeds by hypothesizing that all rational investors hold a market portfolio made up of all investments. This, of course, includes real estate, and must also include all other investment types throughout the world. This need not be an insurmountable objection if it can be shown that relatively small portfolios can be representative of the market. Unfortunately, little or no evidence has been produced to demonstrate this in the context of a portfolio including international real estate.

If, however, we ignore this problem and adduce the return on the market, perhaps by taking the UK stock market as a surrogate market portfolio, then it is necessary to measure β for property investments. The formula

$$R = \mathrm{RFR} + \beta(R_\mathrm{p})$$

where R is the required return on subject investment, β is the measure of relative risk and R_p is the market risk premium (expected return on the market less RFR), enables us to decide whether an investment is under- or over-priced (see Chapter 2, page 45). β is a measure of co-variance of the investment's performance against the market. In the example, would we need measures of the expected return on offices in the USA; or in Texas; or in a part of Texas; or in the particular sub-location; or of the particular office?

We also need forecasts of expected returns. Given that reliable forecasts do not exist, we may be tempted to base expectations on past performance. In order to obtain this, we need records of past performance of offices in Texas, shops in the south of England, and so on. We are unlikely to hold records of sufficient scope and reliability for this purpose.

As a result of these problems, it is not proposed to utilize CAPM in a comparative analysis of the two investments, other than by means of an illustration. Let us assume that we are able to derive β for shops in the south of England and for offices in Texas, that the investor holds a UK market non-property portfolio and that returns on the market have been 18 per cent over the last 5 years and that the RFR is 9 per cent. If the performance of the Texas offices is negatively correlated with the UK stock market, we may find the following βs:

Texas office	-0.3
South of England shop	$+0.18$

The required returns are then (R_s and R_t, for investments A and B respectively):

$$R_s = 0.09 + 0.18 \ (0.09)$$
$$= 10.62\%$$
$$R_t = 0.09 - 0.3 \ (0.09)$$
$$= 6.3\%$$

Given that expected returns are 16.9 per cent and 18.8 per cent respectively, the probable choice is investment B, reversing all previous indications.

It is not yet common practice to choose property investments on the basis of β, and it may never be, but work continues in this field (see, for example, Brown 1991; Baum and Schofield 1991; and Hargitay and Yu 1992).

SUMMARY

Sensitivity analysis showed that a realistic choice of variable parameters produced a much wider range of returns for investment B than for investment A, although the average for B was higher. The conclusion which may be drawn from this is that a higher return is likely for B but at the cost of a higher risk.

Sensitivity analysis produced no simple decision rule, providing the analyst instead with a range of results. We favour this approach in the majority of circumstances: it allows the investor to retain the decision responsibility with the help of the analyst in determining realistic variable parameters.

Risk-adjustment techniques, on the other hand, attempt to provide an objective decision, but only by way of subjective risk adjustment. Three methods were presented. On the basis of the risk-adjusted discount rate technique, investment A produced a higher NPV and a higher margin of return over the risk-adjusted rate, and would be preferred. The certainty equivalent technique, offered as a preferable risk-adjustment method, offered an even clearer decision, as the NPV of investment B became negative and the profitable investment A would have been preferred. The sliced income approach is particularly suited to UK property investment analyses due to the commonality of the upward only rent review at 5-year intervals, and may be an improvement upon the certainty equivalent technique in some cases. In this case it produces a result which makes a choice between the investments marginal.

The fault of risk-adjustment techniques is the probability that the professional analyst will replace the subjective risk–return indifference of the investor by an apparently objective analysis which is in reality subjective to the analyst. This is unlikely to be acceptable to the sophisticated investor, who may wish to base his decision upon separate measures of risk and return. The measures used in the mean–variance criterion are NPV or IRR for return, and SD of NPV or IRR for risk. Investment A would be preferred if

$$\text{NPV (IRR) A} > \text{NPV (IRR) B}$$
$$and \text{ SD A} \leqslant \text{SD B}$$

In this case, as is typical, the mean–variance criterion produced no clear decision. The return of B exceeded that of A: but so did its risk. It is impossible to say which is best, as a choice depends upon the investor's risk aversion. The mean–variance criterion's strict decision rule makes it of little use in many cases.

An attempt to objectify the risk–return trade-off is the coefficient of IRR variation, which measures the risk of an investment per unit of return. Strictly speaking this does not improve upon the mean–variance criterion as a decision rule, as the subjective risk-aversion of the individual investor remains to be interpreted. But investors may have little experience of quantifying their own degree of risk-aversion and may prefer to base a decision on a simple comparison of coefficients of IRR variation. A clear decision may emerge for the typical investor (averagely risk-averse): in the comparison of investments A and B, this was almost certainly true, as B was shown to be around six times as risky per unit of return than was A, and A would therefore have been chosen.

Finally, all of the foregoing analyses may be misleading if the main concern of the investor is the risk of his portfolio, and not of the individual investment. Investment B in the analysis is shown to be much more risky than A; but if it were a US property and US real estate investments can be shown to demonstrate a degree of inverse correlation with UK property investments, the effect of including B in a UK property dominated portfolio may be to reduce the overall risk of the portfolio, at the same time improving return by a greater amount than would be expected by buying A. An analysis of this type requires the estimation of betas of individual properties or property types, and there is no clear consensus that this can be achieved in a reliable and useable manner.

Property investment appraisal remains a developing field. Investors will always be concerned about risk and return, about minimizing one while maximizing the other. How these issues are precisely defined, and how analytical techniques develop in order that they may be measured, will continue to provide rich fields of enquiry for students, academics and investment professionals.

Part five

CASE STUDY AND CONCLUSIONS

9

Value and price: A case study

INTRODUCTION

This chapter describes an analysis of the value or worth of an over-rented City of London office building in 1993. It illustrates the tension between the assessment of worth and a pricing valuation produced by both conventional and contemporary techniques.

In doing so, we attempt to show how the pricing process should be affected by a greater understanding of the purchaser's view, and how changes in economic fundamentals will create changes in worth before market pricing techniques can adapt to new comparable evidence. In other words, there is a short-term deficiency in all pricing techniques which are based on comparable evidence in a changing market, quite apart from the conceptual and mathematical inadequacies in conventional models which we hope to have demonstrated.

THE INVESTMENT

The property

Constructed in 1990, the subject property is an office building of around 15,000 square feet situated on the edge of the central area of the City of London. It was let to a leading firm of solicitors, a partnership, on a 25-year lease in May 1991 at a contract rent of £760,000. The estimated rental value at the valuation date was around £20 per square foot or £296,000 without, or net of, inducements (such as rent free periods and fitting out costs, currently common in the market). At the valuation date of March 1993, it was owned by a small pension fund.

The economic environment

In late 1992, the UK had been in recession for 18 months, and the over-supply of London offices created through the boom of the mid to late 1980s, coupled with a very weak demand side and rents which had reached a peak in real terms by 1989, created a potent mixture. Property companies had been squeezed by interest rate rises in the late 1980s, by a scarcity of debt following the record indebtedness of banks and by a fall in investor demand for property. When rents started to tumble in 1990 and 1991 the final piece in the jigsaw was in place, and the UK saw property company failures, non-performing bank loans and a loss of investor confidence.

In late 1992, the UK withdrew from the European exchange rate mechanism (ERM). As this happened, interest rates fell, gilt yields fell and sterling was effectively de-valued against the German mark.

This marked a turn in investor sentiment. By this time, and after only 2 years, a London office building might have been worth less than 50 per cent of its end-1989/early-1990 peak. Rents appeared to be approaching a floor. Yields were at an all-time high in absolute terms and also relative to gilts and equities and no reverse yield gap existed between gilts and offices and industrial prime property for the first time in 30 years.

The central London office market was now dominated by over-rented buildings, let during the building boom of 1986–90 at rents which peaked at about £65 per square foot on long institutional leases for 20 and 25 years with upwards only rent reviews. Because the rents had fallen so much, these over-rented buildings were not expected to participate in rental growth until their rental values recovered their pre-1990 level. In some cases this was not expected to happen before the end of the lease, as inflation and real growth forecasts were both very low at the time.

The investment: equity or bond?

Investors were now able to buy a fixed income secured on property with the prospect of an equity conversion at some time in the future. Overseas purchasers, especially Dutch and German investors, realized that these investments constituted their natural habitat, fixed interest low risk bonds, at very attractive yields relative both to their domestic bonds and to UK gilts. Not only that, but the currency devaluation meant that a larger building could now be purchased for the same outlay in their domestic currency, improving both the psychic income element of the deal and the prospects of currency appreciation.

This created a radical change in the property investment market. Valuers and investors were locked into thought processes and valuation methods based on the concept of property as an equity investment, that is, one which is expected to benefit from income growth and capital appreciation, from both inflation and growth in the real economy. Instead, property had become a convertible bond.

The distinction between a bond investment and an equity investment is reflected in the two component parts of a valuation. These are the cash flow forecast and the discount rate.

The cash flow

The cash flow from a simple bond is fixed in nominal terms for the life of the investment. The cash flow from an equity rises and falls in response to inflation and to growth and decline in the real economy.

Hence forecasts of the cash flow for a bond do not require a view of the future for the economy or of inflation. Forecasts of the cash flow for an equity require both.

UK property in 1993 might have fallen into the bond category or the equity category. City offices let on upward only rent reviews, subject to both long leases and over-renting, produce a bond which will convert to an equity at the lease end and possibly before. Forecasts of rental growth for offices are not very important in predicting this cash flow.

However, retail warehouses were, in 1993, straightforward property equities. There had been no rent decline of the scale which affected offices, rents continued to rise through 1993 and the cash flow expectation would have been one of rents rising at each review. The expected cash flow would have been driven by expected inflation and expectations of the real economy, especially consumer expenditure growth in those sectors which constitute the retail warehouse occupier market.

Finally, the expected cash flow from a property investment is also subject to two unique factors. The first is the lease terms which determine the payment of rent. For example, the reversionary nature of some property investments will create an income uplift at the next review. The second is the fact that property, unlike any other mainstream investment, is a tangible asset which depreciates through physical deterioration and obsolescence (Baum 1991).

All of these factors combine to create investments which have very different risk characteristics which leads to different discount rates.

The discount rate

The discount rate applied to the cash flow from an investment should be the required return, made up of a risk free rate and a required risk premium. The required risk premium should be determined by the liquidity of the investment and by the sensitivity of the cash flow to shocks created by inaccurate forecasts.

For an equity, the liquidity premium is unlikely to be high or to vary very much between quoted stocks. The sensitivity of the cash flow (the stream of dividends) to economic shocks will be very important indeed. Examples include the effect on oil shares of unexpected changes in the oil price and the effect of a change in the sterling exchange rate on the share price of a company with significant overseas earnings. Default risk is also relevant, an extreme example of the effect of an economic shock on the cash flow. Finally, for those investors interested in the real cash flow (for example, pension funds: see Baum and Schofield 1991), shocks to inflation may be important, although the cash flow is to some extent inflation proof as a result of a generally strong positive relationship between dividends, profits and inflation.

For a bond, the liquidity premium is again unlikely to be high or to vary much between securities. The sensitivity of the cash flow to economic shocks is nil. Default risk is highly relevant, and will be the most important factor in the risk premium. Shocks to inflation will affect bonds more than equities, because the cash flow is fixed in nominal terms and therefore has no inflation proofing quality.

For property, the discount rate will be determined by the extent to which the investment is a bond or an equity. Over-rented offices in central London (bonds) will be sensitive to default risk and inflation. Retail warehouses will be sensitive to default risk, shocks to the real economy and, to a much lesser extent, inflation (remember the fixed nature of rents between reviews).

In addition, all property is subject to two further special risks. The first is the extra illiquidity which affects all property much more than normal bonds and equities and which will lead to an increase in the risk premium. The second is the lease pattern. Long leases and upward only rent reviews contribute to a quality of income stream which will reduce the risk premium.

The property: cash flow and discount rate

It is clear that the subject property is primarily a bond. Its cash flow will be driven by the lease terms, by inflation expectations, by forecasts of the real economy and by expected depreciation.

These factors will all influence an assessment of the worth of this investment. In the section on 'Valuation for worth' (pages 291–2) a full cash flow valuation illustrates how these factors may be accounted for. The following section illustrates an approach to a *pricing* valuation which attempts to account for the factors listed above primarily through the all risks yield.

PRICING

As in all market valuations, the core data is the all risks yield and this was estimated to be 7.7 per cent. Using this as the basis for both conventional and contemporary valuations, the results are as follows.

Conventional core and top slice approach

Current rental value	£296,000		
YP perp. at 7.7%	12.9870		
		£3,844,156	
Overage	£464,000		
YP 23 years, 2 months at			
12.4%	7.5269		
Valuation		£3,492,470	
Net of costs at 2.75%			£7,336,626
Valuation (rounded)			£7,150,000

Notes

1 The term of the overage is dependent upon the valuer's intuitive view regarding whether the real rental value will overtake the passing rent before the final rent review in the lease. The assumption made is that it will not and therefore the overage is taken to the end of the lease.

2 The overage yield is determined in line with the discussion regarding risk premiums in the following section of this chapter dealing with the calculation of worth, and represents a 4 per cent margin over gilts to take into account the additional tenant default risk on the overage as well as illiquidity and normal tenant default risk on the base income.

Contemporary short-cut discounted cash flow

In order to illustrate the contemporary growth explicit approach, a short-cut discounted cash flow (DCF) is also undertaken. The equated yield needs to be determined for a property let at a rack rent and does not include any additional risk premium for the over-rented nature of the asset. The redemption yield on long-dated gilts at the valuation date was 8.4 per cent. Adopting a 2 per cent risk premium generates an equated yield of 10.4 per cent. The valuation is as follows.

Implied rental growth

$$(1 + g)^5 = \frac{\text{YP perp. at } 7.7\% - \text{YP 5 years at } 10.4\%}{\text{YP perp. at } 7.7\% \times \text{PV 5 years at } 10.4\%}$$

$$= \frac{12.987 - 3.7524}{12.987 \times 0.6098} = \frac{9.2346}{7.9195} = 1.16606$$

$$g = 1.16606^{(1/5)} - 1 = 3.1203\% \text{ pa}$$

Will the rent passing be overtaken by rental value before the final review in the lease in just over 18 years' time? $£296,000 \times 1.031203^{18.1667} = £517,267$, so it will not, and the passing rent will remain static until the end of the lease.

Valuation

Rent passing	£760,000		
YP 23 years, 2 months at			
11.4%	8.0526		
		£6,119,984	
Reversion to ERV	£296,000		
A £1 23 years 2 months at			
3.1203% pa	2.0377		
	£603,159		
YP perp. at 7.7%	12.9870		
PV 23 years 2 months at 10.4%	0.10105		
Valuation		£791,573	
Net of costs at 2.75%			£6,911,557
Valuation (rounded)			£6,750,000

Notes

1 The discount rate on the term reflects that some of the passing rent is overage and is therefore a composite yield between the 10.4 per cent applied to the rack rent and the 12.4 per cent applied to the overage. It

is possible to horizontally slice the term income between the ERV and the overage and apply the individual yields.

VALUATION FOR WORTH

Cash flow

The cash flow from the property is determined mainly by the lease terms, which create a very over-rented bond-type investment. With over 23 years of the lease remaining, inflation expectations, real rent forecasts and expected depreciation will together determine the pattern of the future estimated rental value and its relationship with the current contracted rent.

Forecasts of inflation at 4 per cent per annum, rental depreciation at 0.75 per cent per cent per annum and real rental growth forecasts of −13.5, −3.9, −3.9, 17.5 and 4.9 per cent respectively in years 1, 2, 3, 4 and 5, with long-term real growth of 1 per cent per annum after year 5, produce an expectation of an estimated rental value of around £720,000 by the lease end, still less than the contracted rent.

The property is expected to produce a bond-type cash flow until the lease end. After this, it will revert to an equity-type property which can be valued at that point on the basis of the expected rental value and a forecast yield of 7.7 per cent, the same as the rack rented all risks yield used in the pricing valuation.

Discount rate

For a bond-type investment the default risk predominates in the estimation of the risk premium.

Over-rented properties are relatively complex in terms of default risk. The base income is defined as that part of the passing rent which is secured both by the covenant, that is, the contractual lease which binds the tenant to pay the rent agreed, and by the rental value of the property. The froth or over-rented element is defined as that part of the passing rent which is secured only against the covenant.

The base income is doubly secured; the froth income is more exposed to potential default. The risk premium on each element should therefore be different for any other than the most low risk covenant.

Taking the expected redemption yield on a long gilt (8.4 per cent) as the risk free rate proxy, the risk premium for the base income is taken as an extra 1 per cent, to reflect the default risk and the possibility of failing to re-let quickly at the estimated rental value. The risk premium for the froth element is a further 2 per cent. A further 1 per cent is allowed for the illiquidity of all property investments. Hence the base income is discounted at 10.4 per cent (8.4 plus 1 plus 1) while the froth income is discounted at 12.4 per cent (8.4 plus 1 plus 3). (The basis of this approach is the sliced income approach developed in Chapter 8.)

The estimated resale price is discounted at an equity-determined required return, within which the risk premium is set primarily to reflect the real economy risks of predicting the rental value and yield at sale, a premium of 3.25 per cent being higher than the base income discount rate, reflecting the expected difference between a standard equity and a low risk bond.

Discounting the cash flow over the period using these inputs produces a result of £7.4 million.

SUMMARY

The market valuation exercise to estimate exchange price produced valuations of around £7 million. The estimate of worth, using reasonably compatible inputs, produced an estimate of £7.4 million. The building was soon the subject of a bid from an overseas purchaser at a figure approaching £8 million.

The pricing valuations of £6.75 and £7.15 million were based on evidence derived from the market. However, this evidence may have been based on historic transactions or, more likely, on valuers' estimates of what the yields and rents would be if evidence existed. In late 1992, in a changing market, historic transactions would not reflect the ERM exit, lower gilt yields and the new interest of overseas buyers. Changes in such economic fundamentals can only be reflected in traditional pricing techniques intuitively.

With hindsight, the reasons for the underestimate are relatively clear. The value is dominated by the fixed cash flow element underpinned by the upwards only rent review and the ability of the tenant to continue to pay the rent. Once it is decided that the tenant is not likely to default, the bond investor can virtually forget the property risks and concentrate on interest rate risk. In 1993, the prospects of falling interest rates would create possibilities of capital value growth which could be realized when interest rates were forecast to be at their lowest level. By late 1993, the yields on over-rented and rack rented properties in the UK were falling and the risk premium on over-rented properties let to good covenant tenants was substantially less than the 4 per cent used in the valuations.

The price of around £8 million can be achieved by lowering the discount rate on the term within the short-cut DCF to around 9 per cent, only $\frac{1}{2}$ per cent above gilts. This reinforces the view that the investor has purchased a fixed income for a long term with no uncertainty as to the level of income at each future rent review. Apart from illiquidity, it has almost none of the traditional risks of property and it can therefore be rational to accept only a very small risk premium above gilts for the bond element. This appears to be what happened in the UK central London office market during 1993.

The estimate of worth was an underestimate of the worth of the property to the bidder. Nonetheless, it was a better estimate than the pricing exercise and, in addition, the inputs into the valuation are transparent. For example, if the purchaser is not concerned with the illiquidity of property and regards this as a very long-term hold, then the consequent reduction in the discount rate would produce a result close to the bid. The removal of the additional tenant default risk premium on the overage would also produce an answer much nearer to the actual price.

The main reason for the difference between the price and worth valuations is the estimate of rental growth, implied in the market valuation and forecast in the worth valuation. The forecasts of rental growth suggest an average rate higher than the implied rate, which in turn suggests that all risks yields did not fully reflect the expectations of the market, so leading to underpricing. Subsequently, all risks yields did fall suggesting that pricing techniques will continue to move closer to genuine valuation approaches as more analysis of property markets is undertaken. This will introduce rationality, while at the same time improving the chances of accuracy, especially in non-standard property investments.

10

Conclusions

We began this book by distinguishing between market valuation and the valuation of worth, the two specific applications of the skill of appraisal. This distinction continued throughout the text and culminated in separate treatment, in Chapters 6, 7 and 8, of property investment pricing and assessment of worth. In attacking the subject in this way, we reflect the view held by many practising valuers that these are fundamentally different functions, and that as a consequence different models might be appropriate for each. Chapter 9 demonstrates this distinction.

However, the reader will have noted that there is little variation in the basic new models we demonstrate for both valuation and analysis. We propose an explicit cash flow model for worth; and, while we have been careful to make some effort towards an impartial presentation, we have to conclude by proposing (simplified) explicit cash flow models for general use in market valuations. The major technical difference between a market valuation and an assessment of worth is the increase in the number of inputs included in a worth calculation involving the use of forecasts rather than market analysis (implied growth). They are different functions yet they are complementary.

Widespread adoption of our recommendations would be seen as a revolution in the market valuation technique which fundamentally alters the current valuation model. The models we favour appear to replace a tried and tested conventional implicit all risks yield model with a dangerously subjective contemporary explicit cash flow model, forcing the valuer into the hazardous science of forecasting.

We hope we have demonstrated that this is not so. While our examination of market valuation models prior to the appearance of the reverse yield gap (Chapter 3) shows that (in the context of the investment environment and the expectations of investors) conventional techniques had a logical basis, they were at that time explicit cash flow projections, and they were based upon the concept of risk-adjusted, opportunity cost target rates, thereby enabling an investment decision relating property to the alternatives to be made. Our recommendation is not, therefore, a revolution; it is a return to pre-reverse yield gap logic. The revolution that radically altered the logical base of conventional valuation techniques was the creeping and gradual effect of inflation, which replaced the explicit cash flow model by a new, growth implicit, all risks yield technique, riddled (as we show in Chapter 4) with unforeseen errors, irrationalities and difficulties, but made seemingly innocuous by its familiar appearance.

In addition, we reject the afore-mentioned charge that explicit cash flow market valuation models are dangerously subjective and necessitate the use of forecasts. The latter problem is avoided by the analysis of market growth expectations, which we demonstrate in detail in Chapter 5. This does, nonetheless, leave us with the problem that the target rate or equated yield remains a subjective choice, and adoption of growth explicit contemporary models will create a period of temporary uncertainty where valuers are unused to choosing the appropriate equated yield. But evidence will quickly be collected to facilitate that choice; and we have shown in Chapter 6 that, within reasonable boundaries, errors in equated yield choice in the analysis/valuation process for freeholds will be cancelled out by the effect upon implied rental growth and upon the real discount rate. In any case, where (as is typical) the perfect comparable does not exist, the *conventional* model necessitates subjective adjustment. And, as we show in Chapter 6, changing the equated yield in contemporary freehold valuations has much less effect upon the result than changing the all risks yield in a conventional valuation, which lacks the former's inbuilt safety net.

We do not make a case for the adoption of any particular presentation of the contemporary market valuation model. We suggest two alternatives: an explicit cash flow projection with (for freeholds) a cut-off point to simulate resale at the point when the property becomes rack rented; and a real-value/equated-yield hybrid, slightly closer in form to the conventional model.

The former is capable of producing a logical solution and also has the advantage of sharing a common basis with our model for the assessment of worth which is not, as far as we can judge, controversial.

The real value hybrid, on the other hand, has the advantage that it is presented in an almost identical format to the conventional model, highlighting the real difference between conventional and contemporary market valuation techniques (the yield differences within the individual parts of the valuation). Adjusted slightly (to Wood's design), it presents a basis for real return analysis, likely to be of increasing value in future years. Our decision to remain on the fence in this respect is based upon our reluctance to fall back upon the educational method we criticize in Chapter 3, a reliance upon 'rules'. It seems to us that a comparison and reconciliation of the explicit DCF and real value models we present in Chapters 5, 6 and 7 is the source of a thorough understanding of a framework for property investment appraisal, and we must leave it to the reader to choose his/her own means of presentation based upon what we would hope to be an enhanced perception of underlying theory.

The second edition of this text has been written against the backdrop of a recession leading to substantial falls in some property values. It had clearly been imagined that methods developed to deal with rising markets would work in the context of a falling or fallen market. This has proved to be spectacularly incorrect and the recession has provided the advocates of contemporary approaches with enormous justification. Some of the conventional applications to over-rented property valuations have been technically inept and attempts to adjust them to meet the new circumstances have proved woefully inadequate. These inadequacies have been accepted by an increasing number of practitioners. Having re-appraised their techniques, those practitioners have perceived the advantages of the growth explicit alternatives which, having a rational foundation, adjust naturally and painlessly to other situations. Contemporary techniques are now being taken far more seriously than they were before 1990.

The tests of a valuation model are, we suggest in Chapter 1, accuracy and logic. Accuracy has proved difficult to test; the potential for inaccuracy is therefore perhaps a preferable yardstick. Inaccuracy is best avoided by the application of a logical methodology. Conventional valuations are not logical. It is not logical to value a fixed income at a growth implicit yield; it is not logical to value a leasehold profit rent at a rate of return which is based upon freehold yields.

Whether it is logical that investment worth, especially to a group of purchasers, should be distinguishable from market value is a more open question. Short-term variations in price and worth are present in other capital markets where fluctuations in market price can be used to make short-term speculative gains. These speculations can influence short-term movements in market prices which are not heavily influenced by longer term worth as modelled by cash flow techniques.

However, this is not an excuse for adopting irrational models. The contemporary explicit models, applied for their different purposes of market value and investment worth, can and do give varying answers for the same property. If valuers influence market price (short term) through the valuation and negotiation process, they distort the true difference between price and worth by using inappropriate models. This also questions the view of many valuers that explicit models may be appropriate for analysis of price, but not for market valuation.

The role of the valuer/appraiser is therefore founded upon the two functions of assessment of worth and market valuation. One follows the other. As more and more property investment analysis is performed explicitly, the stronger will the motivation become for valuations to be carried out on the same basis. This process has begun: we would like to see the pace of change accelerate. When property investment appraisal becomes rational we shall not only see an improvement in the quality of valuations: at the same time, we shall witness a valuation profession capable of performing comparative investment appraisals, making rational investment decisions and attaining a managerial role. We may even see an improvement in the efficiency of the property investment market.

The adoption of explicit appraisal models by some investors has stimulated a drive for improved information in the property investment markets. Empirical research in these markets has begun to command a premium, and much work still remains to be done. We need to know more about investors' criteria for equated yield/target rate choice; their attitude to risk, and whether it is primarily based upon portfolio or single-asset principles; the impact of depreciation upon return and its relationship to rental growth implications; and, among many other areas for research, the existence of any leading indicators for property investment performance. Research into all of these areas has begun and continues.

But information applied within a faulty model is worthless. Only by the adoption of rational appraisal models will decision-makers in property markets be able to utilize the increasing volume of property market intelligence which is becoming available and be able to command a position of respect within the wider investment community.

Bibliography

AIREA (1984) *The Dictionary of Real Estate Appraisal*, Chicago: American Institute of Real Estate Appraisers.

Baum, A. (1982) 'The enigma of the short leasehold', *Journal of Valuation* 1: 5–9.

—— (1983) *Statutory Valuations*, London: Routledge & Kegan Paul.

—— (1984a) 'The valuation of reversionary freeholds: a review', *Journal of Valuation* 3: 157–67, 230–47.

—— (1984b) 'The all risks yield: exposing the implicit', *Journal of Valuation* 2: 229–37.

—— (1985) 'Premiums on acquiring leases', *Rent Review and Lease Renewal* 5: 212–22.

—— (1986) 'The valuation of short leaseholds for investment', in A. Trott (ed.) *Property Valuation Methods*, London: Polytechnic of the South Bank/RICS.

—— (1988) 'Depreciation and property investment appraisal', in A. MacLeary and N. Nanthakumaran (eds) *Property Investment Theory*, London: Spon.

—— (1989) *A Critical Examination of the Measurement of Property Investment Risk*, Cambridge: University of Cambridge, Department of Land Economy.

—— (1991) *Property Investment Depreciation and Obsolescence*, London: Routledge.

Baum, A. and Butler, D. (1986) 'The valuation of short leasehold investments', *Journal of Valuation*, 4: 342–53.

Baum, A. and MacGregor, B. (1992) 'The initial yield revealed: explicit valuations and the future of property investment', *Journal of Property Valuation and Investment*, 10: 709–26.

Baum, A. and Mackmin, D. (1989) *The Income Approach to Property Valuation*, 3rd edn, London: Routledge.

Baum, A. and Sams, G. (1991) *Statutory Valuations*, 2nd edn, London: Routledge.

Baum, A. and Schofield, A. (1991) *Property as a Global Asset*, Reading: Reading Centre for European Property Research, The University of Reading.

Baum, A. and Yu, S. M. (1985) 'The valuation of leaseholds: a review', *Journal of Valuation* 3: 157–67, 230–47.

Bornand, D. (1985) 'Conveyancing of commercial property investments', *Solicitors Journal*, August 9 and 16.

Bowcock, P. (1983a) 'The valuation of varying incomes', *Journal of Valuation* 1: 366–71, 372–6.

—— (1983b) 'Letter', *Estates Gazette* 266: 87.

Branch, B. (1985) *Investments: A Practical Approach*, Chicago: Longman.

Brealey, R. and Myers, S. (1984) *Principles of Corporate Finance*, New York: McGraw-Hill.

Brigham, E. (1985) *Financial Management: Theory and Practice*, 4th edn, Chicago: Dryden.

Brown, G. (1985) 'An empirical analysis of risk and return in the U.K. commercial property market', unpublished Ph.D. thesis, University of Reading.

—— (1991) *Property Investment and the Capital Markets*, London: Spon.

Brown, G. R. (1992) 'Valuation accuracy: developing the economic issues', *Journal of Property Research* 9: 199–207.

Byrne, P. and Cadman, D. (1985) *Risk, Uncertainty and Decision Making in Property Development*, London: Spon.

Colam, M. (1983) 'The single rate valuation of leaseholds', *Journal of Valuation* 2: 14–18.

County NatWest (1992) *Solving the Risk Premium Puzzle*, Equity Briefing Paper 26, 29 July.

Crosby, N. (1983) 'The investment method of valuation: a real value approach', *Journal of Valuation* 1: 341–50; 2: 48–59.

—— (1984) 'Investment valuation techniques: the shape of things to come?' *The Valuer* 53(7): 196–7.

—— (1985) 'The application of equated yield and real value approaches to the market valuation of commercial property investments', unpublished Ph.D. thesis, University of Reading.

—— (1986) 'Real value, rational model, D.C.F.: a reply', *Journal of Valuation* 4: 16–20.

—— (1987) *A Critical Examination of the Rational Model*, Reading: Department of Land Management and Development, University of Reading.

—— (1991) 'The practice of property investment appraisal: reversionary freeholds in the UK', *Journal of Property Valuation and Investment* 9: 109–22.

—— (1992) 'Over-rented freehold investment property valuations', *Journal of Property Valuation and Investment* 10: 517–24.

Crosby, N. and Goodchild, R. (1992) 'Reversionary freeholds: problems with over-renting', *Journal of Property Valuation and Investment* 11: 67–81.

Crosby, N. and Murdoch, S. (1991–2) 'The legal and valuation implications of abnormal rent review patterns', *Rent Review and Lease Renewal* 11: 130–46, 217–26, 339–52; 12: 25–36.

Crosby, N., Baum, A. and Murdoch, S. (1993) *Commercial Property Leases*, Reading: Centre for European Property Research, University of Reading.

CSO (1983) *Economic Trends* 8: 114, CSO.

Daniels, C. (1981), *UK Commercial and Industrial Property into the 1980's*, London: Economist Intelligence Unit.

Darlow, C. (1983) *Valuation and Investment Appraisal*, London: Estates Gazette.

Davies, T. D. (1908) *Curtis on the Valuation of Land and Houses*, 3rd edn, London: Estates Gazette.

Drivers Jonas/IPD (1988) *The Variance in Valuations*, London: Drivas Jonas/IPD.

—— (1990) *The Variance in Valuations – 1990 Update*, London: Drivas Jonas/IPD.

DTZ Debenham Thorpe (1994) *Money Into Property*, London: DTZ Debenham Thorpe.

Enever, N. (1977) *The Valuation of Property Investments*, London: Estates Gazette.

—— (1981) *The Valuation of Property Investments*, 2nd edn, London: Estates Gazette.

Fisher, I. (1930) *The Theory of Interest*, Philadelphia: Porcupine Press.

Fraser, W. D. (1977) 'The valuation and analysis of leasehold investments in times of inflation', *Estates Gazette* 244: 197–201.

—— (1984) *Principles of Property Investment and Pricing*, London: Macmillan.

—— (1985a) 'Rational models or practical methods', *Journal of Valuation* 3: 253–8.

—— (1985b) 'Gilt yields and property's target return', *Estates Gazette* 273: 1291–4.

—— (1993) *Principles of Property Investment and Pricing*, 2nd edn, London: Macmillan.

Gitman, L. J. and Joehnk, M. D. (1984) *Fundamentals of Investing*, New York: Harper & Row.

Gordon (1958) reported in Brigham, E. (1982) *Financial Management: Theory and Practice*, 4th edn, Chicago: Dryden Press.

Gray, K. J. and Symes, P. D. (1981) *Real Property and Real People*, London: Butterworth.

Greaves, M. J. (1972a) 'Discounted cash flow techniques and current methods of income valuation', *Estates Gazette* 223: 2147–55, 2339–45.

—— (1972b) 'The investment method of property valuation and analysis: an examination of some of its problems', unpublished Ph.D. thesis, University of Reading.

—— (1985) 'The valuation of reversionary freeholds: a reply', *Journal of Valuation* 3: 248–52.

Greenwell, W. & Co. (1976) 'A call for new valuation methods', *Estates Gazette* 238: 481–4.

Greer, G. E. and Farrell, M. D. (1984) *Investment Analysis for Real Estate Decisions*, Chicago: Dryden Press.

Hager, D. P. and Lord, D. J. (1985) *The Property Market, Property Valuations and Property Performance Measurement*, Institute of Actuaries.

Hargitay, S. and Yu, S. M. (1992) *Property Investment Decisions: A Quantitative Approach*, London: Spon.

Harker, N. (1983) 'The valuation of varying incomes: 1', *Journal of Valuation* 1: 363–5.

Hillier, F. S. (1963) 'The derivation of probabilistic information for the evaluation of risky investments', *Management Science* 9: 443–57.

IPD (1991) *Property Investors Digest*, London: IPD.

—— (1992) *Property Investors Digest*, London: IPD.

Jacob, N. and Pettit, B. (1984) *Investments*, Irwin: Homewood.

Jaffe, A. (1977) 'Is there a "new" internal rate of return literature?' *AREUEA Journal* 4: 483.

Korpacz, P. and Roth, M. (1983) 'Changing emphasis in appraisal techniques: the transition to discounted cash flow', *Journal of Valuation* 2: 19.

Lawrence, D. M. and May, H. G. (1943) *Modern Methods of Valuation*, London: Estates Gazette.

Lawrence, D. M., Rees, W. H. and Britton, W. (1962) *Modern Methods of Valuation*, 5th edn, London: Estates Gazette.

Lizieri, C. and Venmore-Rowland, P. (1991) 'Valuation accuracy: a contribution to the debate', *Journal of Property Research* 8: 115–22.

Lofstedt, C. and Baum, A. (1993) *A Comparable Study of Commercial Leasing Structures in Selected European Countries and the USA*, Reading: Reading Centre for European Property Research, University of Reading.

MacGregor, B. D. *et al.* (1985) *Land Availability for Inner City Development*, Reading: Department of Land Management, University of Reading.

Markowitz, H. (1959) *Portfolio Selection – Efficient Diversification of Investments*, New Haven, Conn.: Yale University Press.

Marriott, O. (1967) *The Property Boom*, London: Pan.

Marshall, P. (1976) 'Equated yield analysis', *Estates Gazette* 239: 493–7.

—— (1979) *Donaldsons Investment Tables*, London: Donaldsons.

Mason, R. (1978) 'Versatility in existing method', *Investment and Management Surveyors Conference*, Nottingham, June.

McIntosh, A. P. J. (1983) 'The rational approach to reversionary leasehold property investment valuations', in D. Chiddick and A. Millington (eds) *Land Management: New Directions*, London: Spon.

McIntosh, A. P. L. and Sykes, S. G. (1984) *A Guide to Institutional Property Investment*, London: Macmillan.

Miles, J. (1987) 'Depreciation and valuation accuracy', *Journal of Valuation* 5: 125–37.

Newell, M. J. (1986) 'The rate of return as a measure of performance', *Journal of Valuation* 4: 130–42.

Norris, C. (1884) *The Appraiser, Auctioneer, Broker, House and Estate Agent, and Valuer's Pocket Assistant*, London: Crosby Lockwood.

Patrick, M. J. (1983) 'What use is property performance analysis?', *Journal of Valuation* 2: 137–41.

Plender, J. (1982) *That's the Way the Money Goes*, London: André Deutsch.

Ratcliffe, R. (1965) *Modern Real Estate Valuation*, Madison: Democrat Press.

Reilly, F. K. (1985) *Investment Analysis and Portfolio Management*, Chicago: Dryden.

RICS (1992) *Guidance Notes on the Valuation of Assets*, 3rd edn, London: Royal Institution of Chartered Surveyors.

—— (1994) *Economic Cycles and Property Cycles*, London: Royal Institution of Chartered Surveyors, University of Aberdeen and Investment Property Databank.

Robinson, J. (1985) 'Dual rate D.C.F. analysis', *Journal of Valuation* 4: 143–57.

—— (1987) 'Cash flows and risk analysis', *Journal of Valuation* 5: 268–9.

Rose, J. (1985) *The Dynamics of Urban Property Development*, London: Spon.

Rutterford, J. (1993) *Introduction to Stock Exchange Investment*, 2nd edn, London: Macmillan.

Salway, F. (1986) *Depreciation of Commercial Property*, Reading: CALUS, College of Estate Management.

Senior, H. E. (1975) 'Investment yields in perspective', *Estates Gazette* 233: 1115.

Sharpe, W. F. (1985) *Investments*, 3rd edn, New Jersey: Prentice.

Smith, S. A. (1933) *Curtis on the Valuation of Land and Houses*, 7th edn, London: Estates Gazette.

Sykes, S. G. (1981) 'Property valuation: a rational model', *The Investment Analyst* 61: 20–6.

—— (1983a) 'Valuation models: action or reaction', *Estates Gazette* 267: 1108.

—— (1983b) 'The assessment of property risk', *Journal of Valuation* 1: 253–67.

Sykes, S. G. and McIntosh, A. P. J. (1982) 'Towards a standard property income valuation model: rationalisation or stagnation', *Journal of Valuation* 1: 117–35.

Trott, A. (1980) *Property Valuation Methods: Interim Report*, London: Polytechnic of the South Bank, RICS.

Uthwatt Report (1942) *Report of the Expert Committee on Compensation and Betterment*, Cmd 6386.

Venmore-Rowland, P. and Lizieri, C. (1992) 'Valuation accuracy: a contribution to the debate', *Journal of Property Research* 8: 115–22.

Wood, E. (1972) 'Property investment – a real value approach', unpublished Ph.D. thesis, University of Reading.

—— (1973) 'Positive valuations: a real value approach to property investment', *Estates Gazette* 226: 923–5, 115–17, 1311–13.

Wurtzebach, C. and Baum, A. (1993) 'International property investment', in S. Hudson-Wilson and C. Wurtzebach (eds) *Managing Real Estate Portfolios*, Boston: Wiley.

Index